To Steve, my favourite
who shares my ....
with the Russian people

Jamie Cockfield
2.II.2011

BLACK LEBEDA

J. Rives Childs

BLACK LEBEDA

The Russian Famine Diary of
ARA Kazan District Supervisor
J. Rives Childs, 1921–1923

Edited by

Jamie H. Cockfield

Mercer University Press
Macon, Georgia

ISBN 0-88146-015X
MUP/H701

First Edition.

All photos courtesy of the Hoover Institution Archives,
Stanford University

The paper used in this publication meets the minimum
requirements of American National Standard for Information
Sciences—Permanence of Paper for Printed Library Materials,
ANSI Z39.48-1992.

Library of Congress Cataloging-in-Publication Data

Childs, J. Rives (James Rives), 1893-1987.
Black lebeda : the Russian famine diary of ARA Kazan District
supervisor
J. Rives Childs, 1921-1923 / J. Rives Childs ; edited with an
introduction
by Jamie H. Cockfield
p. cm.
Includes bibliographical references and index.
ISBN-13: 978-0-88146-015-5 (alk. paper)
ISBN-10: 0-88146-015-X (alk. paper)
1. Childs, J. Rives (James Rives), 1893-1987—Diaries. 2.
Famines—Soviet Union.
3. American Relief Administration. 4. Food relief—Soviet Union.
I. Title: Russian famine diary of ARA Kazan District supervisor J.
Rives Childs, 1921-1923.
II. Cockfield, Jamie H. III. Title.
HC340.F3C45 2006
947.084'1092—dc22
2006006613

CONTENTS

It would be a great pity if some District Supervisor who is really gifted with the art of writing does not sit down now and write of his experiences. The true history of the ARA will never be until such experiences...has [sic] been recorded.

—Tom Barringer
ARA District Supervisor in
Ekaterinoslav and Simbirsk[1]

---

[1] Barranger to Page, 13 April 1923, Barranger Papers, 1:11, Hoover Institution, cited in Bertrand Patenaude, *The Big Show in Bololand: The American Relief Expedition to Soviet Russia in the Famine of 1921* (Palo Alto CA: Stanford University Press, 2002) 367.

For Rollin Armour, Douglas Steeples, and Richard Fallis

EDITOR'S INTRODUCTION

In 1921, after the Russian Bolsheviks had killed, driven out, or otherwise cowed domestic enemies and expelled from the Russian land their foreign ones, they suddenly came face to face with a foe more deadly and more difficult to defeat than any the new Soviet state had heretofore endured: A famine of biblical proportions that nearly destroyed the new nation in a way that its physical enemies could not have. Its roots ran deeper than simply the internal chaos brought on by the civil war. A food crisis had begun during the Great War. Farms and estates were stripped not only of the men to work the fields but also of their horses, leaving only the women and children to till the land. Those left performed not only the labor of the men taken into the army but that of the horses as well, since often they were hitched to plows. The disappearance of consumer goods, especially vodka, during the war made the peasants unwilling to exchange what little grain they produced for money, which war-time inflation robbed of its limited value. This dilemma had created urban food shortages, exacerbated by the steady decline in efficiency of rolling stock on the nation's already inadequate railroads.

This early stage of the Great Hunger more than any single thing catalyzed the February Revolution of 1917, but the revolution itself gave the agricultural crisis the decisive shove into the abyss. Peasants across the Russian nation seized the land of the great landlords, and that land often went unplanted in the chaotic political and social situation of 1917 and the civil war years that followed. As the Bolsheviks struggled for supremacy over the Russian land against the Whites and their foreign allies, they introduced an economic system that came to be called "War Communism," which consisted of little more than confiscation of grain and foodstuffs the peasants had produced in order to feed their political base, the working classes in the cities. The peasant classes resisted by planting only what they would need and even destroying fields of grain and chopping down orchards to prevent their falling into the hands of the Communist government. This already bad situation was made even worse as the declining railroad network collapsed almost totally, making it nearly impossible to move to the more desperate areas the scarce supply of food that was somehow obtained by Moscow by the end of the Civil War.

Adding to these famine-producing disorders, in 1921 there befell an act of God, a drought the likes of which the Russian land had never known. It was concentrated in the Volga basin and Ukraine. The winter of 1920–1921 had seen a great shortage of snow, and the spring brought even less rain to the already under-farmed Russian land. Peasants were reduced to eating grass, the bark of trees, old boots—anything that might assuage their hunger. In their desperation, the starving made "bread" from a mixture of clay and the seeds and stalks of a ubiquitous grain-like weed, *lebeda*, creating a ghastly ersatz substitute for the traditional Russian black bread that was then, and still is, the basis of the Russian diet. This "black *lebeda*" might have filled the belly, but it had little nutritional value and was nearly impossible to digest. Conditions were so acute that even *Pravda*, the propaganda rag of the Bolshevik Party, publicly admitted to the nation in June 1921 that a grisly famine stalked the land.

At the end of their tether, Soviet Russia turned to the outside world for help, knowing full well that the nations most capable of giving it were the very nations that had just tried to strangle it in its cradle. Yet the urgency of the situation would permit no other course, and in July 1921, an appeal went out from Moscow, not from one of the Soviet political leaders, but from the great writer Maxim Gorky and the Patriarch of the Orthodox Church, Tikhon. The Soviet government rightly felt that their cries for help would be better received than those of the Soviet hierarchs, who had just repudiated all of Russia's foreign debt. Many groups did offer aid, but the largest and most effective was the American Relief Administration (generally known as the ARA and pronounced as one word by the Russians), an organization chartered by the Congress of the United States on 25 February 1919, to feed the war-ravaged nations of Europe. Its head was Herbert Hoover, a mining engineer-turned-humanitarian, who had first made a name for himself by feeding the hungry Belgians under the heel of the German 1914–1918 occupation. Hoover quickly agreed to give assistance, and the first massive famine relief mission in history was underway.

Negotiations began immediately with the Soviet government, with the ARA demanding a number of conditions, such as Russian non-interference with its work and the free movement of agents within the Soviet state. The Soviet government must have swallowed hard because Hoover's organization had given food to the Whites, its enemies in the Civil War, but they finally reached a consensus, known as the "Riga Agreement," signed in

Riga, Latvia, on 20 August 1921.[2] Soon after, on 26 August, the first American representatives of the ARA crossed the Russian border headed for Moscow to begin feeding Russia's starving millions. Four days later, on 30 August, James Rives Childs himself entered Russia with the second contingent of field workers, bound ultimately for Kazan in the Autonomous Tatar Republic, which was in one of the worst areas of the famine.

In his long and distinguished life, Rives Childs worked in an enviable array of fields. Although primarily a diplomat who spent three decades in the Near East, Childs was at one time or another a teacher, a newspaperman, a collector of rare first editions, a genealogist, a writer of fiction (both short stories and novels), a historian, a biographer, a memoirist, a world traveler, an editor of a serial publication, a leading authority on both Casanova and Restif de la Bretonne, and a recognized expert on the Arab world. He could count many prominent men and women among his friends, acquaintances, and coworkers, both in the literary world and in the world of diplomacy. His broad sampling of life and travel provided much material that later appeared in his writings.

Born in Lynchburg, Virginia, in 1893, Childs began his higher education at Virginia Military Institute but finished his B.A. degree at Randolph-Macon College in Ashland, Virginia. After working as a reporter for the Baltimore *American*, he taught high school, and then began graduate work at Harvard University, where he received a master's degree in literature in 1915. While at Harvard, Childs heard a lecture by the famous journalist John Reed. The man who would later become famous for his *Ten Days That Shook the World* had just returned from the Russian front and inspired Childs, ever the seeker of new experiences, to travel to France and become involved in the war as a civilian ambulance driver. He left in June 1915 and served on the French front for a number of months.

Having been engaged as a private tutor to an intellectually challenged young man from a wealthy family in Illinois, Childs returned in October to America to accept that position, and the following year, he took a post as an English teacher at Lawrenceville School in New Jersey. With the United States on the verge of entering the war, Childs joined the army early in 1917, and on his Easter vacation that year, he found himself in the visitors' gallery of the House of Representatives when it voted for a declaration of

---

[2]See Benjamin Weisman, "Herbert Hoover's 'Treaty' with Soviet Russia," *Slavic Review* 28/2 (June 1969): 276–88.

war against the German Empire. He was commissioned in the US Army on 15 August 1917, and left for France in December. Arriving in January, he was assigned, through confusion with another Childs, to the Cipher Bureau, where he served out the war. For his work in cryptography, Childs was belatedly awarded the Medal of Freedom in 1946. At the war's end, he joined the American Relief Administration and served with it in the Balkans. His work there earned him a commendation from the new Yugoslav government.

Somewhat later Rives worked as a reporter with the Associated Press (AP) in Washington, but when asked to sail to Europe to write a series of articles for the Belleau Wood Memorial Association, he eagerly obtained a leave of absence from AP to do so. Once in Paris, however, Childs vigorously sought a job as a foreign correspondent. No such work turned up, but as Childs later wrote in *Let the Credit Go*, what did turn up "was even more interesting." He learned while in Paris that the ARA was going into Russia, and he signed on and was quickly hired because of his past work with the organization in Serbia. He was sent to the ARA district centered in the Tatar Republic, whose capital was Kazan.

Childs kept a detailed diary throughout most of his tenure there, and after leaving the country, he cleaned up the rough manuscript and wrote an introduction, adding his comments and observations. This "book," as he called it, he titled "My Days in Red Russia," and it is the revised form that I have edited here.

This Russian famine diary is valuable as a historical source for a number of reasons. First, since Childs was in Russia almost throughout the entire tenure of the ARA, his account gives a good picture of the inner workings of the organization that made the greatest contribution to the feeding of Russia's starving. Second, it gives a vivid picture of horrible famine conditions in rural Russia. The ARA quickly established kitchens and orphanages in many places in the Tatar Republic, and an important part of Childs's work consisted of visiting these establishments to make certain that the food was being properly distributed. In these travels, he lived constantly with the grisly skeleton of famine and wrote vivid accounts of what he saw. Third, Childs produced as well a rare view of the functions of local government in the early years of the Soviet Union. Because the Communists had by 1921 established their complete ascendancy over the entire Russian nation, totally controlling all levels of government from the Kremlin down to the smallest district, Childs had to deal with local government officials at many levels and developed a solid working relationship with them. He sat in on their meetings, testified in their system of justice (probably the first American ever to do so), and wrestled with the byzantine intricacies of their local politics and customs. Many of the leaders became his friends. His close association with them led to his presenting these local politicians in a fair light as fellow human beings whose political ideals were born of a sincere belief that Communism would help all of humankind.

Another interesting facet is the work's portrait of the "enemies of the Revolution," the members of the bourgeoisie and the aristocracy that had for one reason or another remained behind in Russia. Their world had been destroyed, and now they had to survive in an environment that was not only alien to them, but hostile as well. Childs interacted with many of the ghosts of the old regime as they came to him to seek employment in their desperation to survive in the new Soviet state. Their histories are both sad and fascinating.

Finally, Childs's account gives an interesting view of the early months of the Soviet government's New Economic Policy (NEP, as it was known), a partial return to capitalism in an effort at economic rejuvenation, which many Communists saw as a backward step. The whole experiment intrigued Childs, and his pages offer numerous observations concerning its early days. Curiously, Childs, a self-styled socialist in those years, found great merit in this partial return to capitalism.

Childs's efforts to turn his diary into a published book were unsuccessful for reasons that still escape us, although we may be certain that, given his dogged determination, he tried. His failure to get it accepted by a press was probably due to the above-mentioned fact that he portrayed the Soviets as people who sincerely dreamed of a better world for themselves and their families and not the horned devils of American propaganda. In so doing he went against the then-prevailing political wind in the West. In the "Red Scare" in America at the time, with terrorists blowing up the US attorney general's home and the sensational trial of Nicolo Sacco and Bartolomeo Vanzetti, any portrait of the Russians in a favorable light would have had a great deal of difficulty finding an audience. Childs's attempt to present the Soviet Russians of his day as human beings was not his last time to swim against the prevailing current.

Since no one is likely to use this work to study Childs the man, I have standardized spellings, used more modern transliterations of Russian names, and corrected typographical errors, misspellings, and Childs's somewhat antiquated punctuation without cluttering the text everywhere with "[*sics*]." I have, however, left an occasional error to give a flavor of the man's work. Those I do so note. Sometimes Childs tended to report too much detail in accounts of how his vehicle was extricated from the mud on a primitive road or provided too much descriptive material about local customs or history. I have omitted many of these sections of the manuscript, or summarized long parts of the text in brackets, generally focusing instead on the parts of the work that deal only with the famine, the work of the ARA and its representatives, and the internal workings—both political and social—of the new Soviet Republic. All footnotes are mine.

The creation of any published work is really a compendium of labor of many people whose names never appear on its cover, and I would like to recognize those who helped me. First, I must thank posthumously the author of this diary, J. Rives Childs. As a graduate student employed part-time in the Rare Books and Manuscripts Division of the Alderman Library of the University of Virginia, I was assigned the task of sorting the forty-four boxes of papers that he had just given the university from his long career as a writer and a diplomat. I did not finish the collection as I left after working on it only two months for my first trip to the Soviet Union, but I was immersed in it long enough to discover the diary, and then and there I decided to try to edit and publish it one day. I must thank Mr. Childs not only for writing it, but for providing a typed copy from which I could work, thus saving me untold headaches in deciphering his inimitable penmanship. I came to know Childs personally, meeting him in 1971 in Charlottesville, and I visited him in his apartment in Nice, France, in 1973. Later I saw him many times in the Hotel Jefferson in Richmond, Virginia, where he came to live in the last years of his life. In our visits he told me stories of his career, of his writing, of efforts to become published, and of his personal life.

A special note of thanks must likewise go to my long-time friend Ann Stauffenberg Southwell, an employee in the manuscripts division in which the Childs manuscript is housed. Ann acted as my "point person" and was instrumental in my gaining permission to edit the manuscript and performed many services from the beginning to the end of the work that were of great value to me. I also owe a note of thanks to Mike Plunkett, Director of Special Collections of the Rare Books and Manuscripts Division of the Alderman Library, who enthusiastically gave me the go-ahead for the project.

A great thank-you must go to my colleagues and friends: William Allison, professor of History at Weber State University; J. Rollin Armour, a former dean of Mercer University and a professor *emeritus* of the university's Christianity Department; my friend Catharine Brosman, professor *emerita* of the French department of Tulane University; and Robert Good, my department chair, all of whom read parts of the manuscript and gave me good advice from their extensive experience. Any flaws in the work are, of course, mine.

I feel that I should thank posthumously two other members of the ARA with whom I passed some time over thirty years ago: Tom Barringer, the District Supervisor of Ekaterinoslav, who had me several times into his home; and Peter Muir and his wife, an agent with whom I spent a fascinating afternoon in the bar of the Claridges Hotel in London. Both men were most kind to share their experiences with a total stranger. Their accounts gave me valuable background information that helped in editing this work.

Finally, I am dedicating this edition to two former deans and our current dean of the Liberal Arts College of Mercer University: Rollin Armour (*fl.* 1980–1984), Douglas Steeples (*fl.* 1994–2000), and Richard Fallis, (*fl.* 2001 to the present). I have chosen to honor these men because they have been, in my thirty-some-odd years at Mercer, the only deans who have vigorously and sincerely promoted research—because they are the only deans we have ever had who themselves have done any. My hat is off to each of them!

ARA Farewell Banquet, June 1923. Left to right, Maxim Litvinov, Lev Kamenev, Cyril quinn, Karl Radek, and the Commissar of Health, N. Semashko Quinn.

Aleksandr Eiduk, representative plenipotentiary of the R.S.F.S.R. with will all foreign relief organizations.

In an orphanage on the Volga River.

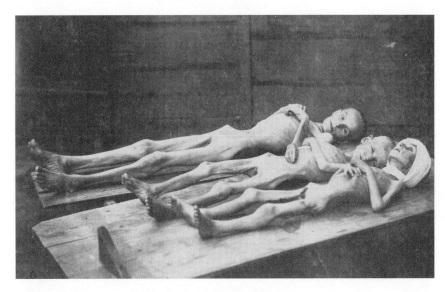

Bodies in a morgue in Ufa.

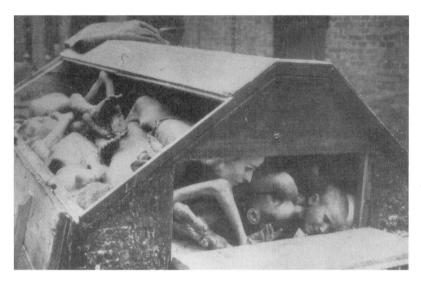

Disposal of corpses from a Tsaritsyn (later Stalingrad, now Volgagrod).

Dealers in human flesh.

CHILDS'S INTRODUCTION

Not long ago when I had made known my intention to a Russian friend to write a book upon Soviet Russia, I received in response a letter in which it was said: "How will you ever satisfy your conscience in writing upon this burning question without having given long and deep study to it? Should it not give you pause in attempting to write the truth about Russia that you have seen but a small part of the life of its people and that you have spent but a few months among us?" Now that the book which I had planned is completed, I have seen fit to take occasion to make answer to this inquiry in acknowledging a very deep sense of humility in approaching my task. What I have written makes no pretense of telling the whole truth about Soviet Russia. Truth is difficult enough to seek out even when circumstances most favor the search. When one confronts that task in the case of Russia of the Revolution and of the Soviets, the obstacles, which present themselves in the way of a clear and critical discernment of the truth, become nothing less than insuperable.

For eight years, or since the days of the gathering clouds of hatred in 1914, the mind of the world has suffered from such a poison of propaganda as to have dulled those perceptive faculties which make it possible to choose between truth and falsehood. Gas poisons the lungs and destroys the body, but propaganda poisons the mind and destroys the integrity of the human spirit. When more than half a century ago Sherman delivered Georgia over to fire and sword, thousands north of Mason's and Dixon's line found great moral satisfaction in the deed. But in 1914, when northern France was overrun and reduced to a like state of waste and desolation, those same ones, who had applauded Sherman, denounced the destruction of a part of France as the work of vandals. Today, when the Soviet government undertakes to confiscate property belonging to the church in order more effectually to wage war against death on the famine front, a wave of resentment arises in the outside world against the Bolsheviki. Yet when the suggestion was made in 1916 by Archimandrite Nicotine that the treasures of Yuriev Monastery, which amounted to millions of rubles, should be sacrificed for the waging of a war against life on the German front, the Allies hailed the idea as one worthy of the sacred cause in which they were mutually engaged with Russia.

This is not to say that Russia, Soviet Russia, is any less responsible than other nations of the world for the making obscure of truth and for even its deliberate falsification. He, indeed, would be a judicially minded one who would attempt to judge as to whether Communists or bourgeois, proletariat or capitalists have sinned most against [the] truth. The one faction has been led, out of fanatical zeal, to represent as existing in reality what was only conceived in theory; while the other, out of panic at the strange ghost which has reared its head in the world, was led to the expression of such unrestrained and chimerical descriptions as would have been impossible for the rationally minded prior to 1914. For this disordered state of mind in which a calm consideration of facts has been made well nigh impossible, there is to be held responsible that breakdown in national morality as a result of the war, that dusk into which the nations have descended through the evasion, as nations, of the same moral discipline, imposed by law and accepted by individuals.

There is no need here to enumerate the fictions, spread by over-enthusiastic Communists who have sought to paint the glories of a paradise upon earth which the Bolsheviki had erected upon the ruins of the autocratic empire of the tsar. There seemed few joys of a paradise to be realized by the people in the substitution of the autocracy of [Vladimir] Lenin[1] for the autocracy of a tsar. The world was not to be deceived by the declamations of Moscow. But the world was not satisfied in the mere rejection of the lies spread in the name of Bolshevism. One lie spoken against the capitalistic

---

[1] Vladimir Lenin (*né* V. I. Ulianov) (1870–1924) was born in Simbirsk in 1870, the son of a bureaucrat who had worked his way up in the tsarist bureaucracy to the rank of noble. Studying law on his own for a year, Lenin distinguished himself on the bar exams in 1891 but soon involved himself in revolutionary politics, joining the Marxist Social Democratic movement. Advancing his own program for the party caused a split in its ranks in 1903 into Bolshevik (Lenin's faction) and Menshevik (the Orthodox Marxists). Leading the Bolshevik overthrow of the Provisional Government in November 1917, he became the first dictator of the Soviet state and a Communist ikon after his death.

world provoked a greater one in return, so that it became as difficult to penetrate beneath this refuse to the root and to the truth in order to persecute Diogenes' search for an honest man. Truths, even in the form of Soviet government decrees, published to the world by the Moscow wireless, rarely found their way into the press of Europe or America, although there were defamatory documents purporting to the official which received wide enough circulation. It is only necessary to mention here the Sisson documents,[2] the decree purporting to nationalize women, and the order alleged to have appeared in the Moscow *Izvestiia*, decreeing the establishment of a Red Terror in Poland and the putting of that country to fire and sword.... [They] had the desired effect of giving opportunity for the expression of all the pent-up scurrility, harbored by the old reactionaries against the "bloodthirsty gang of assassins in Moscow," and of effectually stirring up in mild sections of citizenry, outside the influence of the Department of Justice, fear and apprehension of the horrid bogey of Bolshevism. Proof which was published that the Russian government had never been the author of such decree and that it could only have been fathered by the propaganda bureaus of the Poles or French was never given publication, however, in any but a few newspapers in America so that the greater part of the American public is left to the illusion to this day that it was the intent and resolve of the Soviet government to deliver a nation wholesale massacre....

From the effects of five years of such propaganda, it would be needless to say that it was impossible for me to have kept my mind wholly free before my entrance into Russia. Indeed, my own mind was so poisoned with preconceived prejudices against the existing regime, when I entered Russia a little more than a year ago, that it was perhaps natural that during my sojourn, my attention should have been attracted to that evidence more especially than any other which tended to disprove those ideas which I had

---

[2] The Sisson documents were a collection of papers acquired in Russia in October 1918 by Edgar Sisson, who was serving there as a member of the US Committee of Public Information, that "proved" that the Bolsheviks were the hired lackeys of the German government. Although the Germans were indeed subsidizing the Bolshevik cause for disruptive purposes, those documents were largely forgeries. They were used, however, by anti-Bolshevik groups to catalyze opposition to them in the Russian Civil War.

been led to entertain of life in Soviet Russia. That is I have succeeded in erasing this original bias, I cannot justly admit. But, in the attempt to clear my mind of cant, I have striven earnestly to set down faithfully and impartially only that which I have seen. Where the evidence has been hearsay, it has only been included when I can be reasonably assured of its truth. It has been my especial endeavor to avoid taking the side of any controversial question. To that end I have striven to keep my personal opinions as far as possible in the background in order to make way for the inclusion of every bit of trustworthy evidence which might be judged as illuminating in the slightest degree those perplexing and at all time obscured conditions in the life of a socialistic state.

The year which I have passed in Russia since August 1921 has not been spent as an independent investigator but as a relief worker in the service of the American Relief Administration. In the relations of the ARA with the [Soviet] government and in the administration of relief, there was much which came under my observation to shed light upon conditions. Also, the period of my residence in Russia was an extraordinary one in the life of the new Soviet State by reason of the famine which, in its extent, exceeded not only all previous Russian famines, but one might just say, all famines within historical time.

How then, to combine this three-fold task, to unite in one narrative the facts which I had accumulated of social conditions in a communistic republic with some account of the famine and of the work of the ARA so that no detail would be lost which would help to enlighten inquiring minds? This question, rendered all the more baffling by the rapidity of the change taking place daily in the life of the country, was at length resolved by the decision to leave the material which I had collected in its original form as a diary. Removed from such a setting, which fixed both time and place, it was feared that there might be abstracted from the narrative, in the process of the transformation of it into another form, no small part of the value which had thus been given it.

Most of the facts and incidents related in this diary have been taken from life in that part of Soviet Russia, lying in the basin of the Volga almost directly east of Moscow and centering in and about the city of Kazan and the Tatar Republic.[3] Almost all of the time which I have passed under the administration of the Soviets has been spent in what is known as the Kazan district of the ARA, embracing the following federated states of the Soviet government: Tatar Republic, Chuvash *oblast* (state), Mahri *oblast*, Votskaia *oblast*, and parts of the territories of the governments of Viatka and Perm. These divisions of the territory of Russia have comprised in the Kazan district, the largest administrative unit of the ARA in Russia. This territory, which would seem to be a fair cross-section for the study of life under the Bolshevik regime, I have traversed in and out of season and by almost every mode of conveyance for something more than a year, my work has taken me on brief excursions from Samara in the south to Petrograd in the north, and from Riga and Helsingfors [Helsinki] in the west to the Urals in the east.

From what I have written in the pages which follow, I would not have it concluded that I am in sympathy with either the practices or the aims of the present Russian government. The blunt fact is, however, that I am not prepared to give to Communists indiscriminately the names of thief or rogue as has been the popular pastime since 1917 in the outside world. For I have had the pleasure of meeting communists, as idealistic in their conceptions of life as any men whom I have ever known. Nor do I refuse to give to Lenin the title of statesman, for he is the only politician of the modern world within my recollection who has dared publicly to acknowledge his mistakes. And merely because he is a Jew, I cannot find cause to dispute the opinion that [Lev] Trotsky[4] is a military genius, for only

---

[3] The Tatar (often spelled Tartar in popular works) Autonomous Soviet Socialist Republic was founded on 27 May 1920, as one of the supposedly independent republics of the Soviet state that were based on ethnic considerations in the founding of the Soviet Union. Kazan, where Childs was stationed, was its capital. The Tatars were actually a mixture of the Volga Bulgars, Finns, and Mongols, and their language is one of the Ural-Altaic group.

[4] Lev Trotsky-Bronshtein (1879–1940) was the son of an industrious Jewish peasant whose hard work enabled him to send his intelligent son to private schools. Early involved in radical politics, Trotsky became a Marxist by the turn of the century, first joining the Menshevik faction of the Social Democratic Party. By the time of the October Revolution in 1917, he had become a Bolshevik and Lenin's right-hand man. After serving a short time as the Commissar of Foreign Affairs after the Revolution, he became the Commissar of War, creating in that capacity the Red

a genius could have wielded together the ragged and undisciplined hordes of men, who called themselves soldiers after desertion from the Imperial Army, and have whipped them into a condition which makes the Russian Army the equal of almost any in Europe. I am neither a Red nor a radical, but I am not hesitant in confession that so firmly do I hold to the conviction that the only worship in life of any avail is that of the truth, that I have not refused at any time to set down in these pages facts and impressions of that life which I saw going on about me in Soviet Russia which may not have squared with my personal prejudices or opinions.

And so it is that a year in Russia has brought home to me the conviction that, if the world desires to avoid passing in the future through as great a travail as Russia has suffered these last five years, it had better turn from scoffing to a serious study as to whether the same ailments, which brought ruin and desolation upon Russia, do not exist elsewhere among other countries of the world.

Army. Losing out in the power struggle to succeed Lenin after 1924, he was finally exiled to Mexico, where he was assassinated by a Soviet agent.

The Diary

One day, late in July 1921, I was seated in the provincial Café de Commerce in Chateau Thierry, making plans for a journey to Vienna and Budapest. An American who was by my side and who had been leisurely engaged in the reading of a newspaper turned towards me and casually remarked: "There's a famine in Russia and appeal has been made to America for aid. It seems that the American Relief Administration may go in."

I took the paper which was offered me and read of Maxim Gorky's appeal, of the consideration which Hoover was giving the plea, and of plans which were being projected for a conference in Riga between ARA officials and representatives of the Soviet government. Instantly, my imagination was fired with the idea of going myself to Soviet Russia; for that altogether new world had been a goal toward which my dreams had been directed since 1917. There had been such a conflict of opinions concerning what had taken place in Russia since the Revolution, of what was happening now and of what was likely to occur in the future that, as one pursued by a desire to seek out the truth, I was taken hold incontinently of an impulse to go and see and satisfy myself of the truth or falsity of all that which I had read or heard about Red Russia.

In 1919 I had served with the American Relief Administration in the Balkans, and therefore, upon the conclusion of the Riga agreement a short while later between the ARA and the Russian government, I did not find it difficult to fulfill this desire in receiving an appointment to one of the first of the staffs of the ARA directed to Russia for the organization there of the relief.

August 27, 1921—It was en route from Paris to Riga, soon after passing Kovno in Lithuania, that I made my first acquaintance with citizens of Bolshevik Russia. There were but a half a dozen of them in the *wagon-lit*, and word soon passed around in almost whispers that we had been joined at Kovno by the Soviet courier who was on his way from Warsaw to Moscow.

[Carlton] Bowden,[5] who was also on his way to report to the ARA in Riga for service in Russia, expressed a desire to see and talk with this individual of almost another world. The *wagon-lit* conductor soon brought back word that the courier would be glad to receive us in his compartment.

I found myself a few moments later in the presence of a man like anyone of the other representatives of different nationalities to be found on the train and, in no way resembling a monster. He was attired in collar and cravat and in a suit of clothes which would not have distinguished him in any crowd anywhere in America. He did not growl or show his teeth at the questions which were put to him of famine conditions in Russia but answered them pleasantly and with as much good will as any ordinary human being under the same circumstances would have done.

Riga, August 28, [1921]—Here upon the threshold of the strange new world for which I am bound, I had the good fortune to meet two Americans who have played no minor part in the Russian drama as it has been viewed from American newspapers: ...Colonel Edward Ryan, Red Cross Commissioner for the Baltic, and my old friend and roommate during the Paris Peace Conference, Emmett Kilpatrick. The coincidence in our meeting rests in the fact that I had something to do in America with the part which each has played in Russia.

Colonel Ryan would like very much to return to Russia but is prevented by the displeasure in which he finds himself with the Soviet government and of which I had had something to do, and Kilpatrick only regrets that he was not able to make his exit from a Moscow prison sooner than he was permitted but a few days since, and with that also, I regret to reflect, I had something to do. So soon as I heard that the two were in Riga, I sent word to them that I was at the ARA house on the beach outside the city and was desirous of arranging a meeting, and very soon afterwards I heard from Colonel Ryan that he would call in the afternoon.

Colonel Ryan is a tall, angular man who presents an appearance of having come from the southwest of America and of having spent his early days in taming bucking broncos. He has been in relief work in a half a dozen parts of the globe, having served before the World War in Mexico, China, and later in Serbia, but is chiefly known to the world as the author of a

---

[5] Carlton Bowden became the chief of the Petrograd ARA district.

famous report to the State Department on conditions in Russia which was made in the spring of 1920, when he made a surreptitious entry into Russia with the Estonian Peace Commission. I had always desired to make an acquaintance of Colonel Ryan because it was while engaged in newspaper work in Washington that I had gained access to the confidential report and had obtained authority for its publication.

How the report was obtained and sent out over the wires of a great press association almost at the same hour on an evening in May 1920, when Eliot Wadsworth of the Red Cross was reading it to a gathering of the most distinguished newspaper owners in New York, under the promise that the contents of it would be kept secret, is a story which is too long to be told here. Predicting as it did the fall of the Soviet government within six months and consisting of part of a personal conversation with [Georgii] Chicherin,[6] the report was a temporary newspaper sensation. Its publication, as may be readily understood, created consternation in the State Department and the Red Cross, and I enjoyed the infinite amusement of being subjected to cross-examination by a member of the secret service of the State Department as to the means by which I had obtained the text of the report. The source of my information was never discovered, and that is a further reason for withholding now the details of the manner in which a real newspaper "scoop" was attained.

It was not until that story had been published that I came to realize the dangerously responsible position which a newspaper man occupies in public life. For I have since learned that it was the publication of Colonel Ryan's report and the compromise position in which he was put with the Soviet officials which contributed more than any other one factor to the non-participation of the Red Cross in the great work of Russian relief for which

---

[6] Georgii Chicherin (1872–1936) was an aristocrat with a long, distinguished family history, who joined the Bolshevik wing of the Social Democrats in 1905, but soon switched to the Menshevik faction and became a virulent opponent of Lenin. A somewhat mentally disturbed man, he joined the British Labour Party during World War I and turned strongly pacifist and became once again a Bolshevik. Returning to Russia early in 1918, he soon succeeded Trotsky as Commissar of Foreign Affairs, a post he held until 1930, when health forced his retirement. An accomplished pianist, he spent his last years writing a study of Mozart, which was finally published thirty-five years after his death. Today he is known as the Father of Soviet Diplomacy.

the Red Cross had been preparing since the close of the World War. I informed Colonel Ryan, when he called, of the reason inspiring my desire to meet him. He took my confession, I thought, in very good part.

"I would have murdered you at the time," was what he said. "It placed me in the embarrassing position of appearing to have broken my promise to the Soviet government that I would write nothing or make no reports after leaving Russia. As a matter of fact, and as you know, I wrote nothing, but at the insistence of Colonel [?]Oulds in Paris, I went there and communicated by word of mouth some of the observations I had made during my visit to Moscow and Petrograd. Colonel Oulds saw fit to draw up a summary of what I had recounted and forwarded it to the Red Cross, and this report of Colonel Oulds was in turn communicated to the State Department."

As Colonel Ryan seemed to be under the impression from further conversation that the State Department had deliberately made public the report in order to embarrass him, reasoning that the Department had been annoyed by his unauthorized and unofficial visit to Russia, I proceeded to relieve him of his misapprehension by explaining as well as I could, without however committing myself too deeply, the details of the unofficial means by which the report had been obtained.

"I always thought you should feel grateful to me for the publicity, which I gave you, Colonel," I finally remarked.

"It was enough," was the laconic comment.

August 29, [1921]—I did not see Kilpatrick until today when we had lunch together at the Hotel Frankfort-on-the-Main. Poor boy, the buoyancy and impulsiveness of his Celtic character have been sadly crushed by the months of prison confinement to which he has been subjected. The luxuriant and carelessly brushed shock of red hair was the same, but it was difficult to recognize the "Kil" of rattling spurs and irrepressibly joking spirits whom in our apartment at 18 rue Gustave Zedé in Paris, used to throw the dancing parties from [sic] the Peace conference in an uproar by the drawling southern voice and accentuated bow with which he approached a partner with an invitation to a dance.

It was with the greatest difficulty that "Kil" was held to any continuity in the narrative of his experiences in Russia, from the time that he was taken prisoner on the Crimean front in October 1920 until his release in August

1921. And all was hyperbole. One would have thought from his account that the streams and rivers of Russia were running with blood rather than with water. To judge, too, from his account, it would appear that there were as many people within the walls of prison in Russia as there were without. Prison cells, dungeons and blood; tiers upon tiers of cells; and blood, discoloring the entire landscape: That was the impression which I formed of soviet Russia from Kilpatrick's description.

Occasionally he drew a clearly formed picture as, for instance, when he told of his experiences in the South of Russia and of an interview which he had had with [Semen] Budennyi,[7] the great Bolshevik calvary [sic] leader who had risen from a sergeant in the old army to that of a cavalry commander of Red Army. After his capture in the South, it seemed that Kilpatrick had been accorded singular freedom, and he had himself gained the impression that he had only to report to Moscow as a matter of form in order to obtain his release. On his journey to Moscow, having learned that he was in the vicinity of Budennyi's army, he had requested an interview with him. Boldness and audacity were not the least of Kilpatrick's characteristics.

Upon being conducted before Budennyi, Kilpatrick saluted him as "General."

"I am not a general," Budennyi replied. "We have no titles in the Red Army. I am a commander and that, only by virtue of the wishes and desires of the soldiers who constitute my army."

Nothing abashed, Kilpatrick proceeded to a catechization of the distinguished officer.

"General," Kilpatrick began and was interrupted again.

"My soldiers call me 'Tovarishch' (comrade), but if you please, you may address me as 'Commander.'"

"Then, Commander," Kilpatrick continued, "if you are willing to answer, I should like to know what book in your opinion has exercised the greatest influence on your life?"

"I have never read a book," was the answer.

---

[7] Semen Mikhailovich Budennyi (1883–1973) was the founder and long-time leader of the Soviet cavalry and Civil War hero. He was made a Marshal of the Soviet Union.

"Never read a book?"

"No."

"Hmm, well, General—Commander, to what do you attribute the secret of your great success as a cavalry leader?"

The commander did not hesitate long for a reply: "I never let my men know when they are defeated."

Kilpatrick has always been a great reader and particularly fond of poetry. Before he entered the army in 1917, he had edited a weekly newspaper in Alabama. It was in prison, he said, that poetry became for him his greatest consolation. "I dug up from my memory all the poems I had ever read," he said to me. "And the night I was put in solitary confinement I think I would have gone mad had I not been able to recollect old lines from the "Prisoner of Chillon." I used to tread the cell and strive to repeat for hour after hour poems but dimly remembered and half-forgotten. Many of them came back to me in their entirety, and it occupied my mind to attempt to piece out from day to day a verse which had not been remembered for years." [Called before a Bolshevik judge, he was told that he was going to die and "very foolishly" asked for clemency.]

"The examining judge cast at me a very critical and scornful glance. 'You, a foreigner, an American spy, have the impertinence to ask mercy of me,' he shouted. 'Look about you in this room. Do you know that it has been drenched with the tears of Russian women, and blood of Russian men, people of my race and of my flesh. And do you think that I ever showed them mercy? I do not know what mercy means, you idiot.' In that moment...as I stood there confused and alarmed at what the next moment would bring forth, there recurred to my mind that scene in the courtroom from *The Merchant of Venice*: 'The quality of mercy is not strained, / It droppeth as the gentle rain from heaven / Upon the place beneath.'"[8]...

It was an hour before the departure of the Riga-Moscow train at ten PM that I made my way to the station and pushed through struggling crowds to the first class railway coach which had been assigned to the second ARA party, which I was accompanying to Moscow. Bowden had gone on to

---

[8] Kilpatrick must have received some mercy since he was eventually released and was leaving Russia as Childs was entering.

sweeping the streets. But, aside from these, there was little life to be observed and the depressing atmosphere given the broad avenues through which we passed by this absence of human activity was accentuated by the unkempt appearance of almost every structure of what represented once an exclusive apartment house or a magnificent store.

Arriving at Spiridonovka, we alighted before a great massive grey-stone building which possessed almost the appearance of a prison. "It should be able to withstand a long siege," was the inspiriting comment of Carroll as we surveyed it. And, as we marched into our little fortress, I do not think there was one of us but who accepted the insinuation of our uncertain position with as much seriousness as it had been expressed in however light a mood by Carroll.

There were eleven of us as we sat down to dinner that night by the light of a candle in a bare dirty room and made a meal from canned food. These, the first of us in Russia, included, besides the party which I had accompanied from Riga: Carroll, [Will] Seaforth, [Van Arsdale] Turner, [John P.] Gregg, [John A.] Lehrs, [Columbia P.] Murray, and [Harry J.] Fink.

Moscow, September 4, [1921]—One cannot gain an impression of Moscow in a day nor in several days because the mind is bewildered by the wealth of impressions made upon it. But in a letter written today I have made the first attempt at giving some coherent picture, not perhaps of the city so much as the personal reaction which one forms after life for a few days in it.

[What follows is a direct quote by Childs of the letter mentioned above.]

I wish...that I might give a faithful picture of my impressions of this strange unreal city of Moscow but for the difficult portrayal the extraordinary emotions which it awakens there is demanded the morbidly-minded genius of a Poe or an E. T. Hoffman [sic]. It is like some great city upon which a pestilence has settled and in which the population moves in hourly expectation of death—that is one impression I have formed of it, and yet another is that it resembles a city of another world the inhabitants of which move by motives inverse to those which guide the lives of earthly beings. Two Americans who have lived or somehow subsisted in Moscow through the Revolution, came to our office yesterday, and one, a dentist, declared that when one meets a friend on the streets in Moscow and the question is put as to where one is going, the answer is certain to be, "I have started for home." The implication of course is that no one is free from the fear and constant apprehension of arrest....

One cannot escape the association of this time and period with that of the French Revolution. One seems to be living through the pages of [Thomas] Carlyle.[10] Then Josephine Beauharnais, destined to be the future wife of the Emperor Napoleon [I], was working as a menial in a public house, even as today in Moscow, for example, the Countess [Nadia] Tolstoy, who has come to the ARA as a housekeeper, scrubs her own floors and cuts her slender supply of fuel while who can foretell what the morrow may hold in store for her? For sheer extreme contrasts I doubt if there is a city in the world today comparable to Moscow. One must admit that its streets are clean, there are electric lights, and many of the streets are illuminated at night, but the shops everywhere are boarded up, there is little movement upon the streets, and pervading all, there is such an atmosphere of depression as I never believed it possible for a city to communicate. And there are mysteries to this city of which Eugène Sue never dreamed in the wildest flights of his imagination when he wrote of the *Mysteries of Paris*. There is the Extraordinary Commission, commonly called the Cheka,[11] which passes its judgments and executes its decrees with the dispatch and

---

[10] Thomas Carlyle wrote a celebrated history of the French Revolution.

[11] *Chrezvychainaia Komissiia* [The Extraordinary Commission: Cheka for short] was the first name given to many forms of the Soviet secret police. Founded in December 1917 by the Polish Bolshevik Felix Dzherzhinskii, it quickly became the organization for the suppression of opposition, and it led the government's Red Terror against the real and imaginary enemies. It was disbanded by decree in February 1922, and its duties were given to the Ministry of Internal Affairs. Childs continues, however, to refer to the agents performing these duties by their original name. Suspicious of American motives, the Cheka kept a vigilant eye on the ARA agents.

unobtrusiveness of the Ku Klux Klan. When one speaks of the Cheka, the voice is lowered and the tones of the syllables are hushed.

I went for a walk through the city the other night with an American who had been in Moscow before the Revolution. The main streets were fairly illuminated; the smaller streets, not at all. Care must be taken in traversing the sidewalks of the unlighted streets for there are still unfilled holes made by the shell fire of the opposing forces who fought pitched battles in the city during the Revolution. Upon certain street corners, which one served as strategic points, there are entire buildings which were shattered by artillery fire and whose crumbling walls were literally pockmarked by rifle and machine gun fire. As we passed down what had once been the business center of the town, I was pointed out store after store which once had been cheerfully illuminated and whose windows once had been crowded with a rich display of goods. In some stores there remained the plate glass, but in many the front had been defaced by rough wooden boards to replace the broken glass which had only temporarily barred the entrance of the pilfering mobs of 1917 in Moscow. A darkened corner of a street represented what had once been one of the gayest cafes in Moscow and bare cheerless walls, a once great department store.

But there is a real danger of overdrawing the picture for after all it is not the material poverty of Moscow which impresses one, and that is great, but, if it might be so expressed, it is the apparent absence of a heart and soul with which one is struck so forcibly and pathetically. I think that perhaps the briefest and most just characterization of Moscow would be to say that it is a city without love. It is rare, very rare, that one sees a smile, and it must be because there is rust and corrosion upon the heart and pall of fear upon the soul. This afternoon I took a walk through the Esplanade or park which runs for some distance through the city. It was Sunday and there was a crowd of several thousand people pressing elbows in the path which runs between rows of trees down the center of the street across the city. A woman with the faded face of an aristocrat moves slowly along hawking cigarettes. She wears a magnificent plumed hat, but her skirt and waist and worn-down shoes are those of a scullery maid. Three cossacks in their picturesque flowing skirts [military greatcoats] and great fur caps pass by and give almost the only touch of bright color to the picture. Now a man is approaching in a straw hat and an overcoat. Behind him is a stout Jewess, whose pierced ears are weighted by enormous blue stones which seem to be suspended almost to the shoulders. Alongside are men and women in rags whose delicate countenances betray their former positions of affluence, and there are intermingled with them the scavengers of humanity, the speculators, attired in luxurious fur coats and expensive hats and shoes. Some women have nothing but socks of the length of children's to protect their limbs and others have no stockings at all. An orchestra is playing an air of [Peter] Tchaikovsky from an open air stand, but the tired-faced men and women, seated and standing listlessly about, glance absently before them as if the music of the spheres could not release the spell put upon their souls.

September 10, [1921]—There is a restaurant which we have found on the Arbat,[12] and in which we have been eating dinner, which is like an oasis in this city of dead souls. While it is by no means pretentious, for indeed its surroundings and exterior are quite humble, the food and furnishings and atmosphere of the interior are reminiscent in a way of Furet's in the Latin quarter of Paris or of a quaint bohemian resort I stumbled upon quite by accident one night in Sofia in Bulgaria. There is this difference: That in the Russian restaurant, which is located in the basement of a dilapidated building on a side street, there are one or two superbly beautiful pieces of tapestry, saved from the wreckage of the Revolution, hung alongside paltry chromos.[13] These last, represent no doubt, the only furnishings which the proprietress, wife of a former Russian general, can now afford to buy. And, intermingled with a few beautifully carved oak chairs, there are wooden

---

[12] The Arbat was a street designating an area of bohemian types such as writers, artists, radicals, non-conformists, etc. Today the "New Arbat" is much the same but has developed the air of a tourist trap.

[13] Chromolithographs.

stools. There is a persian rug in one room and matting on the floor of the others. There is obtainable in the restaurant a quite excellent choice of food consisting generally of chicken, veal, beef steak, lamb, potatoes, cauliflower, white bread, excellent tea and coffee, and sweet cakes. A meal of four courses amounts to about forty thousand rubles, or approximately ninety cents.

I am told that this is the first restaurant to be opened in Moscow since the inauguration of the New Economic Policy[14] of the government, and I know that the American correspondents travel across town from the Savoy Hotel in order to be able to avail themselves of the luxury of a meal cooked by some one other than themselves. While wretches outside on the streets are dragging their hungry way along in rags, we sit here, sipping our coffee as in any Paris restaurant. Windows in this restaurant, situated in a basement, arise slightly above the street so that a view is given of some of the side tables to those who are passing overhead on the street. One evening we were startled at the sight of a poor ravenous-looking woman who was staring with envious eyes down at our table, where heaps of food were being piled. I think we all winced as we caught her grimace and the shout of "Bourgeois!" which was flung contemptuously at us as she made off.

There are plain-faced men with the clothes and bearing of workmen who are seated about the tables; there is an occasional officer of the Red Army; and every evening promptly at six there is to be seen making her entrance a young beautiful blonde woman in sables, bediamoned and bejeweled, who looks as if she might have stepped, but a few moments before, from some smart dressmaker's on the Champs Elysées. She is an artist and as such has enjoyed the special protection of the government. A gossip at an adjoining table describes her as the evil genius of a talented young Red soldier who was induced to commit suicide as a result of her caprices; and that infatuation for her and the desire to administer to her

---

[14] The New Economic Policy (NEP) was Lenin's partial return to capitalism, which permitted the opening of such small restaurants and shops. The policy was designed to jumpstart the Russian economy, which was prostrate after a world war, civil war, and foreign intervention. It very much resembled the present-day Russian economy.

expensive tastes brought a Bolshevik commissar to his death at the hands of the ever-watchful Extraordinary Commission.[15]

September 11, [1921]—Tonight I attended my first public gathering in Russia, one of the far-famed gypsy concerts given at the Conservatory of Music. I have always had an especial predilection for gypsy music because for me it is so intimately associated with those great days of 1919 in Serbia and the Balkans when, in every hill town which one visited, there was to be heard the plaintive notes of the music of the Romanies [gypsies], which so captivates the pessimistic, mournful soul of the Slav. But here in Moscow I was doomed to disappointment in the concert, for the setting of the bleak stage chilled the imagination, and the gypsies themselves, if they were gypsies, assumed too artificial a character. But wherever one goes in Russia, there is never the rise of being bored for there is everywhere and at all times interesting observations to be made and reflections over which to ponder. At the concert it was the audience which furnished the dramatic interest and not the stage. The only well-dressed people present were from the foreign missions of Latvia, Estonia, Poland, and Great Britain. But even the correct Britishers felt the necessity of subduing their attire to harmonize with those of the natives and, in order to avoid the conspicuousness which their well-tailored clothes might give, they were for the most part to be observed in colored flannel shirts. With the women generally, it was different, for with truly feminine ingenuity they had found it possible to scrape together nondescript articles of apparel to make a not discreditable appearance.

Upon first glance at the audience, which seems to be composed principally of workers and their families, by fancy, heightened by the accounts in the European and American press of the unruly Communistic citizenry of Moscow, lent itself readily to the apprehension that any moment might be the signal of disorder. But I waited in vain. Except in outward appearance there was nothing to distinguish this audience in the Socialist Federated Soviet Republic of Russia from anyone if hundreds of pleasure-seeking audiences in the United States of America.

September 12, [1921]—Since Seaforth and Gregg left last week, the day after my arrival in Moscow, for an extended inspection tour of the famine area in the Volga, there have come with each succeeding day stronger and

---

[15] The Cheka.

stronger confirmatory reports of the frightful situation which exists in Kazan and Samara. Carroll had announced it as the intentions to inaugurate child feeding operations here in Moscow. But the Soviet government has been so earnest in the expression of the wish that supplies be rushed to the Volga and that all our energy be first directed to that region that, when a brief telegram came from an American correspondent, who had seen but just a traverse of the territory between Kazan and Samara, giving a brief account of some of the horrors of the famine which had been witnessed, it was decided to abandon the original program and to delay operations in Moscow until work had been instituted in the Volga [region].

To me fell the lot of making up the first food train destined for the famine region and which it had been decided to dispatch to Kazan in the Tatar Republic[.] Turner, who had been given temporarily the work of the supply division of the unit, was associated with me. The date fixed for the departure of the train was Wednesday, September 14, or but a little more than two weeks after the arrival of the staff of the ARA in Russia and less than a week after the arrival of the foodstuffs from Riga.

"We'll tell the government we want the train to go Wednesday," Carroll explained with a sly twinkle in his eye, "and that will mean we shall get it out of here Thursday or Friday."

The composition of the train was fixed as follows: Fourteen food cars containing sufficient rations to feed thirty thousand children for one month; three flatcars upon which to place two trucks and an automobile; one cook car and finally two saloon cars to accommodate American newspaper correspondents and the ARA personnel which would accompany the first relief expedition.

September 15, [1921]—Our requirements were submitted to the railroad authorities of the government on Monday, September 12, and the various cars to meet our needs became to assemble in the freight station of Boina on Tuesday. Turner, meanwhile, had been busy attending to the loading of the food from Latvian wagons which were slowly arriving from Riga. Tuesday afternoon everything was in place but the saloon and cook cars, and though I had never had any expectation of having the train in order in time to leave on Wednesday, I hastened to the railroad authorities to press them for the remaining cars. There was much telephoning, a conference of at least seven officials, and at the end [of which] I was informed that it would be possible to supply us with but one passenger saloon car. I enjoyed the further discomfiture of learning that a delay of one day would be necessary in order to switch the train onto the Kazan line and that therefore there was no possibility of dispatching the train until Thursday. After a great deal of parleying I consented to the delay, which had been anticipated from the beginning, but [I] held out steadfastly for the two saloon cars. An answer was promised on the next day.

Upon going to the railroad [yards] on Wednesday the two saloon cars, one of them an International Wagon-lit Sleeper, were found in place, but the cook car was yet absent. This was promised by the evening, together with all necessary cooking appliances. Noontime was set for departure. The hour of noon was fast approaching on Thursday when the cook car, for which I had been so anxiously waiting, was shifted into sight in the yards and [?] Bublikov, [the] government railroad representative, accompanied me to inspect it. The car was found to be horribly dirty and Bublikov, a middle-aged man but radiating with superabundant nervous energy, instantly suggested that if he be given two hours time, the car would be replaced by another one. It did not take a second look at the car to give consent.

This Bolshevik official Bublikov, who I am told is a Lett, offers an interesting study and subject for speculation. He is short and thin, almost with that lean and hungry look of Cassius, wears on his chin the stubble of a goatee and possesses the cold penetrating eye of one devoid of the instinct of mercy. He is ever ready with a smile and subdued chuckle when in my presence, but there is something sinister about his good humor, and of all men whom I have met in Russia, I think I would least of all prefer to be called for judgement before Bublikov. There is ever in view upon his hip an automatic gun which marks him out as a representative of the Extraordinary Commission.

Together we proceeded to the telephone while Bublikov got into communication with the railway department of the Cheka. His conversation, as rapid and incisive as the rat-a-tat-tat of a machine gun, was somewhat as follows as I learned afterwards from my awe-stricken interpreter.

"Hello. Is that the railway Cheka? This is Bublikov. Find a first class cooking car at so and so and have an engine bring it to station Boina not later than two o'clock. Put a representative of the Cheka in the engine cab and notify the responsible railway authorities that unless the car is here within two hours, those responsible for the delay will be placed under arrest. That is all. Do you understand?" There was no misunderstanding about the order, for almost on the dot of two o'clock the car appeared in view and was attached to the train.

The party of ARA representatives and newspaper correspondents for which places had been provided on the train included: Dr. Vernon Kellogg, the chairman of the National Research Council and in Russia as Mr. Hoover's representative; Ivar W. Wahren, formerly of the ARA in Finland and Czechoslovakia, who together with the writer, had been assigned as the permanent ARA representatives in Kazan; Elmer T. Burland, investigator and formerly with the ARA in Austria; B. C. Conger of the Philadelphia *Public Ledger*; Walter Duranty of the New York *Times*, Ralph Pulitzer of the New York *World*; Floyd Gibbons of the Paris Chicago *Tribune;* Isaac Don Levine of the Chicago *Daily News*; Miss Beatty of the International News Service; Varges of the International Film Service; Colonel Lynch, English radical and MP, and Colonel Mackay, Canadian MP.

September 16, [1921] en route Moscow-Kazan—It was not until about noon that we commenced to enter the borders of the famine area where the pinch of hunger and disease was visibly evident on almost every side. All the afternoon we were passing small Russian railway stations into which hundreds of refugees from the famine-stricken villages were crowding with all their earthly possessions. Many of them had pitched their household furniture and furnishings into the form of a rude shelter, much after the form of a pup tent, and into this they had crawled with scarcely any vestige of human expression left to their features. Standing here and there upon the station platform were little girls and boys with stomachs so bloated out of all proportion that they appeared as such unnatural and hideous freaks as are exhibited in museums. I carelessly threw some apple peelings from the window of the saloon car at the stations, and the children, who were standing about outside, scrambled for them as if each peeling represented a coin.

At one station at which we halted for more than [an] hour, a train was standing on a siding alongside us which was swarming with peasants. There were some two thousand of them, it appeared upon inquiry, jammed forty or fifty into a single boxcar. They had been in the same station for two weeks, waiting patiently, while their friends starved and died, for the engine which would come to transport the train to Siberia and to some community where they might find food. They bore with them within the boxcars all the property which they owned on earth. No one was feeding them, and how they contrived to find food for themselves, God only knew. Their bread, which they pathetically held out in their hands for exhibition, disclosed in every specimen examined an admixture of clay or [and?] straw.[16] It was the most repulsive-looking substitute for food which I have ever seen, and Dr. Vernon Kellogg, an authority who had been active in relief work in many starving countries, stated that such bread evidenced the reduction of the population to such extremities as he had never before had witness of.

Although we expect to feed one hundred thousand and possibly two hundred thousand children of the eight hundred thousand in the Tatar Republic, it seems clear that thousands of children are doomed to an inescapable death for want of food, and it is equally evident that the adult population must die like flies unless, by some miracle, the Soviet government, the ARA, or some other foreign agency is able to relieve them. The great surprise of the journey from Moscow to Kazan, however, was not so much the extent and acuteness of the hunger, since I had been prepared for that by previous reports, as it was the relief which the Soviet government was administering. At almost every station passed in the famine area, hundreds of peasants were to be observed assembled with their horses and carts to receive the seed grain which was being weighed out and distributed direct from the sides of boxcars in which the grain had been transported to the locality. The government, it appears, considers that the paramount relief problem of the moment is that of ensuring the planting of a crop. It is not until the distribution of the seed has been affected that the energy of the government will be turned to that of the relief of the population with foodstuffs.

September 17, [1921], en route [from] Moscow to Kazan—The sun had dropped below the horizon and twilight was deepening as we came into sight of the Volga, "Mother Volga," as it is called by the Russians. Looking down upon it from the bridge over which we passed, I could not fail to be

---

[16] Childs describes here the famous *lebeda*, which was the ersatz bread made from clay and straw or grass. The name is taken from a grain-like weed that was often used to make it.

disappointed by its monotonous banks which were unrelieved by any shrubbery or shade. It seemed just another river, that was all, and if I had not been anticipating the sight of it, it would have been passed without claiming my attention. It was after nine o'clock and quite dark when our train of something more than twenty cars was shifted into the station of Kazan. The sight of numberless orphaned children, homeless widows, and despairing old men, hovering like alarmed and strickened birds of passage about the food which he had brought, gave mute testimony of their need and of the famine conditions of the country in which we found ourselves.

A cold drizzling rain was falling to accentuate the misery visible in the mud and cold outside. We were definitely on the famine front, and though there was no pageantry or alarm of arms to distinguish a front such as one viewed on the battlefields of France, I think it struck both Wahren and me at the moment of our arrival of how infinitely more worthwhile it was to engage in peaceful combat on a famine front, which had for its object the saving of life, than that on the battle front, whose major objective was the taking of it.

September 18, [1921], Kazan—Early in the morning word was received that the leading commissars of the Tatar Republic Government, including those who correspond in the Soviet administration to the president and the prime minister, would receive us at midday in the *Sovnarkom*,[17] that is to say, the headquarters of the Soviet of People's Commissars [sic] of the Tatar Socialist Soviet Republic. The automobile, which has been transported from Moscow, had been unloaded from the railway truck in the meanwhile, and therefore, shortly before the hour fixed for the meeting, we set out. Our way led us through what appeared to be the main street of the city and over rough cobbled stones, road over which the chauffeur was obliged to pick very carefully his way since there were among the entire street small but treacherous depressions. The houses which one passed were almost without exception of stone, extending to two, but rarely to more than three stories. As in Moscow every building, which betrayed previous use as a commercial house or store, was now empty and deserted and took on such a forlorn and dilapidated appearance that involuntarily there recurred the line of [the Irish

---

[17] *Sovnarkom* is the short form of *Sovetnyi Narodnyi Komissariat*, the name of the Soviet cabinet.

poet Thomas] Moore: "I feel like one who treads alone some banquet hall deserted." It was not inapt, I considered, for all of this country had once served as the banquet hall for a certain privileged class who had spent their time in feasting or in the lavish display of wealth and now these guests who had lived off the country were gone, and they had left their banquet hall to be reclaimed and restored by their former servants who must now make the best that could be of the disorder.

And what of the new masters? Were they endeavoring conscientiously to restore the wreck and the ruin which had been caused and to discharge truly their responsibilities, or were they the unscrupulous and unprincipled looters of the country which they were represented to be by the press of the outside world?

We drove up to a large amber-colored stone building which, we were told, had formerly been occupied as a residence by the military governor of the military district of Kazan. This was the capitol or state house, one might say, of the Autonomous Tatar Republic. Upon entering, the hall and the rooms of the houses were found bare and neglected in appearance. The only ornament upon the walls were the flaming red propaganda posters which generally depict the Herculean figure of a sooty laborer in the act of toil or a Red soldier in an attitude of defense. As I climbed the stairs to the conference chamber, I recollected that I had viewed such posters previously in the offices of the Department of Justice in Washington, where they were exhibited as the work of a criminal hand. Had crime then been made legitimate in Russia, or was there something awry in the American conception of what constituted criminality?

We entered the simple office room of the President of the Tatar Republic, and a few moments after our entry the president and the prime minister followed us in, together with the various commissars or heads of the different departments of the government. The reception accorded us was quite simple and wholly lacking in an effusive display. Hands were shaken all around and after the soviet officials had taken seats in one corner of the room and the Americans had grouped themselves in the other, the Prime Minister [Keshaf] Muktarov commenced to speak.

It was unnecessary to waste words in any speech-making, he explained in the opening declaration. The government of the Tatar Republic understood that the ARA had come to Kazan for the serious purpose of administering an aid which the country sorely needed. Every facility for promoting this relief would be granted the ARA by the Tatar Republic. Therefore, if the Americans would state their immediate needs, prompt attention would be paid to their fulfillment. These needs were enumerated very briefly by Burland. They included an interpreter, an automobile, at least six trucks for the unloading of supplies from the train which we had brought, a stenographer, and so forth. As Burland's requests were translated by the interpreter accompanying us, they were noted down by Muktarov. At the end of [the notations], the prime minister turned to the group of Soviet officials and in a very brisk and business-like manner issued his instructions. One was directed to attend to the assignment of the trucks, another to the loan to us temporarily of [sic] an automobile, and a third, to the selection of the stenographer and an interpreter for us. When this was completed, Muktarov turned in our direction and stated with the assurance of a field marshal that we might rest assured that our wants would be satisfied without delay. In the general conversation which ensued I had opportunity to observe the outward appearances and physical characteristics of these men who yesterday had been workers and peasants and who today were administering a government. Together they presented a composite picture of an unshaven, rather disheveled, simple, plain workman. The president, [Rauf] Sabirov, of an almost olive complexion and jet black hair and high cheek bones, wore the overcoat of a solider and might have been mistaken for a sergeant in some eastern army. Placed in the vicinity of an Indian reservation in America and one would have identified him as an Indian. Actually he was a Tatar, as were most of those composing the assembly.

It was the prime minister, however, who provoked the greatest interest. Deep piercing black eyes betrayed a strong resolute will which received confirmation in the direct and forceful manner in which he spoke and gave his orders. It was his youth which was of really the greatest interest for he could not have been more than thirty years of age, yet there was nothing lacking in his air of authority nor yet was there any assumption of arrogance in his demeanor. He was attired in a faded blue shirt and wore no cravat. During the course of the conference, which lasted approximately an hour, I do not believe that he gave utterance to one superfluous word. It was the more remarkable since the Russian seems to like nothing better than to talk endlessly about nothing.

I think we were all very much impressed by our first formal interview with the officials of the Soviet government of one of the autonomous republics of Russia, and this favorable impression of the capacity of the leaders was considerably heightened when, soon after our return to the train, we found the trucks and the automobile, which we had requested, putting in their appearance at the appointed hour. So, on this Sabbath day, as the people of America were making their way quietly to church, we had turned in, in our rough clothes, to the work of unloading the train of food and of transporting the supplies to the warehouse which had been placed at our disposal.

Living quarters had already been arranged for Wahren and me by the government before our arrival in what was described as one of the most comfortable homes in Kazan, formerly serving as government offices. We found the house, somewhat in the style of an American bungalow on Lenin Street. With two baths, electric lights, running water, garage, stables and garden, very little was left to be desired. As I was inspecting the house, I was approached by a venerable-looking old man who emerged from the cellar and who inquired respectfully of my interpreter if he might be permitted to speak with me. I signified my assent immediately, and he proceeded to explain that he was the former owner of the dwelling of which he had been dispossessed at the time of the Revolution and that he was requesting that he might be permitted to continue in occupancy of the two rooms in the cellar, where he had made his home during the preceding four years. I learned that he had previously been a very wealthy engineer, and in 1917, as he was about to retire in ripe old age to rest on the fruits of his labors, he found himself dispossessed of everything but two rooms which had formerly been occupied by his servants. I did not hesitate to assure him that so long as the Americans were in occupancy of the house, he might free his mind of any fear of ejection.

[The next full page of the manuscript s is missing and cannot be derived from the rough diary.]

In 1918 Kazan was occupied by the counter-revolutionary forces of Czechoslovaks, commanded by Admiral [Alexander] Kolchak[18] and it was here that the great stores of gold, placed in Kazan for security by the Soviet government, were taken possession of by Kolchak's troops. In the movement of the gold, however, to Siberia, it was recaptured by the Red Army. The city, which now has a population of something more than two hundred thousand, had like Moscow its Kremlin, the palisades of which were built by the first Tatar khan.[19] Kazan was notable before the war chiefly for its Russian leather and the manufacture of candles and soap. I am told that the leather and soap industry has survived to some extent, but to what degree I have as yet been unable to ascertain.

Today, on the occasion of our first drive to the banks of the Volga for the purpose of inspecting warehouses and to superintend the loading of the first boatload of supplies, the weather turned bitterly cold. It was a foretaste of what the cold is likely to be when the thermometer drops to 20 and 30 degrees below zero. The river is some four *versts*[20] from the city, and the sweeping plain which intervenes is barren and devoid of human habitation on account of the spring flooding of the river which brings the waters of the Volga within a stone's throw of the railroad station. As we return from the river, it was a beautiful sight to observe the silhouette of the city drawn sharply against the landscape. Situated as it is upon a slight undulation and thrown into relief by the grey shadows and spectral hues of the fast disappearing sunset, the splash of color of the buildings of the Kremlin, the

---

[18] Admiral Alexander Kolchak (1873–1920), one of the major White leaders in the Russian Civil War, operated mainly out of Siberia, where he gave himself the title of "Supreme Overlord of Siberia." Contemptuous of non-monarchist White elements, he began mistreating leftist groups in Siberia when he seemed to be victorious and was eventually killed by Bolsheviks when his regime collapsed, and his body was thrown into a hole in the ice of the Angara River near Lake Baikal. The Czech force was a contingent of about 70,000 men who had been formerly part of the Austro-Hungarian army but had surrendered to the Russians and switched sides. The Allies were trying to send them to the Western Front through Siberia when an incident led them to seize control of a large part of the Trans-Siberian railroad. They then became for a time part of Kolchak's forces.

[19] King or emperor.

[20] A *verst* is about 2/3 mile.

gilt domes of the Greek Catholic churches[21] and the slim minarets of the Tatar mosques, appeared as if projected upon the great natural canvas of the sky as by the brush of some magic painter. But it was impossible for the attention to be distracted for long to the beauty of the panorama for in our midst, and all along the road to the city were scattered great groups of homeless and hungry refugees, camped under the open sky.

September 19, [1921]—My first interpreter, [?] Antonov, formerly a White officer with the British and American troops in Archangel, was taken from me today under rather unconventional circumstances. We were continuing the unloading of the train of supplies brought from Moscow, and I was superintending it with the aid of Antonov, when two strangers approached the latter and held him in conversation for a few moments. After a few brief words had been spoken, Antonov turned to me and said dryly, "Sir, I am arrested.... It's the Extraordinary Commission, Sir," was the reply in a weary tone, "and there's really nothing to be done. I must go," and with that he was off.

Wahren left today on the steamship [S.S.] *Varlen* with supplies for the cantons, and in the afternoon I was busy in the attempt to get the living quarters assigned us in some order and at the same time to begin the organization of an office staff. In the midst of these tasks I was called upon by one of the young professors of the university, who speaks very good English and who came to offer his services. It seems today that everyone in Kazan, high and low, is coming to call on me for this purpose. However, the young professor was not unentertaining, and we chatted along for some time. The comment of his which interested me chiefly was that which concerned the pleasure given him in the meeting once again with cultivated people. "It has been so many years now since we have been cut off from the world," he continued, "that I feel in talking with you that I am conversing with an individual from another planet."

September 21, [1921]—Wahren left yesterday for three cantons with a boatload of supplies, and with the departure today of Burland and Dr. Kellogg, I was left alone to begin the work of organization of the ARA in Kazan.... However, I was greatly cheered in the afternoon by the appearance

---

[21] Childs uses "Greek Catholic" for "Russian Orthodox" throughout the manuscript.

of an interpreter who had been sent by the government in answer to my request. I came into the office about three o'clock and found awaiting me a very smart- looking young man in the officer's uniform of the Red Army of about thirty-three years of age who saluted sharply, and clicking his heels together, introduced himself as [?] Simson. I almost fell upon his neck as he spoke excellent English, having lived in England for some seven years prior to the Revolution. Indeed, after the departure of the other Americans, I was so pleased to find someone with whom to converse that I kept Simson to dinner....

September 22, [1921]—Although the house is literally swarming from sun-up until sun- down with applicants for work, it is difficult to find speedily the competent personnel for our organization. If one were limited to those who were in need, then it would be necessary to make an appointment of every applicant. This morning the granddaughter of the famous [eighteenth century] Russian general [Alexander] Suvorov, together with her son and daughter, presented themselves for work. All of them speak English as well as French and are attired almost in rags. It needed no second look at their pinched faces to detect the sign of want and prolonged undernourishment. The daughter claims a knowledge of English typing, and I put her to work and gave the son a position as office boy but had nothing to offer the mother. The latter, however, despite her once proud position under the Old Regime as one of the leading hostesses of Kazan and as one who had been received at the Imperial Court, pleaded with tears in her eyes that I find her some work and haunted the offices all day in the hope that I might relent or that something might turn up.

I find these people with nerves hopelessly disordered, and that makes the selection of employees all the more difficult. A Frenchwoman, married to a Russian, and who had been educated in the United States, apparently a very alert and capable person whom I had engaged yesterday, came in today to inquire with much agitation as to whether the Americans intended to remain in Kazan longer than a few months. She explained that a rumor was current in the town that everyone engaged by the Americans would be arrested and that it was certain that if the Americans were only to remain for two or three months, that at the termination of their work everyone who has been in any way associated with them would be subject to arrest. The office was already filled with agents of the Cheka, she said, and if we had no intention of remaining for long, her husband had told her that she must not enter the service of the ARA.

As well as I could, I attempted to calm her fears and also found the occasion an excellent one for expressing my entire indifference to the surveillance of the Cheka. Since we had nothing to conceal about our work, I said, we welcomed the placing of as many agents in our organization as the Extraordinary Commission desired. I represented it as a very desirable action since nothing would more quickly gain us the confidence of the government that the presence in our midst of such secret agents.

September 24, [1921]—Conferences with the government had been continuing every day since my arrival in Kazan, and in the absence of Muktarov, the prime minister, they have been held with Sabirov, the president of the republic. I am forced to bother him with the most inconsequential of details such as concern the needs of the house and office for furniture and the installation of heating and electric lights. Of course, there are questions of major importance to be discussed also and of these, a definite agreement has been reached upon two. The government has agreed to grant us for operating expenses a budget of not less than 500,000,000 rubles a month, or the equivalent of about $10,000. Expressed in rubles it seems a colossal sum, but here in Russia one talks of millions of rubles with as much *sang-froid* as the Secretary of the Treasury in America discusses millions of dollars. This nonchalant attitude of the government towards its paper money puts me in mind of what Carroll had to say of [Maxim] Litvinov's[22] attitude toward this question during the discussions which led to the conclusion of the Riga agreement between the Soviet government and the ARA. When the point was raised by the representatives of the ARA as to the willingness of the Russian government to assume the operating expenses of relief in Russia, Litvinov is said to have extended the stubby fingers of his hands in a magnificently magnanimous gesture and to have declared:

---

[22] Maxim Litvinov (1876–1951) was the assistant commissar of foreign Affairs under Chicherin, and he replaced him when the latter resigned in 1930. As the Russians became desirous of an accord with Germany in 1939, Litvinov, who was Jewish, was removed in March of that year because the Soviets knew that Hitler would never negotiate with a Jew. He died in relative obscurity.

"Money? Vy, gentlemen, ve will give you a carload; ve can put the printing presses on an extra shift if necessary."

An equally important matter about which I have come to an agreement with Sabirov has been the question of the guarantee by the government of immunity from arrest of all Russian employees of the ARA without a cause which may appear satisfactory to the ARA district supervisor. Sabirov has given his assurance personally and officially that the native personnel of the ARA will not be subject to arrest as a result of their connection with the ARA and that further, no employee of the ARA will be arrested until notification has first been made to the ARA and a reason given for the arrest which may appear fully to justify it. This is a matter of paramount importance to the success of our work, as I have seen fit to represent to Sabirov, for as a result of the recent wholesale arrests of the Russian Relief Committees, our employees are in a state of very great nervous apprehension as to the attitude the government may assume toward their association in the work of the ARA.

Indeed, after returning to the office today and after having communicated the assurances which I had received to the heads of departments, I was approached in private conversation and made to feel that very strong doubt existed as to the intention of the government to keep its promise in this regard. And every day I have rumors brought to me that the entire office force of the ARA in Kazan is to be arrested. Of course I laugh at the expression of such fears, but I must confess that the atmosphere of suspicion and distrust and fear which prevails on every side has been sufficient to give me concern and to have contributed no little to the troubles which are accumulating in the work. As I informed Sabirov today, nothing would so effectually demoralize the work of the ARA and make impossible the fulfillment of our contemplated relief as the arbitrary arrest of our employees. If, as it has been stated, the Russian government has small desire for our presence, it will be only necessary, in order to paralyze our work for several arrests of members of the office staff to be made and the resignations of the remainder would be immediately forthcoming.

September 27, [1921]—For some few days,...I have been giving attention to studying the famine situation from the sources at my command. It has required no deep consideration of the material at hand to become convinced that the plight of the adult population is becoming increasingly critical and that unless some outside aid is afforded, the government will be powerless to preserve the lives of thousands of its citizens here in the Tatar Republic. So deeply impressed have I become with the necessity for the undertaking by us of adult feeding that I resolved today that I must take steps to free myself of any of the responsibility which would rest in the future upon those relief workers and observers who failed to give warning of the terrible tragedy which must ensue during the coming months to the now fast-dying population of the Tatar Republic in the event succor is withheld from them. I cannot permit part of the responsibility for the death of thousands to rest upon my head, and I am resolved to do all in my power to see that the acuteness of the situation is brought home to those who have it within their power to give aid. So, with this purpose, I dispatched today the following telegram to the ARA in Moscow after having discussed the situation at length with Sabirov:

> Forwarding this week's statistical report showing severe plight faced by adult population this winter who opinion experts separated from starvation only a few months STOP now exchanging clothes for food which means thousands must perish cold and hunger unless help forthcoming STOP worst manifestation famine conditions breaking down moral fibre people who willing resort anything for food STOP refugee problem temporarily alleviated though thousands children be evacuated Siberia Petrograd next two weeks from Kazan STOP Medical supplies instruments more acutely needed than doctors END Childs. [Telegram *sic*]

Hurrying from the composition of a telegram and even the typing of it—since the single typist I have been able to find is incapable of caring for the mass of work to be done—to an interview with the government and thence to the railroad station to superintend the unloading of a second trainload of supplies, I felt today as if the heavens were about to break over my head and the ground under my feet. But relief came in the form of the arrival of two Americans from Moscow: John H. Boyd and Van Arsdale Turner. Boyd is a young, tall, and engaging Southerner, who saw strenuous relief service in the Near East and who went through the siege of Aintab and who is just from a lecture tour of the United States.... Previously Boyd was in the service of the ARA in London and prior to that he was in France with the Air Service. By his presence in Kazan he is one of the thousands who have answered in the negative that query set to music of "How are you going to keep 'em down on the farm after they've seen Paree?"

Van Arsdale Turner of Maryland is slightly older than Boyd and more sedate in his manner, but he has the language of romance also on his tongue, and though he was not in the army, and though he is the son of a preacher—or perhaps because of it—he too has wandered far afield and has collected reminiscences....

At the first call for relief workers for Russia, he was in Russia and answering the roll call for new adventure.

September 29, [1921]—Now that these sketches of the history and character of the Americans composing the Kazan district of the ARA have been begun, it is appropriate to include that one which holds the greatest fascination of them all and which is concerned with that very remarkable young man, Ivar W. Wahren, District Supervisor, who returned to join us today from his first tour of the country districts. Ten years ago, Wahren, who was but twenty-one years of age, was living in Finland, pursuing a life of idleness and ease on the estates of his relatives. Born in Finland of a wealthy and aristocratic Finnish family, he had been educated in Switzerland and brought up with a knowledge of the Finnish, Swedish, German and French languages. His maternal and paternal grandfathers were the two largest landowners in Finland and upon the establishment of a Finnish constitution in 1907,[23] Wahren's father had taken a seat in the Finnish House of Lords. [Wahren visited America and signed up in the American army.]... In six months he had succeeded in applying himself so successfully to the study of English as well as to his military duties that he was made a non-commissioned officer.... [He served in the army later as an officer, seeing action in France. From there he entered the ARA and was sent to Czechoslovakia and from there to Russia.]...

October 6, [1921]—I left Kazan today on my first trip into the interior of the country for the purpose of transporting a second cargo of food to the

---

[23] Childs is probably referring to the granting of a Constituent Senate to Finland in 1905, not 1907, in an effort to appease Finish nationalist sentiment.

cantons and in order to effect the organization of ARA committees in the cantons of Laishev, Mamadysh, and Elabuga. Accompanying me were: an interpreter, [?] Jacobs, and a representative of the government, Mikhail Skvortzov ....[24]

The ship upon which we are making our journey is the *S. S. Varlen*, an oil burner with some twenty first class cabins, and of about the proportions of the excursions steamers which ply out of Washington to Mt. Vernon and the surrounding resorts of Chesapeake Bay in summer. As we speed down the Volga other boats are passed; heavily laden barges, passenger steamers and oil tankers, these last making their slow way north from Baku on the Caspian [Sea]. The scene of life and movement and activity is hardly the one which I drew before coming into Russia from the newspaper accounts in the press of the complete stagnation of all enterprise in this communistic society.

October 7, [1921]—During the night we were held up at the shallows which lie some thirty *versts* below Kazan and where the banks were lined on every side with a variety of water craft awaiting their turn to be towed through the narrow channel by tug. In answer to my inquiries, the captain of the *Varlen* stated that it might be another day before a tug could be expected to tow us through. With a realization of the pressing necessity of delivering the shipload of food as soon as possible to the famine stricken-districts, I insisted that we proceed ahead under own steam, and inasmuch as I was in absolute charge of the boat, the captain had no other alternative than to execute my order with a reluctance, nevertheless, which he was not at pains to conceal. By skillful maneuvering, however, we were enabled to pass safely through, and in another hour we were at Bogorodsk, which lies almost at the confluence of the Kama and the Volga [rivers].

Bogorodsk is a dreary, mud-besmattered Russian village which seems to have been the work of as artless and uncouth hands as those of children who shape mud pies. Miserable thatched huts have been piled one above another along the slope which descends to the riverside, and along the banks for a distance of several hundred yards, there are outspread rude temporary

---

[24] Mikhail Skvartsov was more than just a representative; he was the Secretary of the Communist Party of the Tatar Republic. He and Childs in time became close friends.

shelters which serve as the homes of hundreds of bewildered hungry refugees. They are lying or are sitting in the mud, surrounded by the few of their personal belonging which they have been able to transport with them and these, when stacked up and covered with a sheet or blanket, afford the only shelter or refuge left to families of five and six. Near the wharf, where these starving homeless human beings were massed, there is a great pile of American foodstuffs which were shipped from Kazan a few days previous intended for the villages in the interior. Every day the refugees dig shallow holes in the mud and slime about them for the purpose of interring some of their number. And each day they look longingly at the food which is piled and stacked so neatly beside them, but they make no movement other than to cross themselves devoutly and to clutch a little more strangely at their fatalistic shadows and conceptions of life inbred through long centuries in the Slavic nature. I glance furtively at the ancient old-styled weapon which the single guard supports upon his shoulder and with which he lounges lazily in his tour of the stacks, and I am moved to wonder whether such a gun would be capable of discharge if it were called upon to serve its purpose. I am inclined to disbelieve that it would and that it is nothing more than a symbol.

I have gone ashore to purchase some provisions, for even in the midst of this scene of desolation and want, there are eggs, butter, milk, and even meat to be bought in the bazaars which line the riverside. As I pass over the landing barge, bales of cotton from Turkestan are being unloaded from the Astrakhan steamer.

October 8, [1921]—Laishev, our first stop for the organization of a committee, was reached early in the evening, and word was dispatched to the authorities of the town, located three *versts* distant from the waterside, to assemble a body of representative citizens on board as soon as possible to permit us to initiate the ARA work. It was pitch dark outside and a cold drizzling rain was falling, and as the hours passed I fell to wondering whether our messenger had been lost. It was not until almost two AM that some twenty or twenty-five men appeared and crowded into the small saloon on board the *Varlen*, permitting us to open the meeting. I presided; Jacobs, my interpreter, sat on my right, and [Mikhail] Skvortzov, the government representative, on my left of the large table about which the citizens of Laishev were gathered. It was pleasantly surprised at the composition of the assembly, for instead of the burly, brutal faces I had been led to expect would be assembled by the local soviet authorities, I found before me a kindly-faced, not unintelligent body of men who might have been representative of some of the more isolated rural communities of America.

I first explained the object of my visit and of the calling of the meeting and proceeded to the reading of the Riga Agreement, which was translated by Skvortzov and its several paragraphs explained by him. That having been concluded I next directed through my interpreter Jacobs some remarks upon the character of the ARA and of what it proposed to do and how its purpose was to be accomplished. The cantonal committee of the ARA which was to be organized would have to undertake the establishment of the necessary kitchens throughout the canton for the feeding of the neediest children. To effect this, subsidiary ARA committees would have to be organized in each of the *volosts*[25] contained in the canton and in each village of a *volost* in which it was planned to feed there would have to be elected an ARA committee. The methods of feeding were carefully expounded and particular emphasis was laid upon the necessity of the exercise by the committee of an absolute impartiality in the selection of the children to be fed and in the election of the committees in the *volosts* and villages. The funds which had made possible the ARA work, I explained, had been collected in America from all classes of society, from the worker as well as the millionaire, and therefore the ARA work would not countenance any discrimination for reasons of class, politics, color, creed, or nationality in the execution and administration of its relief. Finally the assembly proceeded to the nomination of members of the proposed committee and the election was made and then work concluded as the hour of the clock pointed to four AM.

October 9, [1921]—From Laishev we proceeded to the river landing for Mamadysh, located at Sokolky, twenty-five *versts* distant from the cantonal seat. A crowd of about the number which had been assembled at Laishev

---

[25] The word *volost* translates as "district," a level of local government that does not exist in the United States. The tsarist levels of administration were first *guberniia* (Childs refers to them as "governments"), then *oblasts*, (like "states"), then *uezdi* (Childs usually refers to them as cantons; somewhat like counties in the US.), and then *volosti*, which were divisions of the *uezdi*.

drove the twenty-five *versts* to our boat, and the committee was organized in the same manner as it had been the previous day at Laishev.

From these men I heard, as I had heard at Laishev, terrible stories of the hunger and want which existed in the interior of the country, and I was given visible enough evidence of it here, as at other river landings, in the crowds of refugees which were assembled on the shores and particularly in the little armies of children who were to be seen streaming in, under the guidance of one or two enfeebled teachers, to be placed on boats and carried away to the orphan asylums in the large cities. At Laishev we had taken on several hundred of such orphaned homeless children and as many more were given shelter at Sokolky. They were crowded eight and ten into a cabin, and in the evening as I passed the second class saloon there were to be seen fully a hundred and fifty of them occupying every inch of space in the room, lying packed on the floor like sardines in a box and completely covering the tables with their wan, bony bodies. It was the most pitiful sight I have ever witnessed in my life to observe them as they lay relaxed in slumber with their tired, wasted faces contracted into terrible caricatures of humanity. I could not sleep this night for thinking of the faces of those children for there came ever to disturb me the riddle of who was responsible for this suffering. I thought of those children and I thought for some incongruous reason of Fifth Avenue [in New York], the Rue de la Paix [in Paris], and Riverside Drive [in New York]. Was there not something fundamentally wrong with a civilization which had no food for some of its children and toys and trifles for others?

October 9, [1921]—Today is a beautiful Sabbath day, and as we tie up along the wharf at Elabuga, the foliage of the trees, which line the road leading down to the river from the town, is resplendent with rich autumn coloring. I wonder, as I look upon this scene of natural beauty and think of the suffering of the people it masks, whether the religious-minded in the States would object to the holding of the secular meeting which has been called for eleven o'clock in the place of the religious services usually reserved for this hour. I am afraid there are many bigots who would condemn my action, but it is precisely an analogous bigotry which is responsible for the suffering of the people who inhabit that beautiful countryside lying under my eyes. I seem to feel already, after a very short sojourn in Russia, that my estimate of the values of life and its realities are undergoing a radical transformation, and yet I cannot convince myself for that reason that I am any more deeply a sinner. Indeed, it would seem to me that I am throwing off a great deal of useless baggage and that in the stripping of life of its inessentials and in the search and probe for the eternal realities, I am gaining warrant, not for the salvation of my soul, for I dislike and reject that phrase, but for the right to live.

When the body of "representative" citizens from the town of Elabuga had gathered on board our boat, the procedure which had marked previous meetings for the purpose of organizing an ARA committee was gone through with. In all these committees, certain qualifications were prescribed for membership such as, it was thought, would be calculated to give assurance of the election of intelligent, competent workers. Of a membership of five, it was stipulated that a cantonal ARA committee should consist of: one, a representative of the [local] government; two, a representative of public education; three, a representative of the cooperatives; four, a representative of the Russian Relief Committee; and five, a physician.

Of course it would be useless to pretend that the individuals who were assembled in each instance at Laishev, Mamadysh, and Elabuga were representative of all classes of the respective communities. The assemblies had been as obviously packed as any Tammany convention, but one had to go through the form in order that a possibly querulous American public opinion might be satisfied that our relief had been administered in the traditionally democratic manner. It would have been silly to have supposed that in such uncertain times as these that the Soviet authorities would have permitted the collection together of a body of citizens over whom it could not have expected to exercise control. And it would have been an equally silly to have believed that if I had attempted to go out into these communities and to have deliberately selected committee members who did not have the confidence of the government, such a committee could have been expected to work efficiently and to receive the full cooperation of the local authorities. I harbored no such delusions and indeed I was so thoroughly persuaded of the realities of the situation that I was delightfully surprised by an episode which occurred after the formation of the Elabuga committee and which led me to conclude that the Soviet authorities were disposed to show more good faith toward the fulfillment of the spirit of the Riga Agreement than I had credited them with.

The balloting for the election of the committee for Elabuga had been concluded, and Skvortzov had begun the reading of the results at the moment that a rather swarthy-faced and uncouth-appearing individual entered the saloon in which the meeting was being held. The repulsive appearance presented by his unkempt person and [his] gross features had attracted my attention and so there did not pass unnoticed, during the reading of the names of those elected by the committee, the quickened movement of the dark and almost malignant eyes, shaded by shaggy overhanging eyebrows, of the newcomer.

He started to his feet the moment the reading had been concluded by Skvartzov and let loose a nervous rapid stream of words which seemed almost to fall one over another. I needed no interpreter to tell me that his expressions were not the calm and ordered words of thanks of the community to the Americans with which such meetings were ordinarily concluded. A little buzz of excitement had animated all those who were present; Jacobs, my interpreter, was staring at the speaker in frank amazement, while I could observe that Skvartzov had begun the nervous tapping of the table with the point of a pencil. Skvartzov suddenly reversed abruptly the position of the pencil and brought it down in sharp and incisive raps against the wood. Then he held up his hand with a significantly authoritative gesture, and with his forehead drawn in a deep frown he broke into the other's speech, or rant, and delivered himself of a few brief but emphatic phrases. The other attempted once to interrupt, but again that imperious hand flashed into display and after a few words more had been spoken by Skvartzov, there was silence. A few minutes later the meeting was adjourned, and as soon as I was able, I called Jacobs into my cabin to explain the little drama which had been...unintelligible to me. Here is the substance of what had occurred.

Upon the conclusion of the reading of the names of the newly-elected committee, the newcomer...who, it appeared, was an official of the Cooperative Union, had arisen to express his objections to the committee as it was constituted. The members were not all good party men, he had said; some of them were not even Communists. It was in the elaboration of this thesis that he had been interrupted by Skvartzov, who it must be remembered is Secretary of the Communist Party of the Tatar Republic. According to Jacobs, Skvartzov had been by no means restrained in the language which he had used in criticism of the attitude taken by the Cooperative official. "Your remarks are absurd," he had informed this one, " and if you had been present when the character of the ARA work was being exposed, you would have avoided making such remarks. Since you were not here when the non-political character of the ARA work was being discussed, you will have to learn later from those who were present what had been said in this regard by Mr. Childs, as a representative of the ARA, and by me as a representative of the government. Until that time you will restrict any comments you have to make to more sensible ones than you have given expression to, and since that seems impossible, you will do better to remain silent altogether." This incident established my confidence in Skvartzov, and I resolved that whenever I should have occasion to go into the cantons again, I would make special application to the government for his services that he might accompany me as government representative.

I enjoyed other incidents also of my visit to Elabuga, for in making the journey by cart to the town, which was situation [situated?] two *versts* from the river landing, I was engaged in conversation by one of the men who had been present at the meeting and who had offered to conduct me to the town for the inspection which I wished to make of the children's homes and hospitals. This individual who appeared as if he might have been a prosperous farmer before the Revolution and who was now chief of the food supply department of the canton, a kindly-faced, blue-eyed intelligent man of middle age, inquired of me brusquely through my interpreter what the American people thought of the Russian Revolution. "Speak honestly and tell me whether or not they think us lunatics here in Russia?" was another question translated to me before I had been given an opportunity to reply to the first.

It was the first time I had had a question directed to me concerning the political situation since entering Russia, and I was not merely puzzled, I was almost shocked. I glanced stealthily at our driver to observe whether he was showing any agitation, for I was disturbed that my inquirer had not dropped his voice in putting to me such compromising queries. The answers which I gave were put in almost whispers to Jacobs. I did not feel that I was competent to speak for the American people, I said, and as there were differences of opinion among the American people respecting the situation I could only give the expression of my personal view if I gave expression to any opinion. The truth was that I had left my politics at home when I came to Russia; I further explained, as American relief workers, we were supposed to have abjured all entertainment of political opinions for so long as they might be active in relief work in Russia. But my answers were not satisfactory and my interlocutor continued to contrive, as we pursued our way into the town, all manner of pleasant cajoling to induce me to express myself. But I would not and I at length succeeded in turning the subject by an inquiry of my own into the famine situation in the canton and the state of the children's homes and hospitals in the town.

I was first taken to a school and home for children, belonging to families of soldiers of the Red Army. It was as well kept and prepossessing a school and home as one would find in any country. I was struck in particular by the children's work which was exhibited in the form of sketches and drawings upon the walls of the classrooms, and I wondered if children of the same ages, from eight to ten, would be capable of better work even in America. This was the best home in the canton, it was explained to me, but the other two which I visited in the town were equally clean and commodious, and though the ration distributed by the government in those other homes did not equal fully that allotted in the home for children of families of the Red Army, the children did not seem in outward bodily appearance to suffer in comparison. However, I was informed that the canton of Elabuga was in a far better state with regard to the food situation than the other cantons of the Tatar Republic, and I was disposed to agree so far as the comparison which I was able to make of conditions here with those I had gained from conversation with the inhabitants of Laishev and Mamadysh.

October 12, [1921]—After a three day trip up the Kama, during which I touched at the cantonal seats which remained in this vicinity of the Tatar Republic, I have returned on the homeward way and stopped today at the one flourishing town of Chistopol, now, as previous to the war, a rural community of some twenty thousand inhabitants. The evidence of that peculiar decay which one remarks in most Russian town and cites is visible in Chistopol, though it would be difficult precisely to define it. There is first of all an appearance of dinginess and dissolution about even the most solid and substantial stone structures of it for years no hand had been put to repair the inevitably destructive forces of nature. Grass and weeds have grown up in some of the cobbled streets, and all the people one meets seem to wear a saturnine aspect in keeping with the gloomy air and melancholy appearance of their surroundings. I search in my mind for historical similitudes for there is certainly nothing in my experience to draw from for comparison. Presently a cart is to be seen moving slowly through the streets, a cart with a rough cloth flung over its contents. Projecting from the covering are an indiscriminate mass of naked arms and limbs and to my startled inquiry I am informed that it is the death wagon which is transporting the bodies of victims of the hunger to a burial place. And there occurs to my mind the account and illustrations in the school histories of the Great Plague in England, and I wonder if one would not have to go back to that period to find scenes comparable in death and dissolution with those I see going on about me here in the year 1921.

I come to the collecting home in the city for homeless children, and there in a miserable wooden barracks more than three hundred children with the countenances of death are crammed in a space not suitable for one-tenth the number. To say that they are attired in rags would hardly express their miserable state for many have not even the luxury of rags to give their emaciated bodies a little warmth.

Before leaving Chistopol, I called the ARA Committee together and read a bitter indictment not only against them individually but also against the population of the town for what I was persuaded to describe in my indignant state, as the criminal negligence of the city for failure to make better provision for these waifs. I informed them that if I were a citizen of Chistopol, I would not be able to sleep in the presence of such conditions as I had witnessed. I think my words were not without effect for I was assured by every member before my departure that every step possible would be taken to ameliorate the lot of the children.

Dropping down the river, I was brought, as dusk overtook us, to Laishev, where I stopped to go up to the town and visit there some of the public welfare institutions I had been unable to inspect on my previous passage up the river. Among others I had been led to a children's home and passed into a neglected, ramshackle wooden structure which seemed to be inclining to as irresolute an angle as the Leaning Tower of Pisa. Through a pitch black hallway, we ascended creaking steps and were met at the top of the landing by a feeble oil lamp offered us by one of the attendants. Stepping into the room indicated as the sleeping quarters of the children, I halted upon the threshold as I observed stretched out in little tired, pathetic groups upon the floor the children, lying in each other's arms for warmth. There were no blankets, and they were sleeping in the few worn garments which they possessed as clothing. I did not linger but sought the cool refreshing night air outside. As we stepped out into the night, a half moon suddenly emerged from behind clouds and threw into unexpected relief the bold striking outlines of a Russian Orthodox church directly opposite, such as one of these massive finely conceived edifices set down amidst the squalor of a Russian village, as always excites one's imagination by the very incongruity of the scene.

"What a beautiful church!" I ejaculated, fairly taken out of myself in wonder at such unexpected beauty.

"Yes, and what a miserable children's home, that one which we have just left," Skvartzov remarked in a tone of such bitterness and sadness that I was brought back again to reality. "If only some part of the treasure that had been taken to rear this church had been spared and devoted to the building of children's homes and hospitals," he added, "then the usefulness of the church might be more apparent."

Kazan, October 15, [1921]—Tonight the Americans composing the staff of the Kazan District of the ARA took advantage of the theater passes which have been given to us by the government to attend a performance of the opera. The old opera house, a very large pretentious building, was gutted a year or two ago by fire, and the regular winter season of opera, which had continued in Kazan throughout the period of the War, Revolution, and Civil War, has been transferred to the former light opera theater, now known as the Palace of Red Army Soldiers." The interior of the theater well lives up to this name for it is decorated on each side by large and flamboyant symbolical studies of the Revolution. The promenade contains the inevitable portraits of Karl Marx, and in addition those of Lenin, Trotsky, and several other leading figures of the Revolution.

The audience was composed, so far as outward appearance would indicate, almost exclusively of the proletariat. If there were bourgeois present, they had been certainly at pains to conceal it by their dress for the men one saw were universally shabby, and so far as concerned the appearance of the women it could not described as much better. The opera which was offered was *Carmen*, and though I have heard it with Farrar and Caruso from beneath that ultra- conventional diamond horseshoe in the Metropolitan and though I have heard it on more than one occasion at the *Opera Comique* in Paris, I must confess that I have never enjoyed a performance of it such as I witnesses given by a mediocre company on the shabby stage of Kazan in the Russian Socialist Republic.

For while a picture from the bohemian life of Spain of the past as interpreted by a great French author [Prosper] Mérimée, and as set to music by no less famous French composer, [Georges] Bizet, passed before my eyes, I could not but think of that greater drama of which all of us who were present in the "Palace of Red Army Soldiers" formed a part. There before us was a little make-believe tragedy which was being produced in the midst of a great living tragedy, but while the former was enacted upon a few boards, the latter commanded a stage extending from the White to the Black and Caspian Seas. Principals of the greater tragedy were pressing as spectators into the lesser one to forget, in the tragedy of the other, their own. It recalled to my mind old German romantic plays of the early eighteenth century in which spectators of plays within plays were placed upon the stage to take mimic parts before other spectators. How could these poor people about me in their miserable clothes and with gaunt, haggard faces, which betrayed without the accompaniment of any music their tragedy, take interest in romance or love or be attracted by a tale ending in the death to which destiny even now was summoning them? I could not forget or banish these thoughts even under the temporary spell of the superb acting of [the Persian diva] Muktarova as Carmen, nor even under the fascination of her rhythmic movement and great dark flashing eyes, which displayed all their intriguing prowess in that challenge of: *"L'amour est enfant de boheme, / Qui'a jamais connu de loi, / Si tu ne m'aime pas, je t'aime / Et si je t'aime, prends garde à toi."*[26]

---

[26] "Love is a bohemian child / who has never known the law. / If you do not love me, I love you. /And if I love you, watch out." There are some minor errors in Childs's transcription.

I left the theater moved as I had never been before by a performance of *Carmen*, and I cannot think it was the superior quality of the singing, nor indeed the exceptional character of the acting of the operatic cast. It was neither as I came to consider; it was nothing other than the dramatic character of the audience. It was the dramatic performance of the spectators which had so deeply impressed me!

October 16, [1921]—After the consideration of so much misery during the day and when Wahren, Boyd, Turner and I gather about the evening meal, we strive to turn our thoughts as far as possible from the hideous reality of the present. In such a mood and inspired much by the same impulse which draws a hungry man to feast in his imagination, we were discussing tonight beautiful scenes which we had visited in our travels and delightful spots where we had dined....

October 22, [1921]—I left Kazan for the second time two days ago by steamer with a cargo of supplies to be transported to the cantons of the Tatar Republic along the Kama [river], but having been confined during most of this time to my stateroom with ptomaine poisoning, I have had little opportunity for observation. But I did take occasion today to embody some of my general impressions, formed of the socialist government of Russia, in a letter to an old army friend with whom I was associated during the war at the Army War College and afterwards at the Peace Conference:

> My Dear Colonel...
>
> In one way, all my previous notions were swept overboard so soon as I had entered Russia. I had thought that Red Russia implied a chaotic Russia. There is, of course, a certain amount of chaos, the inevitable concomitant of so great and so revolutionary a change as is being introduced, but so far as concerns the ordinary maintenance of law and order, it is as well-regulated as any other country.
>
> Again, I had been led to believe that the authority of the central Moscow Soviet did not extend much beyond Moscow and the larger towns, but that again is, in my judgement, a most egregious mistake, for in all the towns and villages to which I have penetrated along the Volga and Kama and twenty and thirty *versts*

inland, the authority of the central Soviet [government] cannot be questioned.

So far as my six weeks residence in Russia has enabled me to observe, I would say that Lenin continues to be the most popular figure in Russia. His portrait, together with that of Trotsky and other Soviet leaders, may be seen hanging upon the walls in villages, hundreds of miles from Moscow, and they are hanging even where the portraits of officials of the government of the Tatar Republic are absent. I think it would be no mistake to say that Lenin and the Extraordinary Commission are the most potent forces in the government. Lenin offers, I believe, the greatest possibility for the liberal modification of the Soviet doctrines. Were Trotsky to gain absolute control, the government would probably be transformed into a military dictatorship.

Another most interesting fact that I have had occasion to observe, particularly in the organization of the Russian-American committees for the distribution of our foodstuffs in the cantons of the Tatar Republic, is that with very few exceptions the chairman of the local soviet is the strongest and most capable man in the community. That applies also, I should say, to the government officials in Kazan, the seat of the Tatar Republic. One is impressed by their apparent honesty and force and what is lacking in education and refinement is more than made up by a strong and fearless will. They are invariably plain and simple men, but the leaders certainly seem to know how to obtain the accomplishment of what they desire. It is when one goes a little deeper into the Soviet organization and when one encounters the sub-chiefs of bureaus that incompetency becomes manifest. The leaders are here, but they are grievously lacking in competent subordinates to undertake the execution of the tasks conceived by them. I do not think that if Napoleon were to come to the Tatar Republic, he would make so critical an observation as he did when he was in Italy in command of the army there. He said then, "There are six million people in Italy, and I have only been able to find three men." I could find him three men and more here who occupy the positions in the local government which correspond to those of Lenin and [Mikhail]

Kalinin,[27] etc. and whose giving of an order is equivalent to its execution. Who or what were these men before the Revolution— one never asks, but I have learned casually that some were students and others were workmen and peasants. There are almost no strong men of the intelligentsia left because they have either been shot, imprisoned, or have left the country. Those who are left are men broken in mind and body. We have tried to employ some of them in our office, but the older ones have no energy or spirit left for a task requiring initiative.

I am told on most reliable authority that since the Revolution about one hundred and fifty thousand political prisoners have been executed, but I believe this figure low. At the present time it is estimated that in Moscow about ten are executed each day, including those charged with criminal acts, and that the figures for the whole of Russia would reach about one thousand a day. It is further estimated that only about fifteen percent of these are of the intelligentsia and that the majority of those outside the criminal class are Communists. Now that the intelligentsia has been crushed, the government is more strict with the Communists than with any other class. Where a member of the intelligentsia would be only imprisoned for a petty theft, a responsible communist would be shot without mercy. There has been lately what is called a cleaning[28] of the Communist Party. This involves the exclusion from the party of those members of the intelligentsia who have managed to creep in without honest Communistic convictions. There have also been many communists excluded, that is to say, working men and peasants, who the party feels were not possessed with strong enough communistic ideas. Many also have been disciplined by their removal from responsible posts to those of lesser authority.

For the popularity of the government among the people, I would not venture to make any deduction. There are various opinions that one hears expressed, but I believe that the statement

---

[27] Mikhail Kalinin (1875–1946) was the president of the Soviet state from 1919 until his death in 1946. His position, unlike today, was largely a ceremonial one.

[28] The Russian term is *chistka*, a purge.

of a man I consider non-partisan strikes at the heart of the situation
when he said to me this week: "You may hear grumbling and
expressions of disaffection, but let anyone attempt seriously to
criticize the government and one of the workers or peasants surely
will be heard to say: 'That's enough from you. Good or bad
government, it is ours, a government of workers and peasants.'"

Whether the reforms, or I should rather say, whether the
abandonment of the more radical Bolshevik program is improving
conditions, or whether they are going from bad to worse, with my
limited period and sphere of observation, it is of course impossible
for me to attempt to judge. It is certain that the Soviet leaders are
making heroic efforts to adjust themselves to natural law without
entirely compromising their position, and whether there is yet time,
only time can tell.

The army discipline is one of iron. I have become intimately
acquainted with several Red officers and soldiers, and I assure you
that I have never met men of any army in whom the sense of
discipline was any stronger inculcated. As you know, the insignia of
rank has been restored, as also the salute....[29] Troops that I have
seen are extremely well drilled and seem to be well clothed. The
army continues to receive a preferential ration.

So far as concerns the [Red] Terror, that seems to be lessening
as the need for it appears to have passed. Certainly, executions are
much less frequent, and the power of imposing the death penalty
and even of arrest has been considerably curtailed. If one might say
it, I think it would be fair to state that conditions as a whole are
becoming more normal. Of course such a statement is only relative.

The most extraordinary thing in Russia today is by all odds the
Extraordinary Commission. I know of nothing like it in any other

---

[29] After the February Revolution, the Petrograd Soviet, a shadow government to
the Provisional Government, issued General Order No. 1, which changed the
relations between officers and soldiers of the old Imperial Army. No saluting when
off duty was one of these new regulations. In general, the relaxation of the old
regulations led to the disintegration of the old Russian army, which degenerated into
an uncontrolled rabble.

country, though it could be compared I suppose to the old Committee of Public Safety[30] in France during the Revolution. It is an absolutely autonomous body, set up for the purpose of preserving internal order and of maintaining the government. It has, of course, its open organization but by far the greater part of its personnel are secret agents. It can promulgate and execute its decrees wholly independently of any governmental sanction. Theoretically it would be possible for the Commission to arrest any one of the government leaders at any time. I am told, and I believe it a judicial statement, that the Extraordinary Commission has been the one factor responsible for the maintenance of the existing government.

After having been in Russia for six weeks, I believe with all honesty, and after having talked with men of every political conviction, that no greater calamity could befall Russia than the fall or overthrow of the present government. Men who abhor communism and all it represents agree in that opinion, and it is held for the reason that the only strong men left in Russia today are members of the government. Were the present government to fall, it would mean that power would fall into the hands of a set of rascals and desperadoes and that a period of chaos and banditry would ensue which would make the past four years of Russian history appear as a beautiful dream. Every American here in Kazan is convinced of this. There can be but one hope for the regeneration of Russia, and that hope must rest in the political, social, and economic education through practical experience of the present Russian governmental leaders. They have had four years' experience now, and they appear to be adjusting themselves to what I have called natural law. There is no other way out. There is no

---

[30] The Committee of Public Safety was a group of twelve men under the French Revolutionary National Convention, who oversaw and directed the Reign of Terror in France, which ran roughly from July 1793 until July of the next year. Over a thousand people suspected of being enemies of the Revolution were dispatched, including some quite loyal revolutionaries. Their terror was immortalized in Charles Dickens' *A Tale of Two Cities*.

faith in the intelligentsia who have fled from Russia, and there is certainly no faith left among the Russian people in the foreign governments, who through a pitiless blockade, have been responsible for a great deal of the misery and disease which now exists as a result of the absolute deprivation for three years of medicines.

October 27, [1921]—There arrived today from Moscow for a tour of inspection a number of visitors including colonel William N. Haskell, chief of the Russian unit of the ARA, ex-governor [James P.] Goodrich of Indiana, on a special mission of investigation for Mr. Hoover, and Sir Philip Gibbs,[31] famous British war correspondent, who is in Russia as the representative of several British relief organizations. The day was spent showing our guests about the town and in introducing them to the details of our work. Fortunately for us our office had been removed only a few days previous from the cramped quarters of the personnel house to a more commodious building, which made our activities much more presentable.

Colonel Haskell, a handsome man with iron gray hair and firm well-set figure, of distinctly military bearing, served immediately after the Armistice as Allied High Commissioner in the Near East and afterwards was chief of relief activities in Armenia....

Along with these visitors, there came to join the staff of the Americans attached to the Kazan district of the ARA, two additional Americans: [John J.] Norris and [Stephen A.] Venear.

October 30, [1921]—Sir Philip Gibbs and [?] Spray, another British journalist, returned today from a short excursion down the Volga to the canton of Spassk, where they had gone two days previous to observe famine conditions. Until this journey, Spray had expressed himself as skeptical of the existence of a great famine, but he, together with Sir Philip, returned without any false illusions on the subject. They returned indeed so depressed by what they had witnessed that it was difficult to draw them into conversation about what they had observed.

---

[31] Sir Philip Gibbs was a prominent World War I journalist and author of *Now It Can Be Told* and *In the Middle of the Road.*

There was one thing, however, which Sir Philip said had struck him most forcibly upon the occasion of the trip into Spassk, and that was that he had brought home to him as never before in his life the artificial character of money. He told of entering the home of a peasant in which the entire family was starving. The head of the house was lying stretched out upon a bed of rags, and in his weakened state, slowly sinking to death. There was no food in the house, and there had been none for several days, although the day previous some of the members of the family had attempted to derive some sustenance from bread made of straw and clay.[32] The visitors carried no food, but Sir Philip took from his pocket some Soviet rubles and offered the old man the greater proportion of what he had. At first the peasant only stared dumbly at the money and made no movement to take it or to express his thanks. At last he gathered to himself sufficient strength in which to speak and to the interpreter accompanying the party, he said: "I thank him, I thank the *barin*,[33] but his money is of no use. There is no bread to be had here in the village for any amount of money, and though there is some bread in the town of Spassk, you can see I have not enough strength to go there. No, tell him I thank him, good kind sir, but it is easy to see that I must die. My wife has died, one of my daughters has died, and it is now my turn. There is nothing to be done. It is all over with us." And with that he turned his face to the wall in a final movement of exhaustion.[34]

They are dying in Spassk and all over the length and breadth of the Tatar Republic under similar circumstances, and though the famine and disease with which all classes of the population are suffering is not so evident here in the city of Kazan, they are dying here, too. Even our own household has been affected. Only a few days ago, one of the maids was taken ill with the spotted typhus, and now it is our housekeeper who is ill of the same disease. My teacher lost her brother two weeks ago, and now her sister is dying and thus it is with even those who relatively are in the most favored circumstances. People are dying on every side like flies, for the truth is they are so pitifully undernourished that once disease overcomes them they find themselves without any powers of resistence.

---

[32] The famed *lebeda*.

[33] Russian for "baron."

[34] This incident was recounted in Gibbs's *In the Middle of the Road.*

October 31, [1921]—Wahren has gone to Moscow, and during his absence I have been left in charge of the Kazan district as acting district supervisor. This necessitates my meeting each day with the government representative Mr. [?] Slutsky...[unclear] constitute what is known as the executive committee of the local ARA. As the ARA has a semi-diplomatic standing with the Soviet government, the prime function of this committee is, with the Riga Agreement as a basis, to establish a *modus operandi* for the ARA in its relations with the government.

Mr. Slutsky, who is Commissar of Public Education of the Tatar Republic, is a young man with an enigmatical and very mature face. He is a graduate of law of Moscow University and is considered one of the most capable members of the local government. I had the temerity at this, almost our first meeting, to refer to a subject which has given our employees a good deal more concern than it has the Americans, which is: The reported presence in the ranks of the employees of representatives of the Extraordinary Commission.

In the course of my conversation today I state quite frankly that inasmuch as neither the ARA as an organization nor the American representatives in Kazan, officially or personally, had anything to conceal from the Russian government, it was quite a matter of indifference to us how closely we were spied upon and watched. Of course, I said, I realized quite well that our motives in coming to Russia were a great puzzle to many people within the government and that Trotsky himself had declared in a speech that we warranted close watching. Further, I stated that I had brought the question up only for the purpose of demonstrating to him now perfectly candid we desired to be in all our relations with the government. Mr. Slutsky replied by assuring me with great warmth that there were no representatives of the Cheka in our office as employees, inasmuch as the government had never had any doubt as to our trustworthiness or the sincerity of our motives.

Despite my regard for Mr. Slutsky, I have had too much acquaintance with the devious ways of diplomacy to put much faith in the assurances which he gave me. Perhaps I would not be so certain of the presence of agents of the Cheka in our office were it not for the fact that every American has found, on more than one morning, papers disarranged in the drawers of his desk. In fact, Boyd has complained that on two occasions, letters which he had written and left in his desk overnight and which were not particularly complimentary to the state of affairs in Soviet Russia have been not alone mislaid but plainly purloined.

November 5, [1921]—Wahren returned today from Moscow and brought us very encouraging news of the appreciation expressed by headquarters in Moscow of our work and especially by Colonel Haskell, who was represented as being delighted with what we had accomplished in so short a while. According to Wahren, it appeared quite plain that the work of our district was rated in point of accomplishment above that of all others as yet established in Russia. Particularly gratifying to me was the news that Colonel Haskell had expressed a desire to transfer me to Orenburg as district supervisor, but Wahren had been able to persuade him against this. I was exceedingly pleased to learn that my work was giving satisfaction, and I was equally pleased to hear that Wahren had been able to avert my transfer, for despite the classical tradition, I would rather be second in the most successful and important mission in Russia than first in a second-rate one.

Wahren also brought us confidential information that plans were being considered by the ARA to undertake the feeding of adults as well as children, and that in addition, a plan was also being considered whereby seed grain would be imported next spring for use as a loan to the peasants until the next harvest. In preparation for the putting through of such a program, a tentative plan for the division of the work was gone over with us by Wahren today. In this tentative organization, I shall be placed in charge of all child feeding activities in the district; Turner, the adult feeding and seed grain distribution, while Boyd will continue to handle all work relating to transportation and supply.

November 6, [1921]—Today was the fourth anniversary of this altogether strange and bewildering experiment in the reconstruction not only of a government but of an entire social fabric, or what is known as the Russian Socialist Federated Soviet Republic.[35] For four years it has kept its feet in the midst not alone [*sic*] of the taunts of the world but also in the face of the armed blows of more than one half the world. Its armed enemies have included: Great Britain, the United States, France, Germany, Japan, Poland,

---

[35] The Bolsheviks actually overthrew the Provisional Government on 7 November 1917.

Romania, Finland, Latvia, Estonia, and the native forces of half a dozen military leaders. Yet it continues to stand, although foreign chancelleries continue to prophesy its fall. When I consider the virility which the Soviet government has exhibited notwithstanding circumstances which would have caused the overthrow of probably half the governments of Europe, I am reminded always of an observation which Simson is fond of making when I discuss the subject with him: "What is healthy will live and what is corrupt and diseased will die," he constantly repeats when I oftentimes express my inability to understand the basis of support and strength of the Soviet government.

In celebration of the fourth anniversary of the Socialist Republic, Wahren and I were invited to attend in the evening at the Palace of Red Army Soldiers a mass meeting which was being conducted by the local authorities. The theater was crowded to its full capacity with a typical working class audience, which nevertheless was quite orderly and restrained in its behavior. The scheduled speakers included Slutsky, the government representative with the ARA, and [?] Karpov, chairman of the Communist Party of the Tatar Republic.... Contrary to my supposition, the speech of Karpov, I learned, was quite moderate in tone, containing as it did the confession that the Soviet government had been guilty of many mistakes, which however were represented as the natural consequences of an attempt to establish a government for which there was no precedent in the world.

I could not help being struck by a feeling of incongruity that I should be present at a meeting at which the war in which I had been engaged was characterized as one of imperialism and that the American government of which I was a citizen, together with the governments of France and Great Britain, should be described as ["]bourgeois governments,["] united to oppress the workers. As I was led to remark after leaving the theater with Wahren, it gave me a queer topsy-turvy feeling to attend a gathering in an official capacity which the police in America would have "pinched" the instant after it has been opened. But this is one of the novelties of our position here, which is proving so thoroughly enjoyable.

It was this same Karpov, who despite his unintelligent appearance, had been the author of as witty a bit of repartee, a few days previous on the occasion of a dinner party which we had given to the members of the local government, as I have ever been permitted to enjoy. For the purpose of creating conservation, rather than for any other accountable reason, I had entered into an account of the scientific expedition which had recently left the United States for Mongolia for the purpose of discovering the remains of pre-historic man. When I had finished, Karpov smiled in that repulsive and sinister manner of his and said, "One need go no farther than Paris to find the object of such a search."

November 10, [1921]—I have been moved so deeply by the evidence of universal distress with which I come in daily contact here in Kazan, a distress so widespread and of such a magnitude that the little aid which we Americans can afford to dispense seems so pitifully inadequate that I addressed a letter today to the editor of my home newspaper appealing for the raising of funds for Russian relief. [letter below]

> Mr. Walter E. Addison
> Editor, The Lynchburg *News*
> Lynchburg, Virginia
>
> As a citizen of Lynchburg, I wish to make an appeal through you and the *News* to my fellow townspeople who may be disposed to give attention to a picture, drawn by one whom many of them know, of the awful tragedy being enacted there in the Volga basin. It has occurred to me that as the only Virginian so far as I am aware of with the American Relief Administration in Russia and certainly the only Virginian of the Mission in the Tatar Republic, I might be able to establish a personal tie between the Tatar Republic and Virginia or at least with Lynchburg.
>
> We do not know what you have heard of our work, for we have had no news since coming here more than six weeks ago. We have read only the speech of [Fridjof] Nansen[36] before the League of Nations in which we have heard with surprise that he was obliged to deplore the inhumanity with which the world was treating this

---

[36] Fridjof Nansen (1861–1930) was a Norwegian explorer and scientist who became involved in humanitarian causes such as POW repatriation and the Russian famine relief. He relayed Gorky's appeal to the West and coordinated European famine relief to Russia. He received the Nobel Peace Prize in 1922.

greatest of twentieth century tragedies. For myself, I cannot believe that America can stand pitilessly unmoved in the face of what is going on here, that she can be dickering over debts and political opinions while 20,000,000 people are starving. That does not sound like the voice of America.

It may be said that there is distress enough at home to engage the charity of America. That cannot be. There was never a tragedy in America to compare with this.... Along the Kama and the Volga, I have seen orphaned children, streaming in hordes to the refugee centers to be collected and shipped off to Siberia and Turkestan, where they perhaps may find food. Eight thousand of these are crowded in homes in Kazan, where until now they have kept body and soul together with difficulty upon the black bread and grain soup given them once daily by the government. Even this food is now exhausted, and since November first the only food which they, like thousands of other children, are receiving is the single meal being distributed each day by the American Relief Administration. Typhus and other dreaded diseases are the common lot of the population who have not sufficient reserve energy to throw off infection germs. Yet these people are like you and I and others of our fellow townspeople. There have been many lies spread in the name of propaganda but none to equal the lies which have been told of these people. There have been stories published, for example, that out foodstuffs are pillaged. That is a stupid and foolish lie.... I have referred to the fact that it may be said in America that there is a greater need than can be filled for charity enough to be administered at home. To those who thoughtlessly speak thus I would say: For those who are orphaned and homeless in America, there are asylums where life at least may be kept together with food; here there are not even crusts in sufficiency. For those who are out of work, there are surely bread lines in America, but here there is only bread made of grass and slate. For the hungry in America there is always a neighbor from whom food may be had, but here all are alike, foodless and sick....

Now I ask you, cannot you at home who know so little of what hunger and slow starvation means, cannot you help in even a small way to alleviate something of this distress? The American Relief Administration is now instituting a food package system whereby for money deposited in America for friends or relatives in Russia, food may be exchanged here.[37] But there are so many here without friends or relatives in America.

I have thought that it might be possible for those who know me at home to raise a fund which could be deposited with the ARA in New York in favor of the Tatar Republic Mission of the ARA and which we might use in the form of food packages for distribution to those unfortunate ones who come under our personal observation....

November 11, [1921]—Today Wahran and I attended an exhibition of paintings by local artists at the Art Institute of Kazan. Most noteworthy of the artists participating in the exhibition is Nikolai Feshin, a student of the famous Russian portrait painter Il'ia Repin,[38] and now himself probably the foremost portrait painter in all Russia. Feshin's works have been exhibited before the war not only in Germany, France, and England but even at the Carnegie Exhibition in the United States.

---

[37] The ARA developed a program whereby people outside Russia could purchase food parcels to be delivered to individuals in Russia. One veteran of the ARA told this editor that they could gauge the severity of the hunger in a community by how much these parcels brought on the black market.

[38] Il'ia Repin (1844–1930) was one of Russia's most renowned artists. His most famous work is probably *Barge Handlers on the Volga*. His works often had a social or revolutionary theme. He bought an estate in Finland in 1903 and lived there until his death, leaving his home to the Soviet Academy of Art. His student Feshin (which he spelled Fechin on emigrating to the United States) painted many portraits of ARA relief workers, including Childs and his wife Georgina. He later settled in the American Southwest and became rather well known for his landscapes. Bertrand Patenaude, *The Big Show in Bololand: The American Relief Expedition to Soviet Russia in the Famine of 1921* (Stanford CA: Stanford University Press, 2002) 310.

There are some dozen subjects which he had chosen for the Kazan exhibition, and these stood out above all the works of the dozen or more other artists as strikingly as the work of a [John Singer] Sargent distinguished itself, even to the most untrained eye, from the daub of an amateur. Most of the work of Feshin, which was presented, was devoted to semi-symbolical studies of the famine and one of these, a grouping of half-naked refugees making a last desperate effort to cross a bleak plain upon [sic] the way out of death, particularly attracted me, and I was able to purchase it for the sum of six million rubles....

After all I had read in the foreign press of the Soviet administration, I could not avoid being surprised that such an art exhibition was possible in the Soviet republic, and my astonishment was all the more deepened when I came to consider under what handicaps the artists were working who had made this exhibition possible. I know that there is not a family within a radius of a hundred miles of Kazan who, if not in actually want of food today, will be tomorrow and was at some time or other within the past few months. For this famine is not isolated or confined to any particular section or to any certain class; all are victims in one way or another even including the members of the government.

My attention was brought today by one of the women directors of our child feeding kitchens in Kazan to an instance which illustrated how even the most influential Communists may be in need and yet may be by reason of the deep sincerity of their convictions, unwilling to take advantage of their position to improve their state. This woman, who is quite bourgeois herself, had brought to her notice the pitiful plight of the family of a Communist who, though an influential member of the party, was living with a wife and a child on barely enough food for one person. She, therefore, approached the wife of the Communist with the offer of a position as manager of one of the ARA kitchens in the city as she knew from friends that the woman was not only capable but was also distinguished for her integrity of character. News of this offer was communicated to the Communist by his wife who immediately gave answer that even if his family were starving, he would never permit them to be the recipients of aid from the bourgeois organization of the ARA. Later it was learned that he had even refused to permit his little child to present itself for examination with a view to being entered in one of the American kitchens.

I believe this is the most extreme example of Communistic prejudice and class consciousness that I have come upon in Russia, and though I cannot comprehend the pushing of one's convictions to such fanatical conclusions, I cannot yet avoid entertaining a feeling of very profound admiration for anyone capable of exhibiting such strength of will, however misguided, in the preservation of what are conceived to be inviolable principles.

November 12, [1921]—Within the past few days news has been received of two disturbing movements in Moscow; one, the arrest of the leader of the anarchist party [?] Pavlov, and the other an organized escape from prison of many important Social Revolutionaries.[39] In protest against the former there has been a strike of twelve thousand workmen in Moscow. Disturbed by the latter manifestation, it is reported that the Soviet government has proclaimed a Red Terror against the Social Revolutionaries. During the past two days, more than one hundred arrests have been made in Kazan, and last night we received news that our office manager, Salomine, had been arrested.

It is said that when the Red Terror[40] was proclaimed against the Kronstadt rebels,[41] the soldiers [sic] of the garrison were divided by the government into two groups, those formerly bearing allegiance to the Communist Party and those who were non-Communists. The former were drawn up in line and every third was shot while of the latter every tenth was shot.

---

[39] The Social (sometimes called Socialist) Revolutionary Party was founded in 1898–1900 as a socialist party that advocated the rights and goals of the Russian peasant. A major part of their program was terrorism. It won the Constituent Assembly elections in November 1917, outpolling the Bolsheviks by about two to one.

[40] The Red Terror, described in another context earlier, was the efforts of the Bolsheviks to eliminate any opposition to their rule from the time of an attempted assassination of Lenin in 1918 until the establishment of control of the country by 1921. Led by the Cheka, it manifested itself in arrests and executions of suspected enemies of the state.

[41] The sailors of the Kronstadt naval base in the Gulf of Finland, originally steadfast supporters of the Bolsheviks, rebelled against them in 1921, calling for "Soviets without Bolsheviks." Their rebellion was bloodily suppressed by the Red Army.

Tonight Wahren, Boyd and I had gone to the Palace of Red Army Soldiers for the purpose of hearing *Carmen* sung. The first act had been completed and we were settling ourselves down to an evening of enjoyment, free from the nervous cares of our position as bourgeois in a Communistic society, when Turner appeared, the excited bearer of momentous news. He had just been in receipt of a telephone message from an alarmed office employee that Mrs. Depould, one of the organizers of the ARA kitchens in the city of Kazan, had been arrested. Coming as this arrest did upon the heels of the arrest of our office manager, Salomine, it seemed to portend the dreaded general arrest of our employees, which had been our chief concern since arriving to take up our work. We stood a little excited group of four Americans in the forefront of the theater, filled with workers and peasants and Red Army soldiers, a hundred representatives of that power which had challenged that of the one we represented. As we looked into the stolid alien faces, which hedged us about on every side, I [sic] think there must have come into us one and all the same feeling simultaneously of inexpressible isolation. It was Wahren, who spoke first after a few moments of silence brought about by the surprising news.

"Let's get out of here," he said. And we trooped out in single file, with faces so set and determined that the attention of the audience must have been attracted, judging from the stares which were directed toward us. Outside the theater in the security of the darkened street we formed our little council of war. It was Turner, who first spoke, urging that as a retaliatory measure, the ARA offices be closed and that we should leave Kazan in a body for Moscow. Our turn would be next, he said, if further arrests were to be made. It would be useless to attempt to advise the ARA in Moscow of the developments since any telegrams which we might dispatch or any couriers we might send would be detained. In his opinion it was the old treacherous Soviet game all over again which he had witnesses in 1917 and in 1918 in Petrograd.

But cooler heads prevailed and in the end Wahren decided that as a preliminary measure no more drastic step would be taken in the face of the arrests than the cessation of the movement of all American foodstuff within the district. It was the conclusion of the majority of us that the arrests were not the will of the local government, which had manifested itself since our arrival in Kazan was extremely friendly to us, but that the arrests were undoubtedly prompted by the Extraordinary Commission, which while not having shown itself as actively hostile, at least had not exhibited the same friendly spirit of cooperation as the government. Little else was talked of during the remainder of the evening than the course of action which was to be pursued. Finally it was decided that on the next morning, a formal ultimatum should be presented the authorities. It was left that the local government would even welcome such action which would help to support it against the Cheka.

We knew that an altercation had already occurred between the head of the government, Muktarov, and the chief of the local Cheka over the support which the government previously had given us in our opposition to [?] Muskatt, who had been sent down by the central government in Moscow to act as liaison officer with the ARA and who was believed to be in reality a member of the Extraordinary Commission. Accordingly on the following day, November 13th, the following was drawn up by Wahren and by me for presentation to the government:

To the Government of the Autonomous Tatar Republic:

"Gentlemen:

I herewith beg to inform you that all shipments of foodstuffs, medical supplies, and clothing from Moscow to the ARA in Kazan, all food shipments from Kazan to the cantons, and all food deliveries to the kitchens and institutions in Kazan have been stopped by me on this date for reasons herein below stated:

1. Arrest of Mr. Salomine, office manager of the ARA in Kazan, on November 11th in violation of

(a) paragraph twelve of the Riga Agreement, which provides that the ARA shall be allowed to set up the necessary organizations for carrying on its relief work free from governmental or other interference.

(b) Verbal understanding concluded between the government of the Autonomous Tatar Republic that no Russian personnel of the ARA in the Tatar Republic should be arrested without notice first having been given and reasons stated to the Chief of the ARA in Kazan.

2. Arrest of Mrs. Depould, Kazan kitchen manager of the ARA on November 12th in violation of agreement and understanding as set forth above.

You are informed that further movements of foodstuffs into and out of Kazan warehouses of the ARA will be resumed when this office is furnished with exhaustive and satisfactory explanation of violations of the formal and written agreement as set forth in the Riga Agreement, as well as elaborated in the informal and verbal understanding specifically reached personally between the ARA in Kazan and the government of the Autonomous Tatar Republic."

Wahren and I went into a three hour conference with the government representative, Mr. Slutsky, at two-thirty o'clock in the afternoon at which the ultimatum was presented. The conference was most cordial on both sides, and before it was over Mr. Slutsky had informed us that there was no doubt that the release of Mr. Salomine and Mrs. Depould would be effected on the following day. It was quite evident from his conversation that it was the Cheka and not the local government which was responsible for the arrests and further that the Cheka would not be able to withstand the pressure which was being brought to bear by us through the government in the stopping of the movement of all foodstuffs.

November 14, [1921]—In the afternoon as Wahren and I were conferring together, the door opened and our office manager, Mr. Salomine, a very pale and haggard figure, his hair and clothes disarranged, stepped in. As his slender short figure presented itself in motion across the room, I thought he resembled nothing so much as a terrified rat terrier dog who, upon being frightened, scurries to safety with his with his head directed now this way and that. He sat down and commenced a hurried narrative of the events which had taken place from the moment of his arrest until his release a few minutes previously. He had come directly from prison, and as he spoke he kept rubbing his hands together and wetting his lips with his tongue under the stress of the nervous excitement from which he was suffering.

According to his statement, upon being removed from his house to the Cheka [headquarters], he had been questioned as to why he had permitted the employment of a certain inspector who had been recently sent out to one of the cantons by the office. He replied that the man had presented himself as an applicant for work, and he had only done his duty in introducing him to the Americans. Further, he declared to us that he had been presented in prison with a paper in which it was stated that he acknowledged himself as entertaining anti-Soviet sympathies. This paper he said he had signed out of fear. On the same day we heard that Mrs. Depould had been released, and the same afternoon Mr. Slutsky presented us the formal reply of the government to the ultimatum delivered to it on the day previous:

> Council of People's Commissars of the T.S.F.S.R [Tatar Socialist Federal Soviet Republic]
> November 14, 1921
> To the ARA:
> After discussing your letter of the 13 concerning the arrest of the employees of the ARA, Citizens Salomine and Depould, the government of the Tatar Republic has made the following decision: In these arrests the government does not see the reasons that make unavoidable the full or partial stopping of the relief work of the ARA because both of the above-mentioned citizens are called to court according to the law of the country and can be restored to their civil rights by customary trial. And, according to our laws, the above mentioned citizens are to be relieved from their duties during the entire time they are under investigation but will receive the full salary due them according to their positions in the office of the ARA. The government supposes that the real cause of the letter written by the ARA is the question of setting free citizens Salomine and Depould. The government has an especial respect for the ARA and in particular for the work that the ARA is doing in order to relieve the starving, and the government always treats with special attention all requests of the ARA which are directed to furthering the development of the work of the ARA. In this case the government has given attention to the expression of the wishes of the ARA for the setting free of the Citizens Salomine and Depould, and in discussing the question concerning the arrest of Citizens Salomine and Depould has decided to set them free on the

fourteenth of November and has sent a request to the law court to make the investigation as soon as possible.

The government is sure that in [the] future all cases of misunderstanding and discontent will be discussed in the usual way by the representatives of the ARA with the representative of the government of the Tatar Republic, Mr. Slutsky, or by personal negotiation of the ARA with the government. Such a manner of intercourse will lead to mutual satisfaction and mutual trust which are the basis of the present friendly relations that exist between the ARA on the one hand and the Tatar Republic on the other.

President of the Council of People's Commissars, Muktarov

The incident was [therefore] settled by the local government in a manner even more satisfactory than we had anticipated. A few days later, however, we learned from the ARA in Moscow that the central government in Moscow had taken a somewhat different view of the affair. In a letter dated November 20 and addressed to Colonel Haskell by the Representative Plenipotentiary of the RSFSR with the ARA, Mr. [Aleksandr] Eiduck, among other things it was stated:

Parallel with these, shall I say, joyful tidings from the provinces, I likewise receive reports to the effect that in choosing employees for the local bureaus of the RAKPD (Russian American Committee for the Relief of Children) district supervisors collect their personnel exclusively from the ranks of the ex-bourgeoisie, which elements are obviously inimical to the starving children whom they cater to, the latter of course in their majority belonging to the poor classes of workers and peasants. As an example I will quote the following report that I received from one place: "In enrolling its employees from among the Russian citizens, the ARA evinces everywhere a partiality for the class of the bourgeoisie. The latter advances from its midst the most opulent elements; and elegantly dressed women with brilliants on their fingers employ their time in distributing rations to the children. This picture is not very comforting if one takes into consideration that the sole objects of the food distribution are the proletariat and poor peasants. I would therefore count it just if the kitchen employees were recruited from amongst the mothers and the relations of the elements being administered to."

Of course on the strength of the stupendous task which the ARA has taken upon itself in the feeding of one million two hundred thousand children in a territory equal to the size of a few European states taken altogether, it is perfectly in the normal course of events that various irregularities and undesirable incidents occur. Up till now, in order to popularize the organization of the ARA itself, as well as its work, I strove to prevent reports concerning the negative side of the work from entering the press, but to my profound regret these reports are recently ever growing in number, and in certain places incidents have occurred which are most undesirable for me as the Representative Plenipotentiary of the Government of the RSFSR. With the ARA, and I am sure, are no less undesirable for you. For example, in Kazan,...where work of the ARA is showing itself most successful, our organ for forestalling various offenders was compelled to arrest certain Russian employees in the Kazan bureau of the RAKPD. Thus, a few days ago, there was arrested the ex-baroness Depould, who was appointed by Mr. Wahren, your district supervisor of the Tatar Republic, as an inspectress of the kitchens in the vicinity of the powder works, where the said lady made her appearance in diamond rings and bracelets and in *décolleté*, and by her external aspect alone evoked the protest and indignation of the hungry crowd of children and their mothers.

Apart from this, the said lady, before those children expressed herself in a most emphatically anti-Soviet spirit. Resenting this mockery of their starving children as well as the unpardonable attitude towards the Soviet Government, the workers took the necessary steps to inform the local authorities, who eventually ordered the detention of ex-baroness Depould. In the course of further investigations, it was established that the husband of the ex-baroness Depould had at one time fled from Kazan to [Admiral Alexander] Kolchak and had fought in the latter's army against the soviet government, and that Mrs. Depould herself is also an enemy of the Labor [Soviet ?] Government. That she was until now not been detained in a labor house (which is the law in our country with regard to the wives of officers who have fought against the Soviet Government) is only due to the fact that it was believed that Mrs. Depould would not come out actively against the present government, a belief unfortunately which did not justify itself.

The arrest has also taken place of a certain Krasilnikova, a woman employed by Mr. Wahren, who had assisted her husband to escape from the labor house to detention in which he was sentenced. A further arrest was made of Citizen Salomine, an employee of Mr. Wahren's—a Russian subject with an undoubtedly counter-revolutionary past and who was heartily mistrusted both by the local authorities and the central government, by whom the said citizen was kept on a special list as an outspoken enemy of the Labor [Soviet ?] Government, looking out for the first opportunity to carry on anti-government propaganda, which he was not slow of availing himself of when he had joined the number of Russian employees of the RAKPD.

All these incidents would of course have been avoided had your local supervisor, Mr. Wahren, seen fit to recruit his employees to a certain degree in coordination with the local organs, or with my authorized representatives who in accordance with the true spirit of the Riga Agreement, have the right on my behalf to declare a motivated objection. As representative plenipotentiary of the government, with the organization of which you are the head, I consider your humanitarian efforts to be so vast, important, and desirous, not only for us, but also for the American people who have entrusted you, my dear Colonel Haskell, with that task that the arrest or the request for the removal from the staff of employees of the RAKPD. Of certain Russian citizens who, I am firmly convinced, do not tend to promote your humanitarian work, cannot result in any conflicts or misunderstandings between us, and in any case, should not affect the great work of alleviating the terrible pangs of hunger among the children particularly.

To my profound sorrow and surprise, I must state that I was mistaken in this respect. Your Kazan supervisor, Mr. Wahren, in connection with these well-founded arrests, perpetrated on the territory of a sovereign state...[in which] in conformity with the Riga Agreement [you] are working, turned for an explanation not to the proper authorities through our authorized representative in the Tatar Republic, Mr. Muskatt, who knows the English language well, but he addressed the following letter to the government of the Autonomous Tatar Republic on the fourteenth instant.[42]

I am sure, my dear Mr. Haskell, that you will, with myself, disagree with the manner in which Mr. Wahren has dealt with the question, for I cannot by any means reconcile myself to the idea that the great American nation, who of their own free will and in spite of all the counter-scheming of the enemies of the Labor [Soviet] Government, have stated their desire to help the starving children of the Volga basin, and who have entrusted you with that execution of that great humanitarian task, would have placed the question as follows: That the relief proffered to children who are actually dying depends upon the arrest of two of the wives of well-known enemies of the Labor Government, and one or two Russian citizens, whose attitude also is hostile to the present government and who take advantage of their positions as employees of the ARA to carry on anti-government work.

I categorically protest against the manner in which Mr. Wahren has dealt with the question, and I hope, my dear Mr. Haskell, that you will give this matter your serious consideration and see to it that these incidents do not affect the work of the ARA in the region of the Tatar Republic or anywhere else on the territory of the RSFSR.

Hoping that you will kindly inform me as soon as possible of the steps taken by you in the matter, so that I may be enabled to report to my government and issue the necessary instructions to my men in the provinces.

I beg to remain, dear sir,

Yours very sincerely,

Eiduck.

---

[42] Childs omits the letter.

Representative Plenipotentiary of the RSFSR with the ARA

November 14, [1921]—At the invitation of Miss [Zina] Galitch,[43] I
called at her room in the evening at the Second Soviet House to meet two of
her old school girl friends whom she used to know in Petrograd and whom
she had not seen since 1915 until one of them had called at the office in
search of a job. They are the daughters of a former general of the old army,
have the title of princesses, and are now living on memories and what little
black bread they can buy from the sale of their belongings. The oldest, Lily,
had a husband, a White officer who escaped in 1918 from Russia and from
whom she has not heard since. She is now working as a typist in one of the
Soviet institutions. She receives a pound of bread a day which must be
divided among her young son, her mother, and her younger sister, and
herself. Their conversation, which had to do with the old days they had
spent before the Revolution in Petrograd at the [Smolnyi ?] Institute, was
most engaging: Of Monsieur Poupet, who had instructed them in dancing
and who wore such a queer goatee; of M. Bonin, the youngest instructor,
and with whom they were all in love; of the excitement which reigned on the
days when they were permitted to receive visitors. They talked of what had
become of their friends since the tumultuous days which had separated
them, and they laughed when it was told that the proud aristocratic beauty
Stepanova had married a Communist. They took delight in the most trivial
details of that old life and kept expanding and dilating upon it; of the old
general, one of the overseers, who came each week and who never failed to
inquire the family name of each girl he met during his visit, and the regard
which he gave each one in answer seemed to be a measure of his
appraisement of the aristocratic standing of the family to which she
belonged.

They did not draw dramatic contrast between those old days and the
present, but the fact that they did not give greater emphasis to it all. The
contrast which they themselves drew was visible in their gestures, the flash
of their eyes and the tossing of their heads. Adding to the contrast was the
fact that Miss Galitch in the intervening years since those school days had
served as secretary in the Soviet foreign office. I took the girls home and as

---

[43] Zina Galitch was Boyd's secretary.

we walked along the street, Lily told me how greatly she desired to leave Russia for a foreign country but that she and her family were unable to do so as they had no money and nothing left of any value to sell. Almost all of their old friends were gone from Kazan either to the south or out of Russia entirely. Life was a struggle now for the bare necessities. There was little wood for fuel for the few bare rooms to which they were confined, and there was never enough bread these days. They bade me goodbye on the street and disappeared through a door in a fence which surrounded the back lot of a house and which evidently had once been the servant's entrance.

November 16, [1921]—As we went into breakfast we were met in the hallway by the aged engineer,...who was once owner of our house.... With tears streaming down his face, he begged that he be given a job for, as he explained, he has been laid off from work the previous day and now he feared that owing to his unemployment, he would be deprived of the last shelter which remained to him out of numerous estates. He became calmer when he was assured that we would use our influence to see that he retained the use of his rooms even though he might be out of work.

On the same day, Venear returned at noon from his work at the Cafe Metropole with a pathetic tale to illustrate the terrible misery which is about us on every hand. He was passing up the street and met a crowd surrounding a horse, which had been drawing a peasant's cart, and which had fallen through lack of fodder from fatigue in the snow. The owner, an old peasant, was found seated on the sidewalk in utter grief. Three children, thin and scantily clad, were shivering from cold and lack of nourishment under some bags which had been thrown over them in the cart. The peasant explained that a few weeks previously he had lost his wife, the mother of the children, through typhus and that he had then sold his home and set for Kazan with his children in order to put them in an asylum. Now, as he was on the point of reaching his goal, his horse was dying together with his children, and there was nothing left for him but death. A soldier who was passing with a load of hay stopped to fling some to the horse. Some kind Samaritan, but a little degree removed from the old peasant in hunger and in want, took the children away to shelter.

It was found necessary for me to leave this day for the canton of Elabuga, and arrangements were made whereby a special car would be attached to a freight train leaving for Votskaya Poliana from when I would have to proceed eighty *versts* by sleigh. With me went Skvortzov , from the government, and Simson, my interpreter. We left shortly before midnight and we were obliged to make some search of the railway yards before our car was discovered. The station of Kazan was a perfect mob of struggling soldiers and peasants, many of them refugees, moving aimlessly about with no other apparent objective than to depart from the famine stricken area. One was obliged almost to fight one's way through the large rooms and halls of the station in which travelers were crowded from end to end.

Outside the station along one of the tracks there was a pathetic picture of a little boy of no more than twelve or fourteen years, who was making a very desperate and manful struggle to load a child's coffin onto his little sled. In ghost-like lines there stood out opposite, the whitely-painted cars of the German disinfecting train which had just reached Kazan. As I scrambled across the tracks in search of my car, I heard a weary voice bargaining with another for two pounds of bread.

The car given us for our journey was one belonging to the People's Commissars of the Tatar Republic and which from its markings must have had an eventful history. One of the devices painted upon it which had been scratched over and defaced, revealed that the car at one time had been employed by the diplomatic courier traveling between Berlin and Moscow. Later, apparently, the car had been captured by the Poles during the Russo-Polish War [of 1919–1921] for another marking indicated its use by the Polish General Staff in Warsaw.

November 17, [1921]—We arrived at Vatskaya Poliana station about eight PM, and went with Simson, my interpreter, and Skvortzov , the government representative, while the latter got into telephonic communication with the local Cheka in an endeavor to obtain horses and sleighs that we might continue the same evening on our journey. In the telegraphic room of the station, which was a low squat frame building of four or five rooms similar to any other small station of Soviet Russia, there was a single smoky kerosene lamp from the light of which four telegraphers were attempting to work. As I stood in the hallway, a woman stopped to inquire of me when the Americans would begin to feed the children of the Viatka Government, but as I had not sufficient Russian to answer her, I merely shook my head and replied that I didn't understand.

About ten o'clock word was brought to our car to which we had retired that the horses had arrived and would take us to the village of Vatskaya, four *versts* distant, where we would be able to procure other horses for the purpose of proceeding farther. I put on my trench coat with lining and over this a fur-lined coat and with my felt boots and fur hat, and with my revolver, I ventured to start out on my first sleigh journey of any length in Russia. There was a moon which, though not visible through the grey winter sky, gave out enough light for all our purposes. I bundled myself in the basket-shaped sleigh, settled down in the straw, which served as a seat, and gave myself over to contemplation of the strange fate which had brought me to a lonely little station in Red Russia in the winter of 1921. The horse darted forward and my heart lurched to my throat as the sleigh balanced itself on one runner. I thought surely that we had overturned, but I came later to learn that traveling on one runner was by no means an unusual occurrence for a Russian sleigh.

Arriving at the village of Vatskaya Poliana, we were shown into the headquarters of the local Cheka, and for the first time since my residence in Russia I was asked, together with Simson and Skvortzov , to show my Russian card of identity. Two young men were our interlocutors, and they appeared interested to learn whether I was from New York or Chicago. I explained that, contrary to the almost universal impression existing among foreigners, all Americans were not necessarily from one or the other city, and that in my own case I came from a town in Virginia of which it was improbable that either had ever heard. Presently our new horses were brought around and about eleven in the evening we drove off on the first leg of our journey of eighty *versts* to Elabuga....

We rode over a fairly hilly country the first night, dotted here and there with clumps of woods. In the dim moonlight, the groups of stately firs and pines stood out upon the white background of snow like battalions of troops bivouacked in battle array. The stillness of these natural camps was broken only by the crunch of our sleighs upon the snow and the occasional crack of the driver's whip. About one thirty o'clock in the morning,...we drove into the village of Nizhnyi Shuna. The chairman of the executive committee, when found, showed us to the best house in the village, and upon awakening the occupants there gave over to us two rooms. In one of the rooms there was a bed from which one of the members of the family had been ejected and which was offered me. Skvortsov and Simson made their beds alongside upon the floor.

November 18, [1921]—After making a breakfast out of the provisions we were carrying of bacon and beans, we left about nine o'clock with new horses.... [After traveling all morning, they reached the village of Umisk about 1:30 PM.] We went to the home of the village teacher, who was also the manager of the American kitchen, to make our lunch. It was fortunate that we were carrying our own supplies with us, for in the territory through which we were passing, we could never have imposed upon the impoverished people whose guests we were and who had nothing to eat but a little *lebeda* and sometimes a few eggs.

The population of the village of Umisk is six hundred and seventy-six, of whom about three hundred are children. Our kitchen was caring for forty-five children, and the manager estimated that there were at least two hundred other children in the village who were in practically the same predicament as those who had been selected to receive our food, that is, children who were living on grass and weeds and acorns. I visited one home of a mother and three children of whom two are receiving the American ration. The two are boys and appear less hardy than the daughter, who has to depend upon what her mother is able to gather in the form of acorns and grass from the forest. These two, the mother and daughter, I learned from questioning of them, had had no other food for four days than a saucer of milk daily, which was obtained from a half-starved cow, and the bread made of grass and acorns which were gathered from the forest. As I entered the home, the mother was just returning from a visit to the forest where she had been for the purpose of gathering these food substitutes.

The home, which was the ordinary peasant's hut of a single story and of two or three rooms, was simple yet clean and neat in appearance. On one of the walls was to be seen the photograph of a soldier in the uniform of the Russian army who probably had been the late head of this little household. With a face set in no affectation of stoicism and in an expressionless voice, the mother inquired how long the children might expect to receive American food. I assured her I hoped it would be just as long as there was need, and I longed to tell her there was hope that she too might be provided for this winter....

In the fields about Umisk, it is estimated that only about twenty-two percent of the fields have been sown. At present there are no contagious diseases in the village, although there is some sickness from starvation. There is probably enough food on hand to last the general population about one month or six weeks if properly distributed. The American kitchen was located in the village school and appeared well organized and capably administered by the village teacher. I arrived too late to observe the feeding, but from the children pointed out to me in the village as receiving the American ration, I satisfied myself that it was being distributed among those most needing it.

A little after three o'clock we left with fresh horses. My sleigh was driven by a sturdy little lad of no more than fifteen years of age, a bright mischievous boy who, between his lashing of the horses, turned about in his seat to smile or to answer some of the questions I put him through Simson. I was so much taken with him that I asked him whether he would not care to go with me to Kazan to become by coachman. He smiled, gave the horses a cut of the whip, and shook his head.

"My mother and older brother are dead," he explained, "and I have to help my father with the fields. We have fields allotted us for five souls," [44] he added, with a tone of pride in his voice as much as to say, "If you have fields to cultivate, make as good a job of it as I."

It grew dark between three and four and the lashing of the horses increased in frequency. "Hasten!" the youngster would admonish the horses, "The wolves are gathering in the forest and will soon be upon us." Then he would turn his head over his shoulder and grin and wink at us....

Lenino, a distance of twenty-eight *versts*, was reached by six o'clock. The population of the *volost* of Lenino is eleven thousand, of whom three thousand seven hundred and sixty-one are children and the number of rations allotted the *volost* is three hundred. The village of Lenino, ninety rations for the seven hundred fifty children inhabiting the village, have been allotted. While new horses were being prepared we went to the school house to make tea. The villagers explained with every apology that they regretted

---

[44] "Soul" was a pre-revolutionary term for "peasant" or "serf," used mainly before the emancipation in 1861. It would have been somewhat antiquated by Childs's time. The term is best known in the West from Nikolai Gogol's famous novel *Dead Souls*.

their inability to offer us any other refreshment than hot water from the samovar. We still had some provisions left, however, a precaution which experience on the day had demonstrated to be a positive necessity if we desired to eat. The samovar was provided by a very sweet-faced young teacher, whose living quarters were in a room adjoining the school. Her two children were attendants at the American kitchen in the village, and from her we learned that they were receiving nothing else than this one meal a day. The mother, a young woman of about twenty-eight, looked tired and despairing. Asked what food she lived on, she replied that formerly when the school was open, she had received sufficient food from the parents of the school children to support herself, but now that the schools were closed she had nothing. She did not know what to do to save herself from the starvation which, in view of conditions confronting her, seemed to be inevitable.

I turned over to her all the food we were carrying with us, which consisted of only two or three pounds of bread and as many of rice. The gift did not elicit from her tired face even a smile. The only evidence of any human emotion was the glance of tenderness which she bestowed upon her children as they scampered about the bread. Her dull expressionless eyes and careworn face, features which once must have been very attractive in animation, were the image of those depicted in the portrait of a famine-stricken mother I had seen exhibited in the art exhibition of Kazan the previous week.

From such scenes as this, it has become increasingly evident to me that unless some agency undertakes the feeding of the adults in the Tatar Republic, supplementary to our feeding of the children, that it is quite possible that at the end of the winter, our giving of one meal a day to the children in an effort to preserve them and at the same time lift a certain food burden from the parents, will have come to naught, for it is quite apparent that the death of heads of families on such a great scale as is likely to occur unless relief is forthcoming will mean also the death of a large proportion of the children, who, if not now dependent upon their parents for food, are dependent upon them for a sustaining force in life.

We reached Elabuga, which was but sixteen *versts* distant, early in the evening and were lodged at the Soviet Hotel, where I was given a bedroom connected with a living room which might serve me as an office.

November 19, [1921]—Elabuga, which is a town of some ten thousands inhabitants, is one of the most modern and attractive towns in appearance in the Tatar Republic. If differs from almost every other provincial town in the Tatar Republic in the solid substantial stone character of its buildings.... In the morning I visited our central warehouse for the canton, which I found an excellent structure for the purpose and where our foodstuffs were well stored. I had on a previous visit[45] seen the children's homes in Elabuga, which were remarked upon as being in as excellent a state as children's homes in America. However, I repeated my visit to them in order to learn whether it was desirable to ration them. I found that they had not been cut off from government supplies, as the children's homes in Kazan, owing to a shortage of food, and that therefore the committee had acted wisely in excluding them for the present from our distribution. The children's hospital which I visited contained thirty-eight children, almost all of whom were suffering from sickness caused directly by the famine. There were almost no medicines in the dispensary. The doctor whom I interviewed stated that he expected to care for as many as five hundred children before the winter was over and that he placed the figure at this number because that was the limit of the hospital facilities. According to the same doctor, food conditions, which were temporarily alleviated after the crisis of the late summer, took a turn for the worse the last of October and were steadily growing worse and would reach a new crisis about the first of January. Confirmation of this opinion was had by me in all the villages which I visited and where it was estimated that the food stores of the general population would last at most for only six weeks. In the case of many families, of course, the food larder has already been exhausted.

I visited also the public kitchen where five hundred and twenty children are being fed. The kitchen staff consists of five. Another public kitchen is being established in the town to feed a similar number. The children in this kitchen did not appear to be in as bad a state as those observed in the villages, although there is no doubt that without the American food they would be equally badly off within a month.

---

[45] Childs speaks here of a previous visit to Elabuga, but it is not mentioned earlier in the diary. He makes several such references to heretofore unrecorded earlier visits to certain locales.

There is a bazaar in Elabuga, where for the present at least food may be purchased by those who have the price to pay. Almost all of the bread for sale, I was told, came from Menzelinsk, a few *versts* up the River Kama. When the river froze, the price of bread jumped overnight from one hundred and sixty thousand rubles a *pud*[46] to three hundred thousand rubles. Of the four thousand needy children in the town of Elabuga, the committee has made plans to feed one thousand.

After my inspection of the work in the town, the committee was called together in my room for a conference, and I witnessed at this meeting one of the commendable examples of self-sacrifice and honesty of purpose in the election of our work by Russians that I have observed since I began my work in Russia. It came about over a discussion of the proper allotment of rations to be given the new canton of Ariz, which is to be formed out of Elabuga. Thirteen thousand rations had been assigned the old canton of Elabuga, and the rations for the new canton of Agriz would have to be taken from the rations assigned the old canton of Elabuga now comprising Agriz. I suggested a split of three thousand and ten thousand; the former to Agriz and the latter to Elabuga. But the committee demurred. It was not enough for Agriz. I explained that if more were given to Agriz, it would have to come from Elabuga. That was proper, I was informed; conditions were worse in Agriz.... I advanced to five thousand and eight thousand, and I believe they would have permitted an even more adverse division for Elabuga if I had suggested it.

On account of the setting up of the new administrative division, it was decided to go by sleigh one hundred and ten *versts* to Agriz on the railway line running east and north from Kazan, and there to form a committee for the new canton. In order to inform the new Agriz committee what had been done previously in the district by Elabuga, I suggested that one of the most energetic members of the Elabuga committee, a young Russian named Pavlov, should accompany us to Agriz. This was agreed to.... Before leaving we were invited to a lunch at the house of the cantonal commissar of food supplies, whom I had met on a previous visit to Elabuga. [At lunch] the commissar reminded me what it was he who had asked me on my last visit what the American people were thinking of Russia and the Russian Soviet

---

[46] A *pud* is about 36 pounds.

government. I explained again that it had been impossible for me to answer that question as I could only interpret the opinion of a very small body of the population, and it would be unfair to give that as it has been formed on the basis of news reports which were notoriously false. As an illustration of the falsity of such reports, I cited the number of times Lenin has been assassinated in the foreign press and also the report, which had been spread broadcast and which had never died, of the nationalization of women in Russia by the Communist government. We all enjoyed a very merry laugh, especially at this latter....

We left Elabuga about seven o'clock in the evening provided with fast horses belonging to the government and rode...thirty-two *versts* to the village of Kamaevo in two hours and a half. It was the only occasion during four days of driving that I was cold and on this night, upon which a bitter wind was blowing, I would have suffered even more but for a small supply of spirits which I was hoarding for just such an emergency.

We arrived about ten o'clock...and the chairman of the soviet executive committee showed us to the home of a Tatar family where we were to pass the night. The room into which we were conducted was hung about picturesquely with fancy red needle-worked towels and shawls which are peculiar not only to the Tatars but which I used to find in Macedonian homes in Serbia. A low platform, stretching from one corner of the room to the other, I found, served as a sleeping place, and upon this was placed several layers of feather beds. This platform was just large enough for Simson and me, and the other two, Skvortsov and [?] Pavlov reposed themselves upon the floor. Upon our arrival in the village that evening, we had noticed at the post station a group of children gathered about the door of a room in the building. We were told that this was the storehouse of the American food supplies and that, since an adequate storeroom could not be found anywhere else in the village than at the post station, the children from the kitchens kept their turns in standing guard over the food at night.... The child population of the village is four hundred and thirty-eight, and the American kitchen is caring for one hundred and fifty.

November 20, [1921]—We left at nine o'clock with new horses for the next station, Sukman, a distance of thirty-four *versts*, but stopped on the way at Stara Iumia to look into one of our kitchens in the village. Children in this village number two hundred, of whom fifty are being fed in our kitchen.

Families in the village number ninety-eight, and the previous week there had been two deaths from starvation. In order to attempt to alleviate the distress, the inhabitants themselves had collected on the previous day seven *puds* of *lebeda* and seventy-five *puds* of potatoes for distribution among the famine sufferers in the village.

We arrived in the village of Sukman, a distance of thirty-one *versts* from the last post station, at ll:45 AM and drank tea in the house of a Tatar, Zainullin. Zainullin, with the queer bead-like eyes and scanty beard of a typical Tatar, had been in the Russo-Japanese War and had been wounded at Mukden....

We were driven by Zainullin to the next post station, a distance of fifteen *versts* located in the village of Amga, where we arrived at 2:30 PM. On the way he told us that he had met fifteen wolves that morning in the forest at five o'clock, but he had escaped by lighting fires beside him.... Another story was told of a schoolmistress who, while being driven through a lonely stretch of country, was attacked by a pack of the ravenous animals. The driver whipped up his horses but despite the urgency impressed upon them by a whip and their own terror, they were not quick enough to outdistance the wolves. When it seemed as if the woman, as well as the driver and horse, would be lost, the driver turned about in the sleigh and with a push into the snow, delivered the woman over to the wolves. While they tore her to pieces, the driver escaped safely with his horse....

We left at 3:20 PM and arrived at Izhbaiki at 5:00 PM, where we changed horses immediately and left for Agriz, arriving there, twelve *versts* distant, about two hours later.

November 21, [1921]—We were lodged in the best house in the town, a two storey structure belonging to a Tatar, the most comfortable dwelling I found on my trip. The day was spent in organizing a committee for the new canton of Agriz,...and upon the arrival of our car on the railway line from Vatskaia Poliana, we moved to it. It was not until late in the evening that the train for Kazan from Ekaterinburg came by to take us home and on the next afternoon, Wednesday, November 23, we arrived in Kazan.

November 26, [1921]—I learned today that a young and enthusiastic Communist—I need not add also idealist, for the word is almost synonymous with "communist," however incongruous it may appear—committed suicide this morning in the Second Soviet House.... He had grown despondent over the turn which affairs had taken in the Soviet government as a result of the New Economic Policy and was in despair over the difficulties confronting the forward movement of communism which, in this moment, had been forced to make a retreat. So he blew his brains out from being disillusioned over an ideal.

November 28, [1921]—It was made known to me today that the movements of all of the Americans in Kazan are under the closest surveillance of the Extraordinary Commission. So accurate and detailed are the observations of this secret police that it was known to them today that no later than yesterday afternoon I had been to the market to buy two rugs. They are aware of most every article we have purchased since coming to Kazan, and the price that was paid in each instance. Further they have made themselves acquainted with out personal habits to the minutest details.

December 6, [1921]—From several sources it has become known that in our home at 46 Lenin Street the commandant of the house is acting as one representative of the Cheka from among the many that have been set to observe us. In our office it appears that there are at least three: The commandant, one of the technical workers who was recommended us with such urgency by the government and third a woman. Of course, there is a fourth who is well enough known to us but whom it is unsafe to mention.

In the evening I went with Wahren to the dramatic theater to see a performance of [George] Bernard Shaw's *Pygmalion*. It was very well acted and equally well staged. The smartly dressed actors and actresses were in striking contrast to the poorly clothed spectators assembled in the galleries as well as in the pit and in the boxes. The stage property looked as if it might once have formed part of the furniture of some of the more aristocratic mansions of Kazan.

"Loot," I leaned over to suggest to Wahren as our attention was attracted in particular to one setting.

"Loot is right, " was the answer. "The last time I was here, Madam Stepanova (one of the artists of the opera) pointed it out to me as a set which had belonged to her in the days before the Revolution.

December 9, [1921]—Three weeks ago as Skvortzov, Simson, and I sat about a slim meal of canned provisions in a bare cold room in Elabuga, discussing the excellent results we had accomplished in our personal tour of inspection of the canton, the idea occurred to me of a similar journey which would include every canton of the Tatar Republic. Skvortzov, inspired by the ideals of a true and honest Communist and always interested in devoting himself with a fine spirit of self-sacrifice to promoting the ARA work, was enthusiastic. From the map we carried with us we traced our a tentative itinerary. Now, three weeks later, I am about to execute the plan then made, for with Skvortzov and Simson, I am starting off on the first leg of a circuit of the Republic. In addition to the secretary of the Communist Party of the Tatar Republic and my interpreter, there are accompanying me also: [Edwin Ware] Hullinger of the United Press, who had come down from Moscow for the purpose of proceeding with me, and [?] Lambert of the Chicago *Tribune*, who has come to go only as far as Sviazhsk.

Our first jump off was not suspicious as the railway car which we had expected to transport us as far as Sviazhsk was not at the station. While Skvortzov and I were using the telephone in an effort to solve our difficulty by obtaining another car, a member of the Cheka came to our aid and offered to put us in the railway car of the workers. Upon seeking admittance to the car, however, we were met with objections to our intrusion by the score or more of railway workers, already crowded inside. One of them was particularly noisy in the voicing of his objections, but our friend of the Extraordinary Commission took a hand, and upon announcing his identity and taking down the name of the principal objector, we heard no more of the reasons why we should not have been admitted to occupy the car of the workers...

Arriving at the station Sviazhsk at 11:30 AM, horses were awaiting us. I made myself as warm as I could with two fur coats, helmet, fur cap, sheepskins, socks, and felt boots, and behind good horses, covered in an hour the distance of twelve *versts* which separated us from the town of Sviazhsk.

Two public kitchens, two children's homes, two hospitals and the warehouses were inspected, and after we had had lunch with the committee a conference was had with the latter. Lambert obtained horses and returned to Kazan, while the remaining members of the party set out at 4:30 PM on the road to Buinsk, which we had hopes of reaching the next day.

The horses were poor, however, and we had not traversed ten *versts* by 6:30 PM. Upon reaching Umatovo, the *volost* seat of the neighborhood, tea was made and we prepared to feast upon our canned goods which we were carrying along with us while the *volost* committee of the ARA was summoned. By the light of a flickering oil lamp there were presently assembled and with them a curious crowd of onlookers, of old and young and of both sexes. The members of the committee were sturdy, God-fearing honest appearing peasants with dark brown skins and beards which seemed to have taken on the color of the soil they tilled. When one asked them a question so simple as to how the children had been selected to receive the American food, they screwed up their eyes and wrinkled their foreheads in the effort to arrive in their minds at the answer....

We left Umatovo at 3:00 PM and drove by the light of the moon for two hours to Makulovo, ten *versts* distant. In the old days, our sleigh driver informed us, there would have been a crowd of interested villagers to welcome us and escort us to a warm habitation. But the people were too weak and uninterested in life for such manifestations now, he added. As usual, we were obliged to seek out the chairman of the local soviet, who directed us to a Tatar home, where after preparing and partaking of a simple supper, we made our bed upon the floor.

December 10, [1921]—The next morning, as we made our breakfast from the food which we were carrying with us, the door to the peasant's home was opened, and the figure of a middle-aged priest appeared in the doorway, who after having made the sign of the cross several times, strode across the room to greet us. He introduced himself as the manager of the American kitchen in the village. He reminded me of the kindly-faced and very human-looking Greek Catholic priests I used to be acquainted with in Serbia. We invited the priest to our breakfast, but although we had learned from him in the few minutes' conversation we had previously [had] with him that so far as food was concerned, he was no better off than any of the peasants of the village, he declined on the plea that he was observing a religious fast.

The kitchen we found in his home was a model one. Later we entered one of the homes in the village where we found a mother and three children, who had nothing to eat but the black *lebeda*, a substitute for bread made of weeds, which contrives to prolong life for a while. Only one of her children was receiving American food as conditions everywhere are so bad that it is rarely possible to include more than one child of a family in the American kitchen. Before leaving I gave the priest five hundred thousand rubles for charitable distribution. He accepted the money, declaring at the same time that my thanks in appreciation of his work was a thing that was more precious to him than any material gift. He had received many offers, he continued further, from parishes in more prosperous communities outside the famine area, but he preferred to share the fate of the people in adversity, whom he had served previously in prosperity. Departure was taken from Makulovo and the priest at 10:00 PM on a beautiful, cold, clear day, and two hours and a half later we arrived at the village of Kurguza, ten *versts* distant. The American kitchen was found in the village schoolhouse, and when we entered the livingroom of the teacher, alongside we found two members of the family in bed, sick from hunger. It was bitterly cold and on account of the lack of fuel, the school had been closed for some time....

While we made tea in the samovar proffered us, a peasant who had heard of our arrival in the village entered and having first directed his glance towards the ikon in the corner of the room and after having made the sign of the cross, addressed us. He held in his hand some specimens of the inevitable *lebeda*, upon which the entire population is living and with a gesture, which could have moved even the most doubtful of those in France of the existence in Russia of a famine, he state quietly: "Comrades, I can perhaps eat and live on this, but my children cannot. They must die if they are not given help. Cannot you enter all of my children in the American kitchen?" There was no note of complaint in his voice, no whining or the suggestion of a beggar begging for bread. He spoke as a member of the family of humanity in distress to a member in more fortunate circumstances.

I talked with a member of the village committee regarding the general state of livestock. He stated that a year ago he had had two horses, twelve sheep, three pigs, and a calf of which only one horse remains. This case is fairly typical not only of the canton of Sviazhsk but of the Tatar Republic. In the total territory of which since the famine began, about sixty percent of the horses have been sacrificed for food, fifty percent of the cows, and eighty percent of the sheep. So depleted have the livestock in the canton become that during my journey through I was never able to make much more than twenty *versts* or fourteen miles a day.

We left Kurguza at 2:15 PM and arrived at the Ivanovskaia *volost* at 4:00 PM. It was probably the coldest day of our trip, with the thermometer about 39 degrees below zero, and before arriving in town I alighted from the sleigh to take a run in order to get warm again. A drink of the cognac we were fortunately carrying with us brought us to life once more when we had entered indoors. In this village we hoped to obtain horses and leave so soon as we had had a conference with the *volost* committees of the ARA, but after waiting until ten o'clock in the evening I stretched myself out on the floor and at midnight, when the horses had not arrived, I seconded the motion that was put that we spend the night where we were and resume our journey early in the morning.

December 11, [1921]—Leaving Ivanovskaia at 8:30 PM on a very cold day, we drove directly to Verkhnyi Irdinchyi, sixteen *versts*, and in a wholly Tatar village, we were put up in a Tatar home for our conference with the committee of the ARA and the population. From inquiries it was learned that even *lebeda*...sells here for one hundred and twenty thousand rubles a *pud*.

In this village there was to be found the worst children's home which had been viewed in the whole of the Tatar Republic. In what was little more than a barn, something like a hundred children were crowded. There were ties of broad shelves ranged around a single room upon which the children slept. There were no blankets, no beds, no sheets, and the few clothes in which the children were attired were hardly sufficient to keep them warm, even within the interior of the house. It was a pitiful spectacle to observe them in the middle of the day, huddled together in groups about the room in the effort to obtain warmth from the contact of their underfed bodies. I appealed to the committee to attempt to effect some amelioration in the living conditions of these children, and I promised that I would make very effort on my part to obtain clothes for them.

Leaving Verkhnyi Idrichyi at 1:00 PM, the next halt was made at the village of Big Bulatovo, a distance of twenty-five *versts*, which was reached shortly after four o'clock and after the sun had gone down and deprived us even of the little warmth emitted by its feeble rays. It was very cold and we spent almost half an hour in a peasant's home before we felt fully comfortable once more.

Here we had our customary meeting with the village authorities in the effort to learn the famine state of the community at the same time that we conferred with the ARA representatives with a view to ascertaining the progress of the work. The village might be taken as typical of a half hundred that we visited. In the spring the population had been five hundred and eighty, and now it has been reduced through deaths from starvation and through the departure of many families to three hundred. In the month of November there had been ten deaths from starvation. In the spring there had been in the village a total of forty horses; now there are but nine, scarcely sufficient to attend to the everyday needs of the people without reference to the agricultural need of the community.

I interpellated the secretary of the local soviet, a man of early middle age, as to whether there were many families who contemplated emigrating. He said that there would be no mass movement such as occurred in late summer, not only on account of the cold but also on account of a lack of draft animals. The population, he said, at a recent meeting had given expression to the almost unanimous purpose of remaining together in the village, where if one died, it would be among friends.... He himself, however, he said, would have gone but for his duties with the soviet. The attitude of this man as well as of hundreds of others with whom I talked was one of calm resignation in the face of the death, which was looked upon as inevitable. Death might be delayed but there were none of the peasants throughout the Tatar Republic with whom I talked who had more than enough food resources to ensure their lives for more than a month or six weeks. Bread: That is the sole preoccupation today of more than three millions of people in this republic and of how many more from Astrakhan to Moscow, it would be difficult to say. Money's only value today is in the amount of bread it will buy. A man does not complain that you have not given him sufficient money for some service; his complaint is always directed to the fact that with it he can only purchase so many pounds of bread or so many pounds of the bread substitute *lebeda*.

An hour and a half after arriving at Big Bulatovo, we left for Buinsk, where we arrived some three hours later after having traversed twenty *versts*. A room had been reserved for us at the home of the chairman of the local cantonal soviet who was also the chairman of the ARA, and there in a very comfortable home, we passed the night, as usual alongside each other on the floor.

December 12, [1921]—Throughout the first three days of our journey food of any sort had been unpurchasable, and in Buinsk only horse meat was found on sale in the market of the local bazaar. Having foreseen this, I had made arrangements not only to carry food for our needs for a week along with us, but I had had also a second week's supply of food shipped ahead of Chistopol to await our arrival there.

After visiting the kitchens and children's homes in town, the latter of which we found to be in a particularly deplorable condition without blankets, beds, or other linen than the children had brought with them to their asylum, a conference was held with members of the ARA committee and representatives of the population and government. One of the most intelligent of these latter was the head of the Cheka, as usual a young man. He explained that the eating of dogs and cats was general throughout the canton, and it was his opinion, confirmed by others present that only from three to five percent of the population had the food resources with which to support themselves through the winter. [While at the meeting, a telegram arrived stating that a revolution had broken out in America and that the president had fled to the foothills of the mountains.] Instead of betraying as much agitation as those about me, I added to their agitation by smiling incredulously....

Soon afterwards the conference broke up, and we left Buinsk at 2:30 PM with horses to take us to Tetushi. At 6:00 PM we arrived in Chinchurino and went to the home of a peasant to make tea and to warm ourselves.

While we were eating, the usual crowd of curious peasants entered the room and stood about, and as usual, I plied questions at them regarding food conditions. One old peasant, who looked like Father Time and who assumed the role of spokesman for the group, in the course of the conversation stated that two of his children were in the American kitchen and that without this help their lives could not have been preserved. He almost broke down and wept in expressing his simple gratitude. As in all other villages through which I had passed a very large percentage of the population, having reached the end of their resources, were beginning to swell from hunger as a result of the eating of unnutritious food substitutes....

We left Chinchurino after having been conducted by [the manager of the American kitchen] through one of the children's homes where the children in their rags and filth were lying outstretched upon the floor without anything to cover them. Tetushi was reached about 9:00 o'clock in the evening, and we were lodged in a home where for the first time during our journey, we were given beds to sleep on. The only objection that could be made against the room was that it was very cold, and we were obliged to go to bed immediately to get warm.

December 13, [1921]—After making our usual tour of inspection in the town next morning, we met the committee and learned that Tetushi canton was no better off than the others we had visited. Fifteen villages were reported as subsisting at the present time upon cats and dogs, and of the entire population of the canton it was estimated that ten percent were living on no other food than that provided by these animals.

The town was left in a driving snow storm at 3:00 PM and crossing the icebound Volga, the canton of Spassk was entered. Two hours later entry was made into the historic town, now [the] village of Bolgary....[47]

But a few *versts* distance from the village of Bolgary, there was discovered not long ago by Turner of the ARA in the market bazaar of the town of Tetushi a small library of rare old English, French, and Russian books, which to the proprietor of the bazaar, possessed only the value represented by the paper contained within the rich bindings. Many of the books had already been sold for the use to which the pages could be put as cigarette and wrapping paper of which there is a great scarcity. It was possible to salvage from the heap a first edition of the *Letters of Lady Montagne* and a first edition of [William] Robertson's *History of Scotland*. Unfortunately, and despite the search of the entire town by the proprietor of the shop, it was possible to save from destruction but three volumes of a four volume *History of America* published in 1770.

Such discoveries are paralleled almost every day in this country, the preoccupation of which for more than a year has been that of food. At present the government is making an effort through the sending out into the

---

[47] Formerly known as Bulgary, the town was the capital of the early Bulgarians, whose migration here pre-dates the Mongol invasion in the thirteenth century. Their relatives were the ancestors of the modern Bulgarians.

districts of experienced buyers to collect together as much as remains of objects of art or those articles having an historical value. That the harvest in such is still rich, an incident may illustrate. Only recently it was learned that one of the finest private collections of medieval European coins which had existed in Russia before the war had been sold for five hundred pounds of rye flour. Rare and delicate Imperial porcelain is sold constantly as simple table plates and cups, and rich Bokhara rugs have a value only as blankets for bed covering. The finest works of art, the most desired luxuries to the western world mean nothing here unless they can be put to practical use or can be converted into food, since the chief luxuries today in the life of the Russian of the Volga are bread and sugar and meat.

We left Bolgary at 6:00 PM, and although it was only twenty *versts* to Spassk, we did not arrive there until 9:00 PM on account of having lost our way several times on the road, all traces of which had been obliterated by the fallen snow. In Spassk we were shown to the most comfortable and well furnished house I have seen in the Tatar Republic, the home of a veterinary surgeon, Bashkirov, who for some reason has been able to escape with most of his possessions from the Bolshevik levy on property. He took great delight in exhibiting to us his most prized possessions, which included a very old violin, a sword of Peter the Great, and a very fine collection of old coins. He also owns a Victrola and before we went to bed we eased our fatigue, brought on by the constant driving in sleighs, in listening to the music of [Franz] Schubert's *Serenade* and in having more than our usual sip of cognac, which previously we had been doling out to ourselves. Then when we were put to bed in real beds, we forgot all our recent hardships and straightway dreamt of a land where food was in abundance and where the temperature never fell below a hundred degrees in the shade.

December 14, [1921]—It was with real regret that we left such a comfortable lodging [the] next day after Skvortzov and I had made our usual inspection and had had the usual committee meeting. While we were engaged with these duties, Hullinger, at his special request, had been shown by the local authorities the local court and prison and had visited some of the churches. Though there is no code of law in Russia today, he found according to his report justice being administered in a rude though commonsense fashion. In the prison, he found the prisoners being fed despite that a hundred yards outside its walls, people by the score were starving. But the prisoners he interrogated, expressed a preference for liberty and starvation as compared with prison and food.

In Spassk a starving woman whom we questioned stated that she had never heard of [Alexander] Kerensky.[48] She knew that there were some kind of government in Moscow, but she was extremely indefinite in the conception which she expressed of it. Her only real conviction, and in this she represented the mentality of seventy-five percent of the peasants in the Tatar Republic, was that she was starving.

On our way out of Spassk, which we left at 5:00 PM, we passed the Molostvov estate, formerly the home of one of the pre-war landowners of the locality. It has been converted by the Soviet authorities into a children's home and is managed by the children themselves somewhat after the principles government of the George Junior Republic.[49] There is a Soviet control composed of children between the ages of thirteen and fifteen. At five-thirty PM the *volost* seat of Pishtkassy was reached, eighteen *versts* distant from Spassk. People in the village were found to be living on cats and dogs, and as we entered the village my attention was called to a man who was carrying a dead chicken which he had picked up on the roadside and which he evidently intended to eat. This was by no means the first incident of its kind of which I had heard. [Childs continued on over the Kama River to the village of Epantchino.]

The village of Epantchino was found to have been reduced by more than one third since the spring as the result of starvation, and of two hundred and eighty children, fifty already were swollen from hunger, despite the feeding of one hundred and seventy-eight in the American kitchen.

---

[48] Alexander Kerensky (1881–1970) was a prominent lawyer for radical causes and Duma member at the time of the Revolution. One of the founders of the Trudovik Party, a democratic socialist party, he became a Social Revolutionary after the February Revolution, in which he was a major player. He held the positions of minister of justice and minister of war before becoming prime minister in July 1917. He was overthrown by the Bolshevik Revolution in November of that year and spent the remainder of his life in exile in the West, lecturing and writing books mainly on the Revolution.

[49] An American colony for children founded in New York state in 1895 by W. R. George. The governance was conducted by the teenage children themselves, not by adults.

Thirty of a population of seven hundred and fifty had died the previous month of starvation. We slept on the floor of the Tatar home which had been offered us as a lodging, and the next morning rose at 5:45 AM to continue our journey.

December 15, [1921]—A full moon guided us until daybreak, and we had the unusual pleasure of observing the setting of the moon almost coincident with the rising of the sun. We drove along the banks of the Kama and shortly before 9:00 AM observed in the distance the glittering Byzantine domes of the monasteries of the town of Laishev. The beauties of the places of worship of the Russia towns and villages are such as have never failed to afford me an occasion to marvel at the wizardry of the architects and the wealth of the Russian Church. I never remember to have observed among the countless churches I have seen in the towns and obscure Russian villages of the Tatar Republic two which were built alike. And each new one always brings out some unexpected and novel design. Arriving at Laishev we were put up in the rooms of the "Committee of the Communist Party," where one of the first sights which greeted one was a picture of [William "Big Bill"] Haywood upon the wall inscribed with the title of "American Communist."[50]

I did not care to delay my departure from Laishev by going too much into the details of the work of a committee which had conducted its affairs in so uniformly successful a manner and therefore planned to leave at noon. While waiting, however, I visited a kitchen at the local nunnery, which had been turned over by the church authorities to be used as a public kitchen for the American feeding. It was one of the cleanest and best controlled kitchens which I found in the course of my trip. The horses finally appeared at 2:00 PM. We left immediately and made a first stop in the village of Shuran, twenty-one *versts* distant, at 5:30 PM. I found again in this village that people had been known to eat the dead chickens and livestock which were found on the road. We left Shuran at 6:00 PM and arrived at Muzeka in the canton of Chistopol, twelve *versts* distant, an hour and a half later....

---

[50] W. D. "Big Bill" Hayward (1869–1928) was a radical American labor leader in the early twentieth century and one of the early members of the American Communist Party. He emigrated to Russia in the 1920s and is one of only three Americans interred in the Kremlin wall along with the galaxy of Soviet saints.

Leaving Muzeka [several hours later] we arrived at the *volost* seat of
Alexeevskaia, two *versts* distant at 9:30 PM and were put up in a building
which was formerly the post office and in a room which was the filthiest we
had been lodged in since the beginning of our excursion. Hereafter meeting
with the committee, we slept on the floor, and it was here I think that
Simson was bitten by a louse which resulted some few days later in his
falling ill of the spotted typhus.

December 16, [1921]—After visiting one of the kitchens in the village,
we made our departure at 10:00 AM and traveled to Sakorovo-Novosulky,
twelve *versts* beyond, where we arrived at midday. We stopped only long
enough to look into the kitchen and to talk with the authorities and then
made our way on to the *volost* seat of Staro-Ivanaevo, six *versts* distant, which
was reached at 1:30 PM. In the village here we were told that only 262
people out of a population of 14,585 had sufficient food with which to live
through the winter, according to official figures of the *volost* soviet. We
obtained fresh horses here and started out for Chistopol. Skvortzov and I
were riding together and we had a most talkative driver who conversed
freely because he was under the impression that we were both Americans....
His chant was particularly directed to a glorification of the "good old times"
of the past. Land was not owned by the peasants in those "good old times"
but then, after all, according to his versions, the landowners had not been a
bad lot. At least one had had bread then and a sufficiency to eat, but
now...there was nothing, absolutely nothing. He dilated upon this
"nothing," enumerating all that he had formerly had and of which he was
now deprived, and one would have thought from his repetition of it that this
"nothing" was become symbolical to him. Suddenly the old man ceased his
apparently endless plaint to inquire, "Nikolai, the Little Father,[51] is he dead?
So one says, but is it true?" When we told him it was indeed true, he shook
his head and kept his eyes fixed for sometime upon the snow-covered
plain....

[They eventually arrived in Chistopol.]

Chistopol is the largest town of the Tatar Republic outside of Kazan
and numbers about 20,000 in population. It is composed of a large number
of substantial stone buildings. Today a great part of the most pretentious of

---

[51] A reference to Tsar Nicholas II.

these buildings, or more than thirty, are now sites of orphanages. During my stay in Chistopol, I was told that approximately twenty-five orphans were collected from the streets or brought in from the country every day and that this number was constantly increasing. Two months previously I had visited Chistopol and had found the conditions of the children's homes to be exceedingly pitiable and such, so far as concerned sanitary conditions, as were easily capable of correction. On that occasion I had read a bitter act of accusation before the committee for its neglect and for the neglect of the population as a whole, and I was pleased to find upon this visit that much had been done in the way of remedying the conditions which I had pointed out as demanding immediate correctional. In one of the worst children's homes, a distributing center, where the children were brought in from the streets, starving and half naked, the deaths had been at the time of my visit in October at the rate of forty each month. At the time of my visit in December the mortality had decreased to four a month.

The room which we occupied in a former hotel was by no means clean, and we preferred to sleep on the floor rather than in the beds contained in it, which were living nests of bugs.

December 17, [1921]—After performing our usual tour of inspection in the town and after meeting the committee, we obtained horses after several hours delay with which to proceed on to Mamadish. Our driver was a young boy, who instead of leading us by the shortest road, made a detour in order to stop at his home in the village of Buldery. Though it was but fifteen *versts*, it was two hours before we reached it. His mother brought him out a plate of cabbage soup and some *lebeda*, which he ate greedily, although sharing it with the driver of the other sleigh.

A little while later we were on our way again and after crossing the River Kama and passing over into a very wild country, covered over with the underbrush peculiar to flats and marshes and reported the most infested section with wolves of the Tatar Republic, we arrived presently at Vandovka, twenty *versts* distant from our last stop, about 10:00 PM. Here we were fortunate in being put up in the schoolhouse of the village and a very attractive school teacher, who was the kitchen manager of the American kitchen, showed us a comfortable room where we had a meeting with the local committee and representatives of the local population and authorities. There appeared also a member of the Mamadish committee who was on his way from Kazan. He was a young man who before the Revolution had worked in Bridgeport, Connecticut, on munitions for the Russian army. Despite his several years' residence in America, however, he spoke no English.

December 18, [1921]—We arose at 6:00 AM and proceeded to Omara, eight *versts* distant, where we stopped for our usual interrogations of the committee and the population. It was discovered here that some time previously there had been a raid by a bandit on the local warehouse containing American supplies, and although he had been captured and the supplies recovered, the bandit had effected his escape. We left Omara at 9:00 AM and traveled over a flat country, barren for twenty-five *versts* alike of dwellings and trees, until arriving at Mamadish. We had preceded Simson by an hour on account of the less rapid gain of his horse, and when he arrived he was shivering from cold and found it apparently impossible to restore any warmth to his body. We stopped in a private home in Mamadish and there met the committee from whom I learned that the energetic chairman of the committee Dezhin was not giving his entire time to the ARA work without any salary or remuneration. After having inspected the kitchens and children's institutions in Mamadish, the committee asked that I pay a visit to a children's home in one of the suburban villages. We arrived there late and after dark and upon entering care had to be taken that we did not step upon the bodies of the sleeping children who were scattered everywhere about the floor. Here, as in many homes which I visited, there were not only no beds but not even blankets or any bed covering of any kind, and the rags, which the children had to clothe themselves with or to protect their nakedness, were scarcely sufficient to keep them warm during the daytime. In their rags, some crouching, some sitting, and some reclining upon the floor, they resembled, in their dirty garments and in their staring lusterless eyes, the figures of animal rather than human being. There was little that I could do but I gave the chairman of the Mamadish committee two million rubles to buy what few clothes were possible with such a sum. We had expected to leave Mamadish at 3:00 PM in order to reach Elabuga the same night, but no horses appeared, and we were obliged to sit about and wait....

At length after waiting for four hours, the horses were brought around and despite the invitation which was pressed upon us to pass the night in

Mamadish, we set out at 7:30 PM in a bitterly cold snowstorm. Over the snow-covered winter roads, it was difficult to make one's way, and we were lost several times. At length when we had traveled thirty *versts* and found that it was midnight and everyone had become thoroughly chilled, it was decided to stop in the village of Ormaly, in which we found ourselves. Despite a cold wind which penetrated to the very marrow of the bones, I had been sleeping fitfully, crouched as low in the bottom of the sleigh as I could find a place for myself. When we determined upon passing the night in Ormaly, I was obliged to run up and down the road in my two heavy fur boats before the blood regained its customary circulation.

Skvortzov picked out in the gloom the most commodious and substantial of the peasants' huts which were visible and proceeded to knock and call outside the window. There was an interminable pause within, but at length a voice inquired, in a quavering tone, who we were and what we desired.

"Open the door," Skvortzov answered, "and let us in. We are seeking quarters for the night." Evidently such an assurance was not satisfactory, for the voice mumbled something and was heard to confer with other subdued voices with in. After some minutes had elapsed the voice was raised inside again to declare, "There's an American kitchen here and you must go away." The injunction was greeted with a loud laugh, which appeared to puzzle our interlocutor. "That's all right," was Skvortzov's answer, "That is just what we are looking for. I am a representative of the government of the Tatar Republic and with me is an American representative." This last was sufficient to obtain our entrance, for we were greeted with the cordial invitation "to come right in."

When we entered the house, we found it not as comfortable as we had been led to expect from its exterior appearance. There was but one living room in which there were already as many as a dozen people asleep in different corners, and including a young man and his wife, the old father and mother, three young men and a half dozen children, these last upon the stove. However, we found places in the middle of the room upon the floor.

December 20, [1921]—Upon arising in the morning at 6:30 AM, we went to inspect the kitchen which was situated in the cellar. The kitchen manager was already on hand, and we found from him that he had been in America before the war, on board a Russian cruiser which had put in at Newport, RI, for repairs. He boasted with pride of that experience despite the fact that as he confessed he had never been permitted to go ashore during the twenty-nine days that he was in the American harbor.

Upon starting out for Elabuga, we noticed a great movement on the road of peasants, walking and driving in the direction in which we were going. Skvortzov observed that it was the church holiday of St. Nikolai and that the peasants we saw were going to the nearby village of Lenino to attend church there. When we arrived at the latter place, we stopped to have a look inside. There was a great crowd which had already proceeded us within. They were divided into two groups: The women on the left and the men on the right, all standing and continually crossing themselves. Occasionally one would go to the little booth at the entrance to buy a candle to be placed before the image of some saint. The interior of the church presented a mass of ornamental ikons and religious paraphernalia which were illuminated by the countless candles ablaze in every corner of the room. To the right was a little room, a sort of chapel into which the priest in his resplendent robes kept passing. During the ceremony he brought out a censer which he waved and with which I was told he was performing the symbolic task of chasing away the devils. At the time of the reading or singing of the Apostles, Skvortzov made his way to the corner where the members of the church, who were officiating, were gathered and from whom he sought permission to lead the reading. He told us afterwards that they looked at him doubtfully as a stranger, but when he raised his voice and took part in the singing in a very excellent bass voice preliminary to the reading, assent was given. For a moment as he was making his way forward through the crowd to present his request, I was thrown almost into consternation as to his purpose, fearing that he was projecting, as a Communist, some mimicry of the service. But he had been formerly a choir singer, and his father before him had been a priest, and he participated in the service with all the respect which was due it....

At 10:30 AM we arrived at Elabuga and went to the cooperative dining rooms of which my old friend Pavlov, a member of our committee was in charge.... Pavlov gave us the most excellent meal we had found on the entire trip, in fact the only one which had been offered us, and consisting of fish and pelmeny, a typical Russian dish.[52] We had a short meeting with the committee, and then I went to see the local museum while the horses were being prepared. Although the museum was a modest one in size, it contained excellent examples of Tatar costumes and work and also some very good photographs of the special workshops conducted for children, for the blind and for adults in the canton. I do not know what it is about this canton, but in almost every activity it leads the other cantons in the Tatar Republic. Certainly its children's homes are model ones in every respect as also the home for the blind in Elabuga, where they are taught basket weaving and reading.

In Elabuga I found that during the lapse of a brief month a very considerable change for the worse had occurred in this, probably the most favorably-situated of all cantons in the Tatar Republic in food resources. Typhus had broken out within the past few weeks and sickness was increasing alarmingly. Mr. [?] Iskakov, chairman of the cantonal soviet, the ARA committee and of the Russian Relief, stated that ninety-five percent of the population had made application to the Russian relief for aid. Departure was taken from Elabuga at 2:15 PM and in an hour and a half of brisk driving we had crossed the Kama and were in Chelnyi. There we went to the home of the giant, Shakirov, the chairman of the ARA committee for the canton. Standing six and a half or three quarters feet high, a tall slim figure with the Tatar features of bronzed skin and slightly squinted eyes, he presented an extraordinary appearance as a Mongolian Goliath, particularly with the rude sheepskin coat worn by him. We had our conference and we paid our usual visit to the public kitchens and children's homes, and these last we found in no respect better than any we had seen previously on our journey. After a few days of visiting such homes, one is troubled with nightmares at night in which all that is to be seen are thousands upon thousands of children, assembled together as in herds with the wild staring eyes of troubled animals. Not even a nightmare, however, can exaggerate the actual conditions prevailing today in the Tatar Republic.

After horses had been prepared we left Chelnyi at 7:14 PM to traverse the same evening as much as was possible of the distance which separated us from Menzelinsk. Three hours later the village of Elbuktino, where we had

---

[52] Very similar to the Chinese dumpling, the *won-ton.*

planned to stop overnight, was reached, and we were received into the schoolhouse and given over a room by one of the teachers living alongside. That is a fact to be remarked: That in all the schoolhouses that I have seen in the Tatar Republic, there are living rooms, forming a part of the building, which are reserved for the teachers.

December 20, [1921]—There was a bed in the room which was given us, but we preferred to abide by our habit of sleeping on the floor and the next morning we were awakened by the children passing by our room in[to] the schoolroom opposite. The kitchen was in the school building, and the teacher who had entertained us was the manager. After we had made our inspection, we went over to visit a children's home in the village where we found that so many orphans had been assembled that the home was not capable of housing them and almost half had had to be scattered among private homes in town among a population which was not able to take care of itself.

Leaving Elbuktino at 9:15 AM, a stop was made at the *volost* seat, Kuskeevo. Upon going to the *volost* soviet offices it was found that every official had absented himself with the exception of the office boy. Upon inquiring where the chairman of the soviet was to be found, the office boy answered, "At the bazaar." [They then learned that the entire office was there.] Someone ventured to assert that on bazaar days, it was likely, according to the custom of this town, that even the feeding of the children was dispensed with....

"They're Tatar," Skvortzov was at length forced to admit with a wry smile, "and they are incorrigible traders." Meanwhile the kitchen manager put in an appearance, and he spoke so little Russian that Shakirov was obliged to act as interpreter for Simson, to whom I put the questions in English. The latter in turn put them into Russian to Shakirov, and he translated them into Tatar for the benefit of the kitchen manager. In this three-cornered process, there was a good deal of time expended in obtaining the information I desired....

Finally, when we had waited two hours and fresh horses had been brought around, it was decided to leave without the anticipated conference with the officials. We were getting into our sleighs when they appeared. Skvortzov called the chairman, an old patriarchal-looking Tatar, to him. After some bitter comments upon their behavior in leaving their official

duties to spend the day at the bazaar, Skvortzov , in his capacity of secretary
of the Communist Party of the Tatar Republic, informed the chairman of
the *volost* soviet that he would have to go to Zelinsk the next day and explain
his conduct to the cantonal soviet authorities.

[They passed on to Verkhnyi Baliaryi.]

Here Simson complained of being very sick with aches and pains
throughout his body, and so I gave him several generous drinks of cognac,
and we hustled on to Menzelinsk. It was dark when we reached there at 5:00
PM, and after putting Simson to bed, Skvortzov and I started off on a tour of
the kitchens and children's homes and hospitals in order that we might be
prepared to hurry on to the railway point Agruyz, from which Simson might
be taken without difficulty to Kazan. After our meeting with the committee
in the private home to which we had been shown, the medical member of
the committee examined Simson and without attempting to diagnose his
case promised to come to us at 5:00 o'clock the following morning to give
his opinion as to whether he could be moved on without danger.

December 21, [1921]—We passed the night on the floor, and at 5:00
o'clock in the morning, I was awakened by the presence of the doctor, who
had completed his examination and who agreed that we might take Simson
with us. The necessity of getting him, if possible, to Kazan was recognized
by all on account of the very limited attention he might receive in
Menzelinsk or in any other place away from Kazan, if his illness was the
serious one it gave the appearance of being. We set out at 7:00 AM with the
intention of making, if possible before halting, the one hundred and ten
versts of seventy-seven miles separating us from Agryz. Reaching Pianyi
Borg (The Drunken Forest), twenty *versts* distant, a little more than two
hours later, we requested an immediate change of horses, and after waiting
an hour and a half during which we conferred with the local committee, they
were brought us, and we were on our way again. From Pianyi Borg to
Chekaldyi was twenty *versts* which we covered in three hours, arriving at the
latter place at 2:00 PM.

By this time the nerves of all of us were considerably strained as a result
of the driving night and day for the past two weeks and the consequent loss
of sleep from which we had suffered. Officials of the town whom we first
interviewed declared that it would be impossible to give us good horses or
even any at all without some delay, but Skvortzov sent them scurrying by

the declaration that as a representative of the Tatar Republic, he would put
the chairman under arrest and make him answer for his failure to Kazan if
the best horses in the village were not produced within a half an hour. Of
course, we did not expect our command to be executed in less than an hour
and a half, but before we had finished drinking the tea that we had prepared,
the horses were before the door, and they were such good ones that we were
driven to the next village at which we planned to stop...twenty *versts* distant
in precisely two hours....

We were conducted into one of the filthiest homes into which it has
ever been my lot to be introduced and in which we were obliged to spend
two hours awaiting new horses. I was worn out and I desired to lie down, but
when I saw bugs crawling about the floor, I changed my mind. I took my
seat on a bench alongside the wall and was about to put down my coats and
lie upon these on the bench, when I took one look at the wall and felt my
skin creep at the sight of the hundreds of bugs which were disporting
themselves behind me. If not a comfortable [one], it was in every way an
interesting home, for it was the first in which I had seen either children or
even the adults of a family sitting down to anything like an apparently
abundant quantity of food. There were four children, husband, wife, and
grandmother, and they had to eat: Meat soup, cabbage, potatoes, and bread.
The children were fat and healthy-looking and seemed to be gorging
themselves. The head of the house stated that he had returned the same day
from Sarapol, where he had purchased a *pud* of flour for five hundred
thousand rubles or about two dollars and a half. I remarked to Skvortzov
upon the contrast between conditions in which we had been living in the
Tatar Republic for two weeks and those which were observable in this, the
Government of Perm. His answer was: "As a representative of the
government, I have sometimes to blush with shame."

The mother and grandmother, after eating, busied themselves with
weaving by the aid of a handmade apparatus. There was to be observed also
in the room a hand-fashioned cradle, a sort of basket suspended from a pole
which ran latitudinally between one of the walls and the beams supporting
the roof. The children, after having eaten, climbed up by the stove to a sort
of garret, built for sleeping purposes in peasant homes and one side of which
is open and exposed to view from the room. There they lay in the straw with

their chins propped upon their arms, all in a row and looking down upon us like so many little birds perched upon a roof.

We did not receive the same consideration here that we had been accustomed to receive, and the reason given by Skvortzov was that we were not only outside the Tatar Republic but that we were also in a region which was not receiving American help. Horses were given to take us only twelve *versts* or to the first village, which we should enter upon our return to the Tatar Republic. Arriving at this latter point at nine o'clock, I was so fatigued that I stretched myself out on a bench in the Soviet offices to which we were shown and did not awaken until 11:00 PM when I heard Skvortzov 's voice declaring that the horses were ready with which to proceed....

It was 3:30 AM when we arrived in Agryz at the end of our one hundred and ten-*verst* continuous day's ride. The station authorities knew nothing of our railway car, so we sought a lodging at the home of the Tatar, where we had been previously entertained upon our last visit. Even the floor felt soft and inviting on this occasion, and we slept until ten o'clock the next morning.

December 21, [1921]—Simson continued [to be] very sick, but our doubts as to how we would transport him to Kazan were dissipated very early by the arrival of the chairman of our committee in Agryz, who told us that the car accompanied by Victor Sorkin, our general handyman, had arrived and was at the station....

After transacting our usual business in Agryz with the cantonal committee, we moved our belongings and Simson to the car. The station authorities met our request for the coupling of our car to the Kazan train with objections, but they were quickly over-ruled by Skvortzov and threats of the Cheka, and we were pulled out, attached to the train about 8:00 PM.

December 23, [1921]—At noon the next day Arsk was reached, at which point Skvortzov , Victor, and I left the train, sending Simson on to Kazan. I desired to inspect the cantonal organization, and this was completed with dispatch...enabling us to leave the town in sleighs two hours after our arrival.... At seven o'clock we left and covered the thirty *versts* separating us from Kazan in two hours and a half, thus making sixty-five *versts* with the same horses in a total of seven and a half hours. We were at the end of our trip. During fifteen days we had traveled seven hundred and eleven *versts* by sleigh, two hundred and seventy by rail, and had visited twelve of the thirteen cantons of the Tatar Republic. We had held twelve meetings with cantonal committees; fourteen with *volost* committees; eighteen with village committees; had inspected thirty-three public kitchens, thirty-six children's homes, and ten hospitals. This record journey in which [we] three had participated had been made not without casualties for [yet] upon reaching Kazan the illness of Simson had been diagnosed as spotted typhus.

December 25, [1921]—This day of "peace on earth, good will toward men" broke upon me with terrible irony as I sat and surveyed in contemplation those Russian villages through which I had passed a few days previous and where all was death or desolation. I do not think I have ever suffered so profoundly as I have these past days, and when I think of how different the world has proved to this tragedy which will count as a great a number of victims as four years of world war, I wonder to what the world has come and what has become of that thing men and women are wont to vaunt as civilization. And that "good will to men." What has become of it and the other teachings of Jesus Christ? Has the soul of the world been destroyed since 1914?

At least there is some good will left here, even in Bolshevik Russia, for last night the girls from the office stole unnoticed into our house as we were eating dinner and brought a Christmas tree, which they decorated, illuminated and left in an adjoining room without having attracted our attention. With it there was also left a Christmas cake, the gift of our employees, and for the making of which each had contributed from the slender portion of flour which forms a part of the wages which they receive from us. It touched each one of us very deeply, and I think that in all our Christmas recollections of the future this tree, the symbol of the sacred day which all the world celebrates and a token of the love and good will of the greatest of men for humanity and the world, will be marked apart by us as a sign which we were given of the good will in which we were once held by the people of this community....

January 5, [1922]—As a result of inability to control petty thievery among the employees in the kitchens which we are operating in the city of Kazan, it was decided in the last days of December at a conference with the government representative to make use of the Extraordinary Commission in the effort to put a stop to the practice. It was not expected that the perpetrators of such small thievery as we had suspected to have taken place would be apprehended, but it was proposed to enlist the aid of the special secret police of the government for the moral effect which would be produced more than for anything else. It was therefore arranged that on the same day, December 31st, all of the kitchens which we were operating would be visited by representatives of the Cheka, who would make a search of the premises, subject the employees to a cross-examination and if necessary even visit their homes for the purpose of prosecuting the investigation. The result of these Cheka raids, which certainly could not be criticized for any lack of thoroughness, was that no specific instances of the misuse of American foodstuffs were traced to particular individuals, and the moral effect which it was sought to produce was of such a nature as to have nearly caused the ARA the loss of its most capable and conscientious employees. [The Cheka searched both the kitchens and the homes of the employees, even to the point of stripping beds. Only in one household was found stolen food. The description of a typical search follows.] *Kitchen Number Fourteen*: On Saturday, December 31st, at seven o'clock PM, four soldiers entered the room of the kitchen manageress where she was dressing to go out for the evening. She was forced to complete her dressing in the presence of the soldiers. They searched the room and found nothing. They then searched the kitchen and weighed the foodstuffs but found the scales in bad condition. After the search they ate two rolls belonging to the manageress and her assistant (their ration for the day) and two full dishes of beans. Then, although it was after ten o'clock, they began to question the manageress as to how many Americans were in Kazan, what they were doing, and if she thought they really came here only to feed children. Also they inquired as to what kind of children were being fed, children of workers or of the upper classes. They asked her how she obtained a position with the ARA and said that she had a very nice life, as she had plenty of foodstuffs and could invite her friends in to eat. They then left, saying that they would return on Monday, but they did not [do] so, and they left no copy of the protocol....

I recommended that the Cheka be requested to furnish the ARA immediately with a full statement regarding the results of these searches, and that they also furnish kitchens one, five, six and fourteen with copies of protocols similar to those given the other kitchens. I further strongly recommended, in view of the slight results for good realized from these raids in comparison with the mental distress and mortification caused so many of our employees who are innocent of wrongdoing, that they be discontinued from this time on; and that I be allowed to assure the kitchen personnel that they will not be subjected to such treatment a second time.

January 9, [1922]—I have been ordered to Moscow to present to Colonel Haskell in person the observations which I have made of food conditions and of the ARA work during my recent tour of inspection of the Tatar Republic. Departure was made from Kazan at ten PM last night in the private car of the district ARA. Accompanying me were Miss Galitch, interpreter; Mr. [?] Ossipov, editor of the Kazan *Izvestiia*, who together with a representative of the Cheka, had been offered accommodations in the car. I had heard in Kazan of this Ossipov, a young workman, who at twenty years of age had risen to be editor of the only newspaper in one of the most important cities outside Moscow or Petrograd. The chance which had thrown us together during the journey led me to take advantage of the opportunity to enter into a lengthy discussion with him on the subject not alone of communistic theory but of its practice, particularly insofar as concerned journalism and the press....

From him I learned that the press association in Russia which fulfills a similar function to that of the Associated Press in America, Reuters in Great Britain, or Havas in France is the Rosta Agency. Unlike these others, however, the Rosta Agency is government controlled and disseminates both abroad and throughout Russia only such information as suits the Russian government.... All former bourgeois journalists have engaged in a boycott of the Bolshevik press and for that reason it has been very difficult to train the proletariat in journalism.... No opposition newspapers are permitted to be published in Russia at the present time, but so soon as conditions permit it, that is to say, so soon as the government finds itself securely enough established, it is Ossipov's belief that these will be allowed to recommence publication....

I observed that the chief ground of antagonism in America to the Russian government had arisen as a result of the Red Terror, and to this Ossipov replied, "In other words the antagonism to the Russian government has its roots in the Revolution for without the Red Terror, the Revolution would have come to naught." I learned that according to official admissions of the Communist Party, there are only about 550,000 Communists in

Russia at the present time and that during the recent cleaning of the party, some 70,000 were excluded.[53] The presence of so few acknowledged Communists in Russia is frequently advanced by critics of the Soviet government as proof of the rule of a tyrannical minority. But there is never given in such statements any explanation of the difficulties attending admission into the Communist Party....

I asked Ossipov whether or not a letter written to *Izvestiia* by a member of the Menshevik Party would be published. His answer was that the government welcomed constructive criticism but had no patience with destructive criticism of which the opposition parties were all too full. If, in the opinion of the editor, the letter answered the former description, then it would be assured of publication. I must say, however, that I have never had any evidence of such tolerance on the part of the Soviet press, although it may be that I have not taken the pains to pursue a conclusive enough inquiry.... That is like a sign I read recently on the local telegraph office. It ran somewhat as follows: "The political censorship is hereby abolished. Therefore, telegrams in future must bear the approval of the military censorship only[!]"

January 11, [1922]—We arrived in Moscow after a journey of almost sixty hours consumed in traversing a distance of approximately three hundred and fifty miles. There was no one to meet us, but there were plenty of sleighs outside the station awaiting hire. The air was cold and crisp with twenty degrees of frost,[54] and I was happy to have a fur cap to pull about my ears and a fur coat into which I could huddle for comfort. As we sped along over the crunching snow, by the walls of the old town and up the Kuznetsky Most, I was struck with amazement to observe a life and movement upon the streets which contrasted so sharply with the almost lifeless spectacle with which I had been presented of the same city not more than four months previous. Where, in September, there had only been a few scattered

---

[53] Communist Party membership has always been restricted as one of the points of the Bolshevik program, calling for a small, elitist party to lead the Revolution. Lenin derived this position from the nineteenth-century radical Peter Tkachev (1844–1885), who first drew up a plan for a revolutionary party. Lenin paid him the supreme compliment by dubbing him "the first Bolshevik."

[54] Number of degrees below freezing.

individuals dragging a weary and woe-begone figure along dilapidated dirty streets, there were now hundreds who crowded upon the way and stepped briskly and alertly along as if imbued with some hope in life. The outward appearance of the people had changed in more than a physical manner also, for there were many men as well as women who were dressed presentably enough for the most popular thoroughfares in London or Paris.

Nor was this life and movement upon the streets the sole startling phenomenon of the change which had taken place between the Moscow of the autumn and the Moscow of January 1922. For, on every hand along the busy streets through which one passed, the former cobwebbed walls of shops and stores were observed to have been renovated and restocked. Where there had once been unsightly boards and a weatherbeaten sign as the only mark of a once prosperous commercial establishment, there was now to be seen sparkling plate glass windows from behind which a wealth of articles of trade were displayed in neatly arranged windows. Here was an antiquary shop and there a bookstore and yonder a store window, fairly filled with the fanciful and attractive creations of women's hats. It was such a sight as to make one rub one's eyes and to wonder how otherwise than in the rubbing of the genie's lamp by an Aladdin this transformation had been so suddenly effected. There was but one plausible explanation and that was that the genie's lamp was nothing other than the New Economic Policy of the government.[55]

In the afternoon I walked about the streets and entered one or two shops, among others a bookstore. There were heaps of beautifully bound editions of English and French authors in their respective languages, most of them bearing the monogram of some noble family. It was a part of the loot of the Revolution undoubtedly, for they were offered for sale at absurdly ridiculous prices. A beautiful half-leather edition of Alfred de Musset in eight volumes was to be had for two dollars. Further on there was an antique shop which would have made the proprietor rich if it had been located on Fifth Avenue. But of what value were even Gobelin tapestries and imperial

---

[55] It is interesting to note that Childs is here such an admirer of capitalism, since his book *Before the Curtain Falls* (Bobbs-Merrill, 1932), written in the Great Depression, condemns the institution and predicts its ultimate demise.

porcelain when there was not enough bread to be had and when most of Russia was starving?

In the evening I was invited by [Farmer?] Murphy[56] to the mid-week performance of the ballet which was attended, as the ballet is said always to be, by a crowded house.... Between the acts, as I was walking about the large promenade, I passed an old acquaintance, none other than Ludwig C. A. K. Martens,[57] a year previous, "self-styled Soviet ambassador to the United States," and about whom I had written many a line of newspaper copy while assigned to cover his activities in Washington by a press association. He appeared unusually shabby and run down at the heels. In the United States I had often wondered how it was that so intelligent and apparently refined a man could have endured the association of such a one as Santeri Nuorteva, the secretary of his mission, a brutal-faced Finn, uncouth and vulgar in manner and whose character was not only sufficiently revealed by the criminal charged for which he was wanted by the Finnish government but had been such as finally to have warranted the Soviet government into taking him into custody.

Since coming into Russia, I had become more familiar with the conduct of official affairs, and it had become quite clear that while Martens was the representative of the Foreign Office of the Soviet government, [Suteri] Nuorteva was the agent of the Extraordinary Commission, for it is the habit of the Commission to spy upon its own officials, and the spies whom it selects for its sinister work are too often the unscrupulous type of the criminal Nuortseva.

January 15, [1921]—I had been unable to leave Moscow for Kazan on the return journey the day previous as I had intended, for the reason that when I went to the station in the evening, I discovered that my private car had not been attached to the train and therefore I was compelled to wait

---

[56] An assitant in the liasion division.

[57] Ludwig Christian Alexander Karlovich Martens (1875–1948) was an engineer and scientist, as well as a diplomat. A German who grew up in Russia, Martens early became active in Bolshevik circles and was appointed by the Foreign Commissar Chicherin as the Soviet plenipotentiary to the United States in 1919. Never recognized by the American government, Martens operated out of New York, where he promoted US-Soviet trade. His nefarious activities got him deported from the US in 1921. Returning home, he devoted the rest of his life to scientific pursuits.

another day. To make certain that there would be no further difficulty, I went to the station on this day early in the afternoon or some six hours before the scheduled departure of the train. The car was not in the yards, but having knowledge from previous experience of the course to be followed in bringing out expeditiously a desired result, I immediately had recourse to the Railway Cheka or the special railway department of the Extraordinary Commission. Having stated my case and recounted the difficulty which I had experienced on the previous evening, the youthful member of the Cheka before whom I had presented myself, got into immediate touch by telephone with the railroad authorities and gave preremptory [sic] orders that my car should be in the yards not later than an hour before the departure of the Kazan train. With the assurance from him that I need have no further concern about the fulfillment of the order, I left with perfect confidence that I might trust the Extraordinary Commission to relieve me of any more annoyance or delay, for there is no doubt that in Russia, there is one absolutely dependable organization of the government and that is the Extraordinary Commission.

True enough, when I returned to the station a short while before the train was expected to leave for Kazan, I found my car attached but inasmuch as the porter had only been notified a little while previous of my intention to return to Kazan on this day, no fire had been made and I found the car with as low a temperature as that of the open air.

[Ralph] Pearson, a captain in the regular army from Coblenz, who had been detailed to the Kazan district, was accompanying me, and to keep warm we found it necessary to turn in immediately to bed. It was the most bitterly cold and uncomfortable night which I have ever passed, for even with three blankets and a fur coat, it was impossible to preserve any warmth in the body, exposed as it was to the icy draft of the car.

January 16, [1922]—The car was not properly heated until noon and in the afternoon, whether from the sleeplessness of the previous night or the exposure from which my body had suffered, I felt listless and fatigued and spent most of the afternoon in the berth of my compartment, reading for a short while from [Louis de] Bourrienne's memoirs of Napoleon and later sleeping.

January 17, [1922]—Today I felt even more miserable than on yesterday and suffered from such acute pains in the back of my head and such a mistiness of the eyes that I was unable to read for even a few minutes consequently. In addition I found it impossible to keep warm and kept moving between my compartment and the large stove in the opposite corner of the car. But even while I huddled over the stove for warmth, I kept shaking with chills and no matter how closely I crouched over the stove, my teeth chattered with cold. It was almost ten o'clock in the evening when we reached Kazan, and I found myself too miserable and sick even to transport my own portable typewriter to the automobile which had been awaiting us. There was only one thought in my mind and that [was] to get into bed as speedily as possible and if possible to get warm once more.

[Because of the ensuing illness, Childs's diary at this point becomes a memoir as he caught up with the ensuing events almost two months later.]

I did not learn it for some weeks afterwards, or until I had returned to consciousness and was convalescing, that the symptoms of illness from which I had suffered on my trip from Moscow were the premonitions of that familiar Russian disease spotted typhus. Having gone to bed on the night of January 17th, I did not arise from it again until February 13, and it was not for another week that I was able to leave the house to take a few steps.

The intervening days, between the time I fell ill and when I was able to go about again with faltering steps, are now only dimly remembered by me. I remember only that on the two succeeding days after my return from Moscow and as I was lying in bed with high fever, I was disturbed with the thought that my indisposition was occasioned by the dreaded typhus, and I plagued [sic] the doctor during these days for some information about my condition. But he was skillful enough to parry my questioning and to put me off with the reply that nothing could be known until the result of a blood test had been communicated to him. Then, I recall also that the thought occurred to me that I should write or dictate a letter home in case there should be necessity for a valedictory, but the apprehension lest such action should betray to my friends a fear of death which was very alien to me, induced me to abandon this purpose. Besides I had not the strength for it or indeed for any act which required the concentration of the mind upon any fixed subject. For two days, as I was told afterwards, I hovered between life and death, during the time of the crisis, when the germs of typhus were making a concerted and desperate effort to obtain victory, or death for the human being and life for themselves.

During the week or ten days my mind was far from lucid, and I suffered from the most terrible hallucinations. So vivid and deeply imprinted upon the mind were some of these that it was not until weeks after I had recovered and until after I had been fully restored to the use of all my faculties and entirely normal in health again that I was able to persuade myself that these conceptions which I had formed during my illness were false. For example, I remember that I came out of the delirium of typhus fully convinced that my parents had died during the Christmas holidays, and it was not until I had actually received letters from them dated in the month of January that I could be assured that they were alive.

On February 22, although scarcely able to walk on account of the weakness with which typhus inevitably leaves one in the legs, I left Kazan for western Europe for convalescence and proceeded via Moscow and Riga to Berlin [and from there to Paris]....

[In Paris] for the first time in six months I saw men and women laughing heartily, eating and feasting to their fulness [sic] and showing no trace of concern for those fellow men of theirs in Russia from whom they were separated by only a few hundred miles. I could take no part in gay and frivolous distractions as I once might have in Paris after coming from the front. For some reason, the vulgar noise of the variety theaters and the gay laughter of the *cafés chantants* repelled me. I could not stomach what, in my abnormal state, I took to be an evidence of the unfeelingness of human nature. So I cut short my vacation for I could not rest until I was on my way to Helsingfors [Helsinki] from which point I had chosen to re-enter Russia.

They were dancing there in the Hotel Societets Fuset in Helsingfors on the last night which I spent in the outside world previous to returning to Russia. I sat and watched the smartly groomed couples as they came into the dinner dance. The orchestra was playing softly the *Valse Caprice* of [Anton] Rubinstein, but it was no palliative to my nerves for I was fretful with impatience to be on my way and back again to those lonely villages in the Tatar Republic. Thank God, there were tasks left in the world worthy of men....

[At the Soviet border], I was fortunate in having to wait only six [hours]. There was only a boxcar to accommodate the few assembled travelers into Petrograd. But I did not bother; I was content for I was back again in Russia.

Petrograd, March 24, [1922]—Upon my arrival the previous evening in Petrograd, I had found quarters in the comfortable home of the staff of the ARA on the English Prospekt. It was here that I met Mrs. Eleanor Franklin Egan, who had recently been admitted into Russia as the representative of the *Saturday Evening Post* for the purpose of writing a series of articles on the work of the ARA. Mrs. Egan, who was one of the four women delegates on the American advisory commission of the Washington Conference,[58] is large and florid faced. She is one of those women who has a habit of injecting herself into any conversation within hearing and speaks authoritatively and dogmatically on any subject concerning any corner of the globe, whether it be Novi Pazar, Saghalien, Mount Althos, or the Peloponnesian isles. She has probably "done" in tourist fashion most of these places, for in a certain fussy manner she gives the appearance of having been eternally and nervously moving up and down the world with a Baedeker in one hand and a notebook in the other. As the wife of a partner of J. P. Morgan and Company, she came into Russia with a mind, wholly impartial and unbiased toward an experiment in socialistic government, a mind indeed which impresses one as being as open as the vaults of her husband's bank. When I met her, she had kept it so far free and open and receptive that although she had been in Russia but two weeks, she boiled over with indignation when I let fall the innocent suggestion in her presence that not all Communists were thieves and murderers.... And indeed, I gained the impression after being shown her purchases that she was much more interested in collecting porcelain and antiques than in the collection of any notes for the writing of the articles which had been presented as the motive which had gained her permission from the Soviet government to enter the country....

March 25, [1922]—While in the offices of the ARA in Petrograd my attention was attracted by a young girl [Georgina de Brylkine-Klokacheva],[59]

---

[58] The Washington Naval Conference of 1921–1922 resulted in a number of naval treaties among major maritime powers determining relative sizes of navies among them.

[59] Georgina de Brylkine-Klokacheva (d. 1964) became Childs's wife in August 1922. The daughter of a French mother and a well-to-do Russian father, she was widowed by the war. Curiously Childs, who was often ready to inject personal information into any of his writings, does not mention either her name or the fact

whose smile and beautiful brown eyes would have commended attention anywhere. There were streaks of grey in her hair, which I was to learn afterwards had resulted from the suffering and worry to which she had been subjected during the Revolution. I was informed that she had proved herself one of the most capable employees of the ARA in Petrograd, although four years previous as a member of a noble Russian family, she had never had to lift her hand for herself.

An opera party was being made up on the same evening of the young lady, her mother, and two of their relatives, which I was invited to join. The opera was [Tchaikovsky's] *The Queen of Spades*, and we occupied a box in the lower tier of the house. The eagle, surmounting the former imperial box, had been covered with a red flag and the box of the former emperor, that of the grand dukes and aides of the tsar, were now filled with orphaned children who were present as guests of the new republic. An elderly lady in our company, who had not been to the opera since the Revolution, after an observant survey of the audience with a lorgnette, remarked in a tone of sadness and surprise: "I do not see a single familiar face." Poor lady, from the groups of Communists and workers who filled the theater, it was not likely that there would be present any acquaintances of hers. As one of the bourgeoisie, she had lived far removed from these....

Madame and her daughter, previous to the Revolution, had been very wealthy. The daughter had been educated in England and in France and spoke half a dozen languages fluently. They had traveled widely and had enjoyed every luxury which wealth could obtain....

How terribly the spirits of the people have been broken can only be faintly realized by those who today live in security and comfort in New York, Boston, and Richmond, or in London, Paris, or Rome. I have heard of people who have not ventured from their homes into the street from the time of the Revolution in 1917 until but a few months ago. They are broken in spirit as well as in body, but bourgeoisie and the aristocracy, and one may detect almost an abnormality in their mental processes. It is true that one cannot judge them by ordinary standards of life and of conduct. Their morale is gone and their spirit is crushed so that one must give credit to the

---

that his "very young girl" with the "beautiful brown eyes" became his wife five months later.

Bolshevik government for having very effectually achieved at least one of its aims, that of stamping out the bourgeois elements of society in Russia. That is why today there is no possibility of the formation of a counter-revolutionary movement against the government from any political elements of the Right. The bourgeoisie have been beaten, one might say, into insensibility. Never was the spirit of any class of people any more completely subdued....

Kazan, April 5, [1922]—The Soviet ruble continues to fall in value at the rate which seems to be accelerated with each succeeding day. Since last August the value of the ruble in dollars has depreciated from forty-five thousand to the present low level of two million. Notes of the lowest denomination, which Americans found in Moscow when they arrived in that city last August, were for one hundred rubles, and there was much complaint at that time against the necessity of having to carry around a receptacle for the paper money which one needed in the course of a day. The same complaint is now being voiced against the note most generally employed in circulation, a note of one hundred thousand rubles, although bills of the denomination of ten million are now in evidence and will no doubt take the place of the one hundred thousand ruble notes for general use by the time bills for a billion are appearing from the printing presses....

The precipitancy with which money depreciates has brought with it a number of unusual regulations of the banks and of the business world which give for the first time to many people some insight into its intangible character. Interest at the rate of four percent per month is paid by the State Bank on all deposits and all business, when not done on a cash basis, is transacted with the understanding that the amount involved will be paid at a later date, not at the purchase price stipulated, but for a sum equivalent to it when converted at the old ruble rate. That is to say that if a payment on a purchase be delayed for one month, the debtor is bound to fulfill his obligation with a sum equivalent to the purchasing power of the ruble when the transaction was made. A Soviet decree has recently legalized the right of a creditor to exact this of a debtor....

Of course the swift course which the depreciation of money takes has enormously stimulated buying and selling. Once an article is converted into cash, the seller turns at once to place the money realized into some article of stable value. Here in the Volga region it is natural that the chief desideratum of all merchants of whatever class is food, for food has almost taken the place of gold as an artificial basis for the very artificial paper money. In bargaining for any article of dress or in the haggling over the making of any desired purchase such as is the custom, the proffered price, made after the seller's price has been given, invariably will bring forth the expostulation: "But that sum will only buy so many *funts*[60] of bread. Rye flour with which to make a coarse black bread is selling today for six million rubles a *pud* so that cab drivers turn a deaf ear when solicited by a fare unless an amount of Soviet rubles equivalent to four pounds of flour is offered them for a short journey. Of course he will not eat four pounds of flour, but he must consider that the forage for his horse will account for the equivalent of a good many pounds. Recently, merchants have been known to refuse to make a sale of articles of particularly stable value in lieu of anything but actual flour. Whether this is an indication of a definite trend toward the ancient principles of barter has not yet become sufficiently general to make definite conclusions possible....

April 8, [1922]—Professor [Nikolai F.] Katanov,[61] master of one hundred and fourteen different languages and Russia's greatest oriental scholar, is dead here of starvation. He died by one of life's ironies, succumbing to undernourishment at the moment that his situation was being brought to the attention of the American Relief Administration. Before food could be given him, news of his death was published in the newspapers, and it is only his wife and daughter who are left to be the recipients of the food which might have preserved for the scientific world his erudition for a few more years....

April 11, [1922]—I visited Kazan University today, one of the great institutions of higher learning in Russian and which, despite all ravages and hardships imposed by famine and pestilence and eight years of civil and foreign war, has shown this year a greater student enrollment than in any

---

[60] A *funt* is roughly a pound.

[61] Nikolai F. Katanov (1862–1922) was a prominent ethnographer and linguist, a specialist in Turkic languages. Graduating in Oriental studies from the University of St. Petersburg, he was a professor at the University of Kazan from 1893 until his death.

previous years since 1914. Alma mater of Nicolai [sic][62] Lenin and of Count Leo Tolstoy, both of whom for one offense or another were dismissed from the student body, Kazan University yet manages to keep alive the light of learning through its professors and students with difficulty preserve an existence on the miserable diet upon which for many months now the people of the Volga region have by some means subsisted....

Constructed in 1906, [the university library] was found most modern and arranged much after the manner of any modern American library. A card index for both author and subject revealed that among the American authors in English, the library possessed an edition of James Fenimore Cooper, published in Paris in 1837, and an almost equally old edition of Edgar Allen Poe's *Tales of Mystery*, published in London. The name of the ubiquitous Walt Whitman was absent in the English index but was to be found in the Russian along with Frank Norris and Upton Sinclair. There was no opportunity of ascertaining the American medical journals to which the library had subscribed before the war, but there were in abundance American journals of political science and economy. They included: *Annals of American Academy [of] Political and Social Science*; *Journal of Political Economy* and the *Quarterly Journal of Economics*, and there were besides, the *American Law Review* and the *Yale Review*. The former existed in a complete set from 1883–1917 and the latter, like all the other foreign periodicals, was brought down and stopped abruptly and significantly in the number October 1917. The librarian, huddled in a threadbare overcoat owing to the lack of heating facilities in the room,...begged that he might be permitted to make a request. It was somewhat disconcerting, therefore, to hear from him the plea that "we need so much the old American magazines and journals and if possible a few books. Can't you see what could be done for us in this regard. With the ruble more than two million to the dollar, it is obviously impossible for us to hope to subscribe to these regularly for a very long while."

A professor of the highest standing in Kazan University is paid today hardly the equivalent of five dollars, and the government ration, though it is a preferential one, is scarcely sufficient to enable a single individual to live,

---

[62] Lenin's first name, Vladimir, was frequently given incorrectly at the time as Nikolai.

taking no account of his family. As to how they live, that question may be better answered by considering the means by which any of the population of the Volga basin has survived the past winter. Suffice it to say that it is no uncommon sight to see in the market places of Kazan, professors of the university mingling with the peasants and the proletariat, and the old bourgeoisie, offering for sale books from their private library, pieces of household furniture, or maybe at times, even a scientific instrument, the purchase of which had only been achieved after long years of professional struggling.

Since the Revolution, Russian universities have been accorded, in comparison with other institutions of the Old Regime, a singular freedom by the Soviet government. Although the Soviet government was very quick to establish faculties for instruction of students, recruited from the proletariat, in which Communistic theory formed the main curriculum, there has been little if any interference with the old faculties. Professors of history and political science and economy are privileged to continue their instructing under a certain academical freedom. The autonomy which was granted Russian universities by the old Imperial government and which was always been a precious tradition in academical circles despite the various abridgements of it which was made by one or another of the tsars, has been recognized by the Soviet government. Immediately after the Revolution of October 1917, this autonomy, while recognized in theory, was virtually restricted by the appointment of a commissar to each university as a representative of the government, but these commissars have since been removed. The present rector of the Kazan University has held the same office under both the Imperial and Soviet governments. Until the present time, or it would be better to say, under the old economic policy of the Soviet government, students have been admitted to the universities without charge and have in addition been provided with subsistence. Under the New Economic Policy there has been worked out a plan for the division of the students in four groups. The poorer applicants for admission to the university will be placed in the preferred group and will not only be admitted to the university without charge but will be provided with all necessary living expenses. A second group will be granted admission without charge and will be accorded certain limited living expenses. The third group, though not granted any living expenses, will nevertheless receive free tuition. It is through the fourth group, those who are capable of paying their expenses, that it is hoped to derive an income for the university. This group will not only be charged tuition but will be required to meet all living expenses to which they are subjected.

April 14, [1922]—There is a family in Kazan, formerly noble, one of whose members after having served in the Kolchak army and having witnessed the debacle of all military efforts to overturn the Soviet government, entered the Red Army as an officer. That this is by no means an unusual occurrence in Russia is a fact which has been somewhat perplexing to the outside world which for these past five years has depended largely for information of Russia upon those reactionary Russians who fled abroad at the first signs of dissolution of the old Imperial government. The truth is that most of the higher commands in the Russian army are held by the old imperial officers, and without their aid it is doubtful if Russia would ever have been able to repel the assaults made upon her [by the Whites, the Poles, and the Allies]....

The military commander in Kazan is a former general of the old army and that his loyalty to the present government is no mere lip service is evidenced by his familiar and intimate intercourse with the members of the Soviet government of the Tatar Republic. At the first dinner given by the government to the American Relief Administration staff in Kazan, this former general of the Imperial army was one of the honored guests present. The commander of the division stationed in Kazan is also a former officer of the old army.

Of course the world knows of [General A. A.] Brusilov[63] and of the part he played in the campaign against Poland, but I doubt if the outside world has any realization of the extent to which the higher ranks in the present Red Army are occupied by old army officers. The Whites abroad have

---

[63] General A. A. Brusilov (1853–1926) was Russia's most successful general in World War I. Commander of the Southwestern Front, he masterminded the highly successful Galician offensive of 1916 that essentially destroyed Austria-Hungary's ability to play a major role in the war. He remained neutral in the Russian Civil War, but he came out of retirement to join the Soviet Army to oppose the Polish invasion of 1919–1920. He remained "with Russia" after the Soviet Union became stabilized and served in the Soviet army as the Inspector of Cavalry, earning him the enmity of the White Russian émigré community.

attempted to counteract the impression made by those individual cases which have attracted publicity in the foreign press, by the explanation that the families of such men were held as hostages by the Soviet government or that they were forced into the Red Army under pain of death. It is quite probable that individual instances have occurred in which the service of old officers was obtained under some such compulsion, but the very state of efficiency to which the Red Army has risen from the disordered mobs of deserters in 1917 should restrain the drawing of any general conclusion which would make it appear that intimidation was the chief means by which the service of the old officers was obtained....

April 23, [1922]—There is no throwing of rice or old shoes as a part of the ceremony of a Russian wedding, but there are other customs connected with it in Russia which are equally bizarre and strange to the foreigner. The ten Americans, composing the Kazan district of the American Relief Administration, had occasion today to participate in their first Russian wedding when one of the Americans, John J. Norris, attached to the mission as secretary, was married to a Russian widow, Mrs. Pankratov.... Although the four American members of the wedding party had great difficulty in assembling anything like suitable dress for the occasion here in the famine stricken area of the Volga, what was at length mustered into service obtained the complete approbation of the more than a thousand young and old of Kazan who attempted to crowd into the church to witness the unusual spectacle of the marriage of an American to a Russian. The bridegroom, after having scoured the town, seized upon a dress suit of the pattern of 1910 which was offered him, as did the best man while two of the witnesses were obliged to depend upon tuxedos. A third wore a cutaway....

Norris has the distinction of being the first native-born American to contract a marriage with a Russian bride under the laws of the Soviet government. It was in the study of Russian that the present marriage had its inception, but almost before Norris was able to learn the language of romance in Russian, rumor has it hat he had reverted to English; a neglect of study, however, which plainly did not prejudice him with his teacher as it might have done if he had been a little younger....

April 28, [1922]—I have come down to the boat, the first to leave for the cantons with corn since the breaking of the ice, and am now aboard awaiting the necessary documents to be obtained which will enable us to leave. It is three PM, a warm, bright, cheerful day, so much so that is difficult to believe that the river only ten days ago was filled with ice. It is equally difficult to believe that only a few miles away the existence of thousands of human beings depends upon the swift dispatch of the food contained within the boat. Each hour lost means the sacrifice of so many more lives to the famine....

Across the road from the river landing, where the corn is being transported from a railway siding to boats and barges, there are gathered a hundred or more wretched specimens of humanity. There are aged men and women and there are children hardly able to toddle. The same object directs them, however, and they are motivated by the same impulse, an empty belly. They hover like birds of prey around the cars and boats, kneeling in the dust and dirt to pick from the ground the grains of corn which fall from the sacks as they are borne upon the backs of laborers. Each carries a small bag into which the grains are collected. Occasionally, as one of the number approaches close to one of the railway cars to within forbidden territory, the rifle of the guard from the Red Army speaks out. There is a sudden shot, a whiff of smoke, and two legs are seen scurrying to safety. The shot is rarely more than a warning one in the air, but during the first few days in which the corn was unloaded, there was such a frenzied rush of starving humanity that several were killed.

On the Volga, April 29, [1922]—Instead of leaving Kazan yesterday as had been expected, the boat was pulled out into midstream and lay anchored outside Kazan until early this morning. I arose after the start had been made and after having passed a very chilly uncomfortable night.... This time, however, I have profited by my typhus experience and have brought cot, blankets, and even typewriter. One fatal mistake was made, however, that of not investigating before my departure the two food boxes which I had ordered the housekeeper to prepare. Upon investigation they have been found to contain little else than breakfast food. There is enough Quaker oats, Shredded Wheat, Grape Nuts and Corn Flakes to stock a country grocery store, and I particularly detest that typical American institution, breakfast food.

Bogorodsk—It is now six o'clock in the afternoon, and the captain of the boat has come in to tell us that inasmuch as there is no tug, we cannot proceed farther tonight. The tug, which brought us from Kazan, has been diverted to Spassk with several barges, and there is not sufficient fuel to enable the boat to continue to Tetushi under its own steam. There is fuel on the hill just above us but no way of transporting it, so we have both sent impatient telegrams to Kazan and must bide our time. Simson, who is something of a wag, suggested to the captain that the fuel be placed in barrels and rolled down the hill, but to this the captain replied quite seriously that there was no means of preventing the breaking of the barrels if this method were adopted. Simson and I went off the boat to shore in search of caviar, meat, and honey. Mutton was the only one of these commodities obtainable, and that was purchased at the rate of four hundred thousand rubles a *funt*, or about twenty cents a pound.

A hundred nomadic Russian peasant men, women and children were seated on the banks opposite the landing surrounded by their belongings. They comprised the same types one saw last fall at every river landing and in every railway station, waiting endlessly to go anywhere and everywhere. One woman was seated industriously knitting while another was pursuing a very excited search of her garments and after having located the object of her search was crunching it between thumb and forefinger. Having returned to the boat from Bogorodsk, I sent Simson to the official in charge of the waterways to learn what could be done about getting us to Tetushi. In answer to Simson's representations a tug was found for us which took us off the same evening and brought us to Tetushi the next morning.

Tetushi, April 30, [1922]—There was considerable maneuvering necessary to bring our boat alongside the shore where it might be discharged, and while this was taking place there was a call through a megaphone from shore as to whether or not I was aboard. Just opposite us there were a dozen or more warehouses, set against cliffs which resembled those of Dover, and about which there was a crowd of peasants, whom I took to be workers, gathered in readiness to unload the corn.

As soon as we had approached close to the shore, [?] Pribytkov, one of our inspectors from Kazan, came aboard and informed me that everything had been prepared for the reception of the corn according to my wire. Representatives from all the *volosts* in the canton had been awaiting my arrival for two days, and together with the cantonal committee would be shortly on board. Very soon thereafter, [?] Nikanorov, chairman of the Tetushi Committee, put in his appearance. As soon as the other representatives had been assembled on the boat, they were gathered in one of the larger cabins and the meeting was opened. They presented a curious assembly, this score or more of peasants who seemed, like [Emile] Zola's tillers of the soil in *La Terre*, to have absorbed in the texture of their skins something of the earth which they cultivated. Simson remarked that there were probably half a dozen tribes and nationalities represented including Russians, Tatar, Chuwashi, Bashkirs, Cheremis, and Votyaks. Some of the physiognomies might readily have been mistaken for those of Americans while others inclined sharply, in their high cheekbones and queer twist of the eyes, to their Mongolian brethren, the native American Indian.

I made them a short preliminary speech and afterwards had Simson read them the instructions which had been prepared on the handling of the corn. Of course a speech in acknowledgment had to be made by one of their number and for this [?] Valveev, chairman of the cantonal soviet and of the Russian relief, assumed the task. He made a speech which touched me very deeply because from the tone of his voice, I knew that, however plainly and simply he expressed himself, what he had to say came from the heart. He said he wished to express the thanks of the Tetushi canton to the American people, the American government and to the Americans of the ARA in Kazan, whom the people of Tetushi had learned to love and esteem very greatly, for the generous assistance which had been extended the canton in its distress....

I was much struck by the incident which occurred at the close of the meeting when a stolid old Tatar arose and in the Tatar language, which had to be put into Russian by Nikanorov, and thence into English by Simson for me, declared that he had come to Tetushi promising to bring back with him food for his *volost* and that he would not and could not return to face his people until the committee was ready to give him the corn. The meeting having been concluded, I found that Nikanorov's wife had been so good as to prepare a delightful surprise for Simson and me, a lunch which had been sent down to the boat and which consisted of *sterlet* [a small sturgeon], caviar and cabbage salad. After living almost exclusively for two days on breakfast food, it was a great treat....

By three o'clock in the afternoon a gangplank of some twenty-five feet had been constructed to our boat from the shore and the unloading of the corn into an adjacent warehouse had commenced. Delivery of it to the *volosts* had been arranged to begin the next day, despite the fact that it was May 1st, a great revolutionary holiday,[64] and it was expected to be in the hands of the people in the villages within five days. It was yet light at eight-thirty PM when the expected steamer to take us to Spassk was sighted. A soup or ragout, which we had ordered to be cooked for supper, was just being brought to our cabin, but at Simson's suggestion we took the bowl and two spoons into a rowboat, which was to take us, together with our baggage, half a *verst* down stream to the steamer landing.

Nikanorov and the captain of the boat, which had brought us from Kazan, were hugely amused at the unconventional mode we had adopted of eating what might have been termed our ["]communistic supper.["] they stood on the bridge and shouted down to us: "You should hoist a sign to advertise your floating Volga restaurant." In a more serious parting vein, Mr. Nikanorov added, "Mr. Childs, the people of Tetushi will never forget that the American people have saved their lives."...

We rowed down and climbed aboard a very trim little steamer of the Samara-Kazan line. Upon hearing that Americans were aboard, the captain sent down word to us at our places in the lower forepart of the boat that a cabin had been placed at our disposal. As we only anticipated a journey of an hour and a half, the proffer was declined, I preferred to remain out in front where I might enjoy a beautiful spring evening and follow the tortuous course of the Volga....

The boat was speeding along at the merry rate of thirteen to fourteen knots an hour; it began to grow chilly and I slipped inside where a hundred or more peasants were spread out upon their floor with their belongings, some sleeping, some smoking, some scratching. One long-bearded old fellow was showing to a group of admirers a photograph album which appeared to contain portraits of pre-revolutionary times to judge from the cut of the garments in the illustration.... We did not arrive at our destination until eleven o'clock, and to our disappointment it was found

---

[64] First celebrated in Warsaw in 1890 during a workers' strike, 1 May became thereafter the Russian "Labor Day," when the working classes in tsarist times showed solidarity with their movement by strikes and demonstrations. After the Revolution, it became a legal holiday, when workers demonstrated their unity with the international workingmen's movement.

where we had landed that we were still some twelve *versts* from the town of Spassk and that we would have to traverse the intervening distance over flooded fields by boat the next day. The question arose as to where we might sleep this night as apparently there was no other shelter in the vicinity besides the floating barge which served as a landing stage. Simson went off to see the agent of the river station, and I sat ruminating upon our belongings. He returned a little later to say that the agent had offered to give us for the night the use of a small office room on the barge adjoining the ticket office. There was just room sufficient to put up my cot and to allow Simson sleeping space upon the floor....

[The next day Childs and Simson get a ride aboard a tug to Spassk.]

While I stood on deck waiting for the tug to push off, an amusing comedy was being enacted between the crew and a group of peasants. These latter had some twenty sacks of potatoes they desired to be transported to Kazan, and they had begun to dicker with the crew as to the bridge which would be acceptable. The captain and pilot had taken a hint and had gone below to permit the transaction to be made. Finally a price was settled upon, and the crew fell in to a man to assist the peasant in loading the potatoes. Of course neither passengers nor freight were admissible to the boat according to regulations, but that did not prevent a number of others from being taken aboard. Once the boat had put off, one of the members of the crew made his way about among the passengers and approaching Simson said, "Well, what are you to pay?" Simson began to joke with him but the other continued seriously, "Anything you have to offer will do." Finally when it was made known to him that we were from the ARA, he made his apologies and went about the business of collecting from other passengers....

An hour's ride and we were in sight of Spassk. We had been steaming for some time over nothing more than a flooded meadow when suddenly there was a slowing down of the boat as it grated and staggered on the bottom. We had run on[to] a bank, and it later developed that the unskillful piloting had been the work of a substitute pilot who had taken the place of the regular one while the latter had gone below with the captain to supervise the apportionment of the day's bribes. It was an hour before the boat had regained its necessary draft of water and this was only made possible by the united efforts of all on board, who with a dozen long-sounding poles, at length succeeded in pushing the boat off the shoal. The barge of corn, which we had brought down from Kazan to Bogorodsk, had already arrived when we reached Spassk and despite the rain was being unloaded. As it was the only shelter available from the unpleasant weather, we found refuge in the cabin of our transportation agent, and there made tea while word was sent to [?] Tersky, chairman of the ARA committee and the cantonal soviet, of our arrival. A horse and carriage having been sent for us, our nine pieces of baggage were loaded, and we started off for the home of Bashkirov, veterinary surgeon, where I had stopped in December on a trip through Spassk....

Almost the first question directed at me by Bashkirov was for news of the Genoa Conference.[65] All Russia is a-tip-toe over the conference and has been since it was first announced as a possibility. Bashkirov explained that the latest news received over the governmental wires was that France had threatened to leave the conference and that she was preparing for war. I said I thought she would have slight sympathy from America, whose patience had been exhausted by her late ally.

In the afternoon I met with Tersky and representatives of the ARA committees from the *volosts* of the cantons, going over the details of the corn feeding as I had done at Tetushi, and afterwards returned to Bashkirov's to play his very excellent imported Victrola (made in the USA). He has a very good repertoire of records including band marches, gypsy and Russian national songs, airs from Russian and Italian operas, and Russian dance music, but thank God, no Jazz!...

Spassk, May 2, [1922]—I had asked Tersky the day before for horses to enable me to visit one of the nearby *volosts*. On account of the condition of the horses in the country, he was obliged to give me government horses and a driver to take me to my destination and return. We left at three o'clock in the afternoon with very good horses and a *tarantas*, a Tatar vehicle in which

---

[65] At the Genoa Conference (10 April–19 May 1922), held in the Italian city of that name, thirty-four nations assembled to discuss a means of jumpstarting the European economy. It was significant because both Germany and Russia, both international pariahs, were invited as equals. The United States decided not to attend. The conference collapsed, however, when the German and Russian delegates stole away to the nearby resort of Rapallo on Easter Sunday morning and signed the Rapallo Treaty, recognizing each other diplomatically and rejecting mutual debts and war claims, thereby ending each nation's total isolation.

there is only one seat, that for the driver. The rear is filled with straw and that affords a seat for two travelers. We carried with us a box of food, blankets, a cot and sufficient hay and oats for the horses....

Romadanovskaia *volost*, our objective, was reached about eight o'clock in the evening while it was yet light, and the secretary of the local ARA committee was found at the local soviet. He begged to be excused for not being able to show us to our lodgings, but his foot, which was swollen from starvation, prevented him from walking. We were introduced into a very clean dwelling place, where the samovar was quickly prepared and an evening meal of canned bully beef and cocoa was had. After a ride of forty-five *versts*, I was rather tired and immediately after eating I put down my cot, rolled out my blankets, and went to bed.

Romadany, April 3, [1922]—After breakfast Simson and I were called upon by one of the members of the ARA *volost* committee who conducted us to *volost* headquarters for the conference I desired with the *volost* authorities.

Though the population and officials of the *volost* seemed greatly heartened by the arrival of the American corn, there are general forebodings entertained as to whether it will be possible, even with the seed which is being received from the government, to cultivate sufficient land to ride the population over ten months to the next harvest.

Of the five thousand, five hundred *desiatins*[66] of winter [wheat] fields, there were planted last fall but one thousand eight hundred and twelve *desiatins*, and of this only one hundred and forty-one *desiatins* were planted with the seeds of the peasants. The seed supplies by the government, which went to the planting of one thousand six hundred and seventy-one *desiatins*, suffered badly from frostbite on account of the lateness of the time at which they were planted, and this spring the fields thus sown are showing up very poorly.

Of the four thousand seven hundred and eighty-one *desiatins* of land devoted to summer cultivation, there have been received in the *volost*, seed sufficient to plant but one thousand and twenty *desiatins*. These seeds were distributed April 23, and the *volost* authorities estimate that not much more than five percent of them have been diverted to food by the peasants in their extremity of hunger. As this will enable only twenty-five percent of the fields

---

[66] A *desiatin* equals about 2.75 acres.

to be planted, the peasants are attempting to find seeds for the cultivation of kitchen gardens, but for this purpose it has only been possible for the *volost* to obtain seven *puds* of seeds.

Of a population in the *volost* in December 1, 1921, of ten thousand seven hundred and eighty-seven, there were left on May 1, 1922, but eight thousand eight hundred and sixty. Some few former refugees have begun to return to their homes at news of the distribution of the corn and seeds. Horses, which numbered one thousand seven hundred and fifty-one in September of last year, have been reduced to eight hundred and eleven....

The American kitchen, feeding one hundred out of one hundred and sixty children in the village, was found located in a peasant's hone, and at the moment that I visited it there were present a score of children receiving their food. I remarked to the manager upon the number of rations which were being given over to parents to be taken home to children, and she explained that since the shortage of child feeding supplies had necessitated the feeding of a half ration, fifty percent of the children had become ill as the American food was all that they had to depend upon....

There seems to be a quite universal impression in the outside world that the old homes of the estate owners and landlords in Russia have been appropriated for the personal use of avaricious Soviet officials. I have been at considerable pains to investigate the use to which such former landlords' homes were being put by the Soviet government, and I have yet to find one which has been appropriated to the personal use of anyone. Just outside of the town of Spassk, there is a very beautiful white-stoned building, formerly the Modesto estate, which has been converted into a children's colony. In Kazan, a magnificent building, formerly the club of the nobility, has been turned into a receiving station for orphaned and refugee children found in the streets. The best children's hospital in Kazan is located in what was formerly the home of a nobleman, while the president and the prime minister of the Tatar Republic occupy respectively two rooms in a very modest apartment house of the city.

The Soviet high school, which I visited in Romadanyi, housed sixty-five pupils drawn from various villages in the *volost* and who now are living on the premises. A class in elementary physics was being conducted at the time of my visit and was being instructed from a textbook published in Moscow in 1918. Another class was occupied with the history of Greece and

Rome and were following a textbook published in Kazan, also in 1918, the work of Professor [Maxim or Osip?] Kovalevsky. In comparison with the average country high school of Virginia, I should say that this Soviet school was no better nor worse. Among the subject in which instruction was being given were: Russian, French, German, physics, botany, geometry, natural history, geography, history, agriculture, carpentry, horse-shoeing, singing and dancing. Nine *versts* distant from the village there is a school called Novyi Mir, New World, where instruction is given in the doctrine and theory of Communism. I did not have the opportunity of visiting this school, but I learned that it was open to anyone without qualifications as to previous education or political affiliations. There had been a year previous a plan for the establishment in the village of Romadanyi of a school for adults up to forty years of age, but economic conditions had made this impossible.

A little after one in the afternoon, we left for Pitchkassy on the return journey to Spassk. As we left the village, corn was just arriving, having taken five days to reach this village after its dispatch by barge from Kazan. From Romadany, forty-five *versts* into Spassk, the road appeared to be one long stretch of horse carts bearing American corn. Here and there along the way a temporary camp had been formed while the drivers consisting of both men, women and children, cooked a meal and gave their ill-conditioned horses a rest. Three hours later and we were at the *volost* seat of Pitchkassy, where a halt was made to permit of the making of a few inquiries. Here, as in Romadanovskaia *volost*, both Simson and I were very much impressed by the earnest character of the local soviet officials. They seemed to be "dirt" farmers and to have for that reason a very keen appreciation of the peasants' plight and of their problems.

Out of a population of twenty thousand six hundred and five inhabitants on March 1, 1920, there were in the *volost* on March 1, 1921, eighteen thousand and eighteen and these had been reduced on March 1, 1922, numbered two hundred and forty-two; in February, two hundred and three; March, two hundred and forty-five and in April, three hundred and seventeen, of whom in this last month two hundred and fifty-nine had been children. Yet this *volost* is considered to be in a more fortunate position than any of the other *volosts* in the canton.

On March 1, 1922, there had been in the *volost* two thousand one hundred and forty-nine horses, and these had been reduced on March 1,

1922, to one thousand and two hundred eighty-four. Likewise, of cows, which had numbered one thousand eight hundred and forty-one, there were on March 1, 1922, but one thousand one hundred and sixteen; of sheep, which had numbered three thousand two hundred and twenty-seven, there were left a scanty remnant of five hundred and thirty and of two hundred and eighteen pigs, only twenty.

Last fall, out of six thousand three hundred and sixty-seven *desiatins* of land devoted to winter [wheat] cultivation, there had been planted one thousand seven hundred and fifty-four *desiatins*, of which only eighteen *desiatins* had been planted with local seeds. As in Romadanovskaia *volost*, the one thousand seven hundred and twenty-six *desiatins* planted with the seed distributed by the government were showing very poor results. Of nine thousand eight hundred and forty-three *desiatins* of land capable of cultivation this spring, seeds have been received for only two thousand one hundred and fifteen *desiatins*. Only a very small part of this has been converted into food.....

We were in Spassk by seven o'clock. Our host Bashkirov was unusually communicative and discussed any one of a dozen subjects. It was an excellent opportunity to learn something of the opinion of one of the intelligentsia of life in Soviet Russia. Here briefly is the substance of what I gleaned from him. Elections to the village soviet are not controlled by the Communist Party but are left to the inhabitants to determine without outside influence. Those of the *volost* soviet are also free and unhampered, and the *volost* soviet chairman is always from the community from which he is elected. There was one instance known to Bashkirov when Tersky, the cantonal soviet chairman, had attempted to have a friend elected to one of the *volost* soviet committees, but he had been voted down by the assembled village representatives. As for the cantonal soviet chairman, he is rarely if ever a native of the canton to which he is appointed or elected. The names of such chairman are presented to the canton by the Communist Party of the Tatar Republic, and they go through as a matter of form. The chairman of the Spassk cantonal soviet, Tersky, is supposed by various conjectures to have been previously either a sailor or a workman. He is often seen attired in a sailor jacket and sailor's trousers and is understood by some to have been an ordinary sailor in the Volga service. I inquired whether the elections were open to all and whether he, Bashkirov, had ever voted. The reply was that the elections were open to everyone but that none of the local intelligentsia ever exercised this privilege. The reason given for this abstention from voting was that the intelligentsia were not free to vote according to their convictions but were liable to every form of coercion should they attempt to exercise an independent right of franchise....

I asked Bashkirov if it were not his opinion that the times were improving and if it were not true that less violent measures were being manifested by the government at present towards non-party citizens. His reply was an emphatic "No," and he instanced the five day search of his house by the Cheka, which had been made only last November. However, this opinion of his is in contradiction to that of every other Russian I have spoken to since entering Russia. Bashkirov personally believed that conditions in every way were growing worse, and he thought that the famine would be worse the ensuing winter than it had the last. It was also his opinion that the central authority was growing weaker and that authority was becoming every day more localized. He stated that he knew of several orders which had been issued lately by the Kazan government which the local cantonal government of Spassk had disregarded although such inattention to orders from the center previous to 1922 and since 1918 had been known....

Spassk, May 4, [1922]—In the morning I went to the post office and got into communication with Boyd in Kazan over a direct telegraph wire. I informed Simson of what I desired to have said, he translated it to the operator, and it was ticked off. Then followed Boyd's reply, which came ticked off in dots and dashes of the type employed by the Russian telegraph system. Later I went to the cantonal soviet to inquire into means of transportation to Tetushi. We were offered a rowboat to take us to Spassky Zaton, twelve *versts* distant, but were informed that if we were willing to wait, the tug which had brought us to Spassk would be in town in the evening, and we accordingly decided to wait for that. Three of the ARA kitchens in the town were visited and found to be in excellent order and apparently very capably administered.

Afterwards I took a look in at the local bazaar and found there, as in almost every other bazaar in Russia, quantities of old books being sold for cigarette paper. From a number I picked out the fourth volume in Russian—the others doubtless having gone up in smoke—of Walter Scott's

Woodstock. The title page stated that it had been translated into Russian from the first French edition, and as the Russian edition was dated 1812, I daresay that it too was a first edition.

[Childs left Spassk by tug at 4:00 PM, but the boat ran aground, and after spending all day on the tug, was finally returned to shore at 10:00 PM.]

Old Bashkirov was entertaining two Communist friends: One, the head of the local finance department of the government and the other, secretary of the Communist Party of the canton. He explained afterwards to us that they were both of the intelligentsia, but he neglected to offer any explanation for his inconsistency in representing to us the day previous that there was no participation by the local intelligentsia in the Soviet government.

Spassk, May 5, [1922]—We have our troubles, Simson and I. So soon as we had eaten breakfast, Simson went out to learn the state of affairs of the transportation system to Zaton and discovered that the tug had been released and had gone without us. Today is Karl Marx's birthday and therefore a holiday, and it was afternoon before he was able to locate the soviet chairman. Zaton was reached by this latter by telephone, and Simson was informed that so soon as fuel could be obtained, the tug would come to Spassk for us. Our cantonal inspector, [?] Bergman, came in from a visit to the *volosts* in the meanwhile and gave a very depressing picture of conditions which he had found on his trip. It is his opinion that it will be five years before food conditions are in any way normal on account not alone of the scarcity of horses for the tilling of the land, as well as the scarcity of seed grain, but by reason also of the unfamiliarity of the Tatar portion of the population with agriculture. The Tatar have always been accustomed to earn their livelihood at trade, but since there is no business they have nothing to turn to but agriculture of which they have little knowledge.

The seed grain of the soviet government, it seems, is being distributed in favor of certain classes by order of the center in Moscow. In the preferred category are the families of those now serving in the army and those who have the horses and equipment necessary for tilling the soil. The second class comprises those who, while they may not have at the present time the requisite equipment, nevertheless last fall had prepared the land for cultivation this spring. The third class consists of those who have made a cooperative agreement with neighbors who have the necessary means to assist them in bringing the land to a state of cultivation. Such peasants who, with the necessary equipment of horses and implements, have entered into agreements with those who are not in possession of such resources will receive from the government a bonus of two *puds* of seed grain for each *desiatin* which they assist in cultivating and in addition will be entitled to claim twenty-five percent of the harvest of the neighbor whom they have assisted. A fourth class includes those without any horses or equipment and who have made no collective agreements but to whom seed will be given for the small cultivation which they may be capable of undertaking. In a fifth class are placed those who are in possession of their own seeds. There could hardly well be a program which was less communistic; surely a far cry from the creed to which the government was committed by the old economic policy. And yet there was never a time when a people's only salvation was more dependent upon the adherence to a cooperative or communistic program.

The famine, as if to mock the soviet government, has awakened the most individualistic instincts of man. There seems very little desire on the part of the more fortunate inhabitants of the villages to assist those who are in greatest distress. According to Bergman, a real enmity had developed between the two classes; the more fortunate peasants actually nursing the hope that others will die in order that more land will accrue to those who remain alive. Since, according to the plan of the government's seed distribution, the greatest harvest will be reaped by those who are in the most fortunate circumstances, the result will be that thousands are doomed to die in the future who, having no horses or equipment, will receive but a small quantity of seed. Those who are dying from hunger can hope to receive no assistance even from members of their family. When one is compelled to take to bed from weakness due to hunger, he is left undisturbed and unaided. Since the warm weather has set in, it has become the custom for those who feel themselves thus seized to go out of doors and place themselves along the road in the hope that some Good Samaritan may pass by who will be able to render them some help. But no one ever does and when Bergman passed a village some distance out of Spassk, he viewed six such individuals lying outstretched apparently asleep, all swollen from hunger and with skins the color of yellow parchment. "The sanitary people will be after them tomorrow," the driver remarked with an indifferent flick of the whip, so common has death become along the Volga.

After the discussion with Bergman and the serious situation which he represented as confronting those who, being without horses or farming implements, would for that reason receive an insufficient quantity of seed grain from the government and therefore would have small hope of restoring themselves to a normal economic life, I determined to get in touch with the local authorities to learn if we could not settle upon some plan which might offer a solution of this difficulty. As I saw it, the main purpose of our work, to return the country again to a self-supporting basis, would be defeated if a large proportion of the population was destined to die so soon as we withdrew our relief operations. At a conference held with the sub-chairman of the cantonal soviet, the chairman being ill, it was admitted that the gravity of the situation as presented me by Bergman was fully appreciated by the local authorities. He was quite overcome when I suggested that the ARA would be willing and even anxious to cooperate with the government in order mutually to restore the economic independence of those citizens who had suffered most by the famine and who now appeared helpless to regain their foothold in the economic life of the community.

We passed to a consideration of the various possibilities which might be taken advantage of in cooperation between the government and the ARA in the distribution of the seed grain and corn. Finally I merged the best features of several proposed plans and suggested that from the lists of those peasants selected to receive the corn there be stricken out en masse the names of those in possession of horses. Reinstatement would be made possible for those who agreed to engage in the transportation of corn or seed and for those who signified their willingness to cultivate a certain portion of the fields of those not in possession of the necessary equipment. The plan met with the hearty approval of the government representative, and it was thereupon transmitted to Kazan by telegraphy.

Spassk, May 6, [1922]—We were up at six o'clock in the expectation of leaving on the tug at eight, but there was an inevitable delay consequent upon the towing of a barge from Spassk to Zaton, and we did not arrive at the latter point until after midday.

As there was presented no immediate possibility for continuing the journey to Tetushi, and as I was determined that I would arrive there without further delay, I went to the manager of the local waterways and sought to have the tug continue on with Simson and me to Tetushi. This was found impossible owing to previous orders having been received for the return of the tug to Spassk, but in the meanwhile, the Kazan-Astrakhan boat having put in, the manager promised to hasten its departure so that we might be subjected to no further vexatious delay....

Quarters had already been prepared for us in town, and although three large boxes of food had been sent down to me from Kazan, Nikanorov, chairman of the cantonal committee, insisted that we have dinner with him. As the head of public education in the canton and as a professor of literature, I enjoyed a delightful chat with him on Russian prose. Like Nikanorov, most of the teachers of secondary education under the Imperial government in the provinces, have continued at their posts under the Soviet government, but great difficulty has been experienced by the authorities in finding the necessary personnel for primary education as a result of the great expansion of the educational system of Russia by the present government.

Having made the request of Valeev, chairman of the cantonal soviet and a member of the ARA committee, for any of the old Zemstvo stamps which might come under his notice, he informed me that the central government had officially ordered the local authorities to set aside a week for the collection of all old stamps, which were to be forwarded to Moscow. From such as he was able to collect, he promised to reserve some for me....

Tetushi, May 7, [1922]—Having heard from one of our inspectors that the representatives of the canton of Buinsk were showing an unaccountable delay in unloading the corn from the barge consigned to them, I called the representatives together and gave them four days in which to complete the work under penalty of having what remained unloaded after that date taken from the cantonal allotment. At eleven AM Simson and I set out in a *tarantas* with two horses and a driver for Buinsk, forty-five *versts* distant. The only break in the journey was made at the village of Chinchurino for the purpose of inquiring into the feeding and general economic conditions. The corn had arrived and had been distributed the day previous, and the inhabitants thronged around me to express their thanks to the American people. The chairman of our local committee insisted that we have tea with him, and that done we were off again.

Between Chinchurino and Buinsk, hundreds of men, women and children were encountered on the road feebly dragging or pulling small, low, two-wheeled handcarts containing corn which was being transported from the river to interior villages, many of them a hundred miles distant. Probably half the corn destined for the canton of Buinsk is being conveyed to its village destination in this manner owing to the scarcity of horses. The average horse on account of its weakened state, is limited to one third of a normal load. Human beings are capable of moving one tenth the load of a horse, although this itself is but one third the capacity of a healthy individual. Arriving at Buinsk before sundown, we found rooms in the excellent two-storied home of a Tatar, who had entertained us upon a previous visit in December. A meeting was held with the local committee, and arrangements were made whereby two horses, a driver, and a carriage would be given us on the next day for a tour of the canton.

Buinsk, May 8, [1922]—Inspection of four of the children's homes in town in company with the committee revealed a quite considerable improvement in them since my last inspection when their miserable conditions provoked a very bitter rebuke of the local authorities by me. Not only had the former managers of these institutions been discharged, but a reorganization had been effected of the committee itself which now showed itself energetic and resolute. Shortly after noon, Simson and I set out in the vehicle placed at our disposal for a fifteen *verst* circuit of a *volost* adjacent to the town. Returning at five o'clock we found a dinner of rice, carrots, potatoes, and roast veal had been prepared for us at the direction of the chairman of our committee and of the local soviet. When he appeared, I gently admonished him for a courtesy which I knew the community could ill-afford and represented to him that I always carried my own food in order that, even where some little food was to be found, I might not be a burden upon the locality. Bashkirov, the chairman of both the ARA committee and of the cantonal soviet, who had come lately to the latter post from Kazan, replied that even the famine could not relieve the Russian from the obligation imposed by the presence of an honored guest.

Throughout the present trip I have found among government officials and local dignitaries that a certain formal spirit with which the ARA was first received has been succeeded by one of apparently whole-hearted trust and confidence. For the first time in my experience in Russia, I have had local officials express publicly the thanks of the Russian people not only to the American people but also to the American government. On this particular occasion Bashkirov found the opportunity to remark that if it should ever happen that the American people were to find themselves in a position of national distress, they might count not only on the sympathy but on the practical support as well of the Russian people.[67]

At seven o'clock in the evening, we set out on another journey into the canton, proceeding eight *versts* to the *volost* Runginskaia, where a halt was made for the night. Here we found shelter in the hut of a Chuvash family from whom for four million rubles—a little more than a dollar—I was able to buy some of the interesting[ly] colored needle work of this old race whose ancestors had been pushed northward centuries ago by the Tatars. Today most of the Chuvash are converts of the Greek Catholic Church, but there are some who remain steadfast to the pagan faith and nature worship of their forefathers....

Rungin, May 9, [1922]—Before our departure the sub-chairman of the *volost* soviet waited upon us and made known his desire to learn something from us of the progress of the Genoa Conference. Newspapers, he said, were received very infrequently, so that the community had little reliable information to depend upon of events in the outside world. The inquiry, directed of me in a simple naive manner, as to why America was not participating in the conference, put me in some embarrassment for an instant. But when I replied that America was sick of the quarrels of Europe and impatient of the delay which some of the European nations were displaying toward the all important question of disarmament, I was instantly relieved from my momentary discomfiture at the perception that I had struck a popular chord. "Ah! This is it," he ejaculated, his dull face brightening with understanding. And without any hint on my part, he continued, "It is France, who is today disturbing the peace of the world.''...

Like many Russians whom I have met, he had found it difficult to appreciate why America is willing to help Russia with food and yet is not willing to sit down with other nations of the world at a conference table with

---

[67] As a result of the US-Russian friction in the Soviet era, the work of the ARA was obliterated from Russian history. Note editor's comments at the end of the manuscript.

her and help to work out a plan for her economic regeneration. I find it difficult myself to understand, but I must need offer to Russians what explanation I can to the end that the good name of the United States shall not suffer; as Lodgeism[68] is no part of my philosophy....

From Rungin we proceeded seventeen *versts* to the *volost* of Timbaiavo, and although the local committee was not to be found, we profited from our visit by conversation with a member of the seed campaign committee for the *volost* and another for the canton, both young and energetic men. The former opened the conversation with the blunt question as to whether the ARA was sending food into Russia to foster the ancient Russian institution of bribery. It was only the earnestness of his character, which had led him to phrase the inquiry in such a manner, and became apparent after our assurance had been given that it was anything but the intention of the ARA. The question had been provoked by the fact that a month and a half previous he had investigated for the local authorities a report that a kitchen manager in an adjacent village had been accustomed to accept bribes from the children for their admittance into the ARA kitchen. He had made a report of the circumstances to the *volost* ARA committee, but the committee up to the present time had taken no action. I, therefore, ordered the kitchen manager discharged and his corn ration taken from him and left an order that the committee should make a report of the reason for its delay to the cantonal committee.

From here we passed on to Entuganovskaia *volost*, where lunch was had and thence on to Ubeevskaia *volost*, in all a distance of twenty-four *versts*....

From Ubeevskaia *volost* to the *volost* of Malo-Tsilnyi, there remained but six *versts* to traverse. It was nine o'clock in the evening when we arrived and the authorities were most cordial in the reception which they gave us. Having been conducted to the home of a Tatar, a clean and well-kept peasant's home... Formerly this house of two small rooms had been the only schoolhouse in the locality for a community numbering as many as five thousand. One of the officials who was accompanying us, a tall handsome

---

[68] Childs's coinage "Lodgeism" is a reference to the Republican US Senate leader Henry Cabot Lodge, who led the movement to prevent the ratification of the Versailles treaty. This move is considered an early sign of the isolationism that prevailed in America's view of the world between the two world wars.

man of splendid physique and of some thirty-five years of age, exclaimed impetuously as he called our attention to the educational limitations of the past: "We have been kept a dark people, and it is only now that we are beginning to move in the direction of enlightenment. You have had educational advantages and you cannot appreciate the repressive influences surrounding us. For myself, I never learned to read nor write until after the Revolution, and then you may imagine with what clumsiness and difficulty."

Malo-Tsilnyi, May 10, [1922]—In this *volost* it is estimated that one third of the seed distributed by the government this spring has been eaten by the inhabitants prior to the receipt of American corn. This is greater by thirty percent than any previous estimate I have been given in other cantons.

The frightful mortality of children, ten percent, which has prevailed in the *volost* since the closing down five weeks previous of the American kitchens owing to a breakdown of transportation, coincides with estimates everywhere given me on this trip and bears testimony to the fearful rate death of which the country would have been the sufferer in the absence of American aid during the winter.

From here it was forty *versts* to Buinsk over a fairly good road, and we continued on with but one intermediate stop at the *volost* of Staro-Studenetsko. At this latter *volost*, I was attracted, in the office of the local soviet, by the sight of a comparatively young man attired in the blouse of an American soldier. Simson remarked that the man probably had been at Archangel in the Red Army and the blouse had very likely formed part of the stores taken from the stocks of British and American forces at the time of their evacuation. There had been enough taken at the time, he said, to supply the Red Armies on the northern front for more than a year, a superfluous comment of his, I thought, and specifically designed to rub in a rather inglorious page of American history. The Russian young man who, it developed, was the chief of the local militia, vouchsafed the explanation, however, that he had been one of the forty-five thousand Russian prisoners of war whom the American forces had liberated in their advance into Alsace-Lorraine in 1918. These prisoners had been completely reequipped with uniforms and supplies by the Americans for a period of four months, he stated. Upon the evacuation of the area by the Americans and the entrance of French troops, these latter had despoiled the Russians of practically everything given them by the Americans....

He did not deem it necessary to refer to France even in scorn, for the name of France itself is a sufficient expression of anathema today in Russia. It is a lesson in sarcasm to hear the inflection given the word by the average Russian.

It was only five o'clock when we returned to our temporary home or headquarters in Buinsk; and Maleeka, the charming Tatar girl, the wife of our host, welcomed us with a steaming samovar....

According to Maleeka's childishly naive testimony, her husband actually was the possessor of but one wife, herself. This she explained by the fact that the wife, whom she had supplanted, had been relegated with two children to the lower floor of the house and enjoyed now only the drudgery and duties of a servant, maid, or housewife. Her husband might marry again by Tatar law, she said, but in that case, she remarked, with a proud toss of her hair, she would refuse any longer to live with him and would return to the home of her parents....

Buinsk, May 11, [1922]—We were promised horses for eleven o'clock or so soon as we had had the opportunity of indulging in a Russian bath in the special house for that purpose which was attached to our temporary dwelling place. But there was such a dearth of horses in the town that it was not until five o'clock in the afternoon that two were found. Before the New Economic Policy, the government was privileged to go to a citizen's home and commandeer his horses, but apparently that policy has been abandoned along with a good many other arbitrary restrictions on personal property.

[While waiting to cross the river, Childs held a conversation with the Tatar driver.]

How did the Soviet government compare in his estimation with the Imperial government? It was all the same, he said. He didn't care. He had only one concern and that was a desire to see good times. If he had been acquainted with American life, he would have undoubtedly added "and a full dinner pail." He had no complaints to make of the Soviet government, he continued, despite the fact that he owned two horses and was a bourgeois. *He* [Childs's italics] had been left alone, and *he* [Childs's italics] had never been reduced to the necessity of eating any bread substitutes such as *lebeda*. It was difficult to compare the two governments in his opinion. Under the government of the tsar the authorities had deliberately attempted to stir up dissensions between the many tribes and races composing the Tatar

Republic. The Soviet government had given the Tatar a measure of autonomy. But the old Tatar thought the ideals of the Communist Party were too high for them to be realized through the agency of the too often weak Communists upon whom the Party and government were obliged to depend. "The Communist Party demands men for governmental positions who are strong and incorruptible," was his manner of expressing this thought. "But," and he regarded us with that perplexed air which, if he had been a Frenchman would have provoked an instinctive shrug of the shoulders, "but, tell me, you who know this canton, where are they to be found?"...

[Childs asked him what he thought of a man who had two wives?]

"Two wives?" he repeated. "Better to have two dogs."

Tetushi, May 12, [1922]—After a visit to several of the excellent kitchens in town, I made arrangements to leave by the first boat putting in to Tetushi for Kazan. I went meanwhile to the *Altai*, upon which we had come from Kazan with food, and which was lying close into shore, having been promised by the local manager of waterways that I would be communicated with as soon as a boat had arrived.... The boat was the *Valodarsky*, newly painted in excellent condition with a restaurant aboard—though offering a slim bill of fare—and commodious first-class staterooms with electric lights and running water. There were four classes and for the first and second classes there were provided two almost elegant saloons....

May 16, [1922]—One of the most novel of my experiences in Russia befell me today when I was called upon, together with Simson, to testify in a Soviet court. So far as I know, I am the first American of the ARA in Russia to have had the benefit of this experience. A communication was received in the morning from the government inquiring as to whether Simson and I were in the city, and if so, we were requested to appear at one o'clock at the Commissariat of Justice to testify concerning what was described as "the improper activities of M. Skvortzov."

Skvortzov was, until his transfer recently to the Ukraine, secretary of the Communist Party of the Tatar Republic. The responsible position which he occupied in the government as well as the integrity of his character I had thought to be such as to have protected him from such an accusation as this. Yet it is true that no one in Russia can really be said to be safe from suspicion hauled to court as was demonstrated in the Tatar Republic last summer before our arrival when the prime minister was arrested and imprisoned.

At the appointed hour accordingly, Simson and I made our way to the office to which we had been directed, that of "the Examiner of Important Matters of the People's Commissariat of Justice of the Tatar Republic," commonly known as the Revolutionary Tribunal, the highest judicial institution of the government. Upon entering the office we found ourselves, instead of in a court as I had been led to expect by the summons, in an ordinary and rather bare office room containing two officials seated at tables in opposite corners of the room. These were the examiners "of important matters."…

When it came to my turn, he requested that I reply to certain questions which, as they were answered, were filled in in a form which was before him for that purpose. There were the usual interrogatories such as name, nationality, home address, present address, and present occupation. When this latter had been answered, he further inquired into my permanent occupation. It was the final inquiry, however, which drew me out of my abstracted mood.

"What is your political faith?"

I could scarcely suppress a smile and felt that I was on the point of being cited for contempt of court when I was reassured and brought to a sense of the unconventionality of the proceedings at the lighting of a cigarette by the magistrate.

"Tell him I'm a progressive Democrat, if there's such a thing," I said to Simson.

The examiner screwed his eyes up and puckered his forehead.

"Into what category does a progressive Democrat fall?" was the next query directed of me: "Menshevik, Bolshevik, Social revolutionary or what?"

Again I smiled. I remembered that in the past, Communists with whom I had discussed politics and to whom I had expressed my political faith, had described me as a Social Revolutionary.

"Tell him we haven't such political divisions in America," I replied, and the magistrate duly and solemnly recorded my answer.

That done, he came to a statement of the purpose of the examination into Skvortzov at the station of Viatskaia Poliana last November, and whether I remembered if there had been any difficulty experienced there in the sending of a telegram, signed by me, to the ARA in Chistopol. I said that I recollected having sent a telegram from Viatskaia Poliana and that I recollected having sent a telegram from Viatskaia Poliana and that there had been some difficulty about its transmission but as to the nature of the difficulties, I was obliged to confess to a hazy memory. According to the charges as represented by the examiner, Skvortzov , having been refused permission to send the telegram, had used very strong language, representing among other things that he was an official of the Tatar Republic, as he was, and that as such his orders should be carried out. In the end the telegram had been dispatched, but the telegraph authorities had complained of Skvortzov's conduct to the central government in Moscow, Viatskaia Poliana being under the jurisdiction of the central government itself and not under that of the Tatar Republic. My final answer as to whether I recollected any unusual scene as having taken place was that I did not and I could not believe that it could have been extraordinary or I would have been sure to have set it down in the diary, kept since my entrance into Russia. That completed the proceedings after my answers had been read to me in Russian and translated into English by Simson, and after I had duly signed the affidavit.

As I left, I could not help thinking of that formidable sign which marked the outside of the door and which bore in impressively colored letters, "Examiner of Important Matters." That embodies an incongruity which strikes one in so many relations with the Soviet government that, what is deemed as important by the Soviet authorities would be, in another country, hardly worthy of notice or of the distraction of a government's attention.

May 17, [1922]—An attractive little girl, still in her teens, whom we have known since our arrival in Kazan and who is in the ballet of the Kazan Opera, called at the house this evening upon Wahren to recount to him in fear and trembling the peculiar circumstances in which she had been placed this day. In the morning she had received a note from the Extraordinary Commission, directing her to appear at a certain hour before that body. It was explained in the communication that should she fail to put in her appearance, a guard would be sent to her home to escort her forcibly to the interview. [At the interrogation, she was asked about the behavior of the Americans and her relations with them.]...

But all their inquiries were in vain, and she was finally told that she might leave. But it was not before she had been enjoined to disclose to no one the circumstances connected with her visit to the Extraordinary Commission or else harm would befall her. This is by no means the first time that we have learned directly of the activity of the Cheka in keeping a strict surveillance over the American personnel of the ARA in Kazan. It has been brought to our knowledge by several during the period of our residence in the city, and there must have been many more who have been called up to testify concerning us who, through intimidation, have never felt it safe to make a disclosure of it.

May 18, [1922]—A general of the tsar's Imperial Army, a tall, erect, gentleman of the old school, was admitted to the office today, coming with an application for work. His patrician face was half hidden by a closely cropped beard, and he wore his old military coat, stripped, however, of all insignia. Standing a figure of six feet in height, it was apparent that his shoulders were stooped a trifle under the weight of years and the ordeal of the Revolution. He stated in a few words and quite simply that, though he was all alone in the world, he had himself to support and must find work in order to live. Since his military service in the war against Germany, he had served neither in the White nor the Red Army. I could think of nothing which might be offered one of such advanced years until after searching my memory, and moved by the sympathy which his dignified bearing aroused, it occurred to me that we were in need of watchmen for the kitchens in town.

Could I suggest such a position to him or not? I hesitated in doubt, notwithstanding that I had come to understand that the desperate struggle of these people of the old aristocracy for existence had suppressed, however, temporarily, much of their old pride. But scarcely had I made the suggestion, as delicately as it was possible, when I perceived my mistake. It seemed to me that the old general rose a little more erect in his chair, and I know that the tears formed in his clear intelligent blue eyes. If the eyes were the windows of the soul, I was sure that a great soul shone within those stained windows. His voice faltered and I though that he would not be able to collect himself. But by a superb evidence of self-discipline, he broke the strained silence to inquire in almost a matter-of-fact tone into the conditions of work. So soon as these had been explained to him, he arose with decision from his chair and bowed, not an indignant bow but with a turn of the head as if to say, "Young man, I pardon you your mistake. I cherish no malice for ignorance. But if you had known, you would have hesitated long before inflicting such a wound upon an old man."

I shall never forget that bow and that face; one moment, calm as a Grecian Olympus and the next, twitching and torn as if by the lash of some whip. What a moment in life of parades and reviews that must have been for him! I was left wondering after he had left which of us must have suffered the most?

May 23, [1922]—Last December the Kazan district of the ARA was extended to include the two autonomous states of Mahri and Chuvash, which adjoin the Tatar Republic in the West. But owing to my illness in the winter, I was prevented from making a visit to this new territory until today when, with Simson, I set out by rail to Shikhranyi, from which point I planned to make a brief trip across the Chuvash *Oblast*.

May 24, [1922]—Arriving at Shikhranyi, there was not much business to be done aside from a meeting with the committee and the inspection of the kitchens in the town, and that completed, we were given an excellent pair of horses, which took us off on our way to Tsivilsk, a cantonal center, forty-three *versts* distant. Halts were made at the *volosts* of Shinkhonosanov and Shelbugin, where conferences were held with the *volost* committees. In the former *volost* village I was shown an old Chuvash national costume of the women which I bought for two million rubles. The young girl who sold it to me explained that it had been made by the grandmother of her mother. In the latter village I had the good fortune to find one of the ancient and now rare headpieces of the Chuvash women, ornamented with silver coins. This one was extraordinary for the number of silver coins attached to it and which amounted to more than five hundred, many of them dating from the time of the old Russian princes who reigned in feudal state over the territories now comprising the Russian Republic before the establishment of a central authority in Moscow.

Here in the *volost* village of Shelbugin, I met an inspector of the cantonal ARA committee, who in the course of a discussion, stated that the greatest difficulty to be overcome in the ARA work in the villages was in the transportation of foodstuffs. There were not only an insufficient number of horses for the work, but there was also met with quite frequently difficulty in persuading the peasants who possessed horses to give them to the task of hauling without recompense in money or foodstuffs. The peasants for the most part had been willing to undertake the transportation of the food for the children without payment, but it was not so easy to induce a similar cooperative spirit as concerned the food for adults. The problem was complicated by the fact that it was very rare that a peasant in possession of a horse was in sufficient need as compared with the rest of the population to warrant his inclusion in the ARA corn list.

I said that the American people would be most assuredly disinclined to aid a people who were not willing to do what they could to help each other and that the burden of transporting the corn without payment was nothing more than a duty which those in possession of horses owed to their less fortunate fellows. The inspector agreed but adduced the ignorance of the peasants as making it almost impossible to bring about in them an appreciation of the cooperative spirit necessary to enable the country to attain its former economic footing.

Yes, I said, that was the most sorrowful part of it all, not the selfishness which made itself evident but the appalling ignorance and unenlightenment which existed. And this, I reflected, the Soviet government is beginning to recognize: That Socialism may only be put into practice in a thoroughly enlightened community or state. For, until a people are taught better, avarice and greed and selfishness like the other base passions will continue to remain the controlling principles of conduct....

The days are long in this part of the world, and it was not dark, although close to eleven o'clock, when we arrived in Tsivilsk. A very comfortable room with two beds was assigned us, and it was not long after eating a supper, prepared from the food which we carried with us, that we were asleep.

Tsivilsk, May 25, [1922]—After a visit to the ARA kitchens in town and after [acquiring] certain statistical data which I desired had been obtained from the local authorities, I returned to the headquarters which had been established for us and found there a man who had been awaiting me for an interview. He entered the room with uncertain enfeebled step and sank heavily into a chair. At first glance he appeared to be an elderly man of some sixty years, but upon closer examination and from a knowledge gained by contact with many starving people, I was able to perceive that his aged appearance was due to hunger and privation and that in reality farther advanced in life than forty or fifty years. In the depths of a gaunt face, which was partially screened by a thin beard and hair, left long uncut, there were disclosed a delicately cut mouth, firm chin and frank, steady eyes.

The conversation was opened with the announcement in slightly labored English that he was a German subject and that for the purpose of stating the object of his visit, he was able to speak English but preferred German or French. I replied that it would be agreeable if he spoke French, and he accordingly proceeded to the narration of his story.

In 1914 he had been captured by the Russians and had passed some months in Kiev in prison. In 1915, along with other Germans, he had been sent to Tsivilsk, and here he had remained for seven years. His other comrades had been exchanged or repatriated before the October Revolution, but he had remained with the intention of repaying certain debts which he owed Russians. The Revolution had not only made this impossible but had made it also impossible for him to return to Germany. By 1918 he had learned sufficient Russian to enable him to obtain a position in the local high school as instructor of French, but an illness, which he had contracted in the army, forced him to abandon the only occupation which permitted him to earn a living. To exist he had been therefore compelled to sell one by one the few possessions which he had been able to collect together since his stay in Russia until, with the coming of the hunger, he had been driven under the desperation of the times to find shelter in an asylum. Now he found himself without means of making his way to Moscow to seek repatriation while confronted on the other hand by the alternative of remaining to starve. Twice he had been granted permission to proceed to Moscow for repatriation, but each time he had been prevented from doing so by the lack of funds. Once he had had sufficient money for the expense of the railway journey, but he had found himself too weak to walk to the nearest railway station, forty-three *versts* distant.

In support of his identity, he produced first citizenship papers taken out by his father in the Superior Court of New York n 1854, the American passport with which his father had returned to Germany in 1859 to become a German citizen, a card of identity carried by his grandfather, a citizen of Düsseldorf, when the citizens of the Duchy of Berg were enrolled in the armies of Napoleon, and finally, papers belonging to him from the late war. [Childs fed the man and loaned him the money to reach Kazan, where he could gain further help, and then Childs proceeded to Chebekaryi.]

Simson and I were directed to the home of the leading officials of the community where we were made welcome and a room given over to us. The house, which was a modest wooden construction, was in some contrast to the many handsome stone dwellings contained within the town and in which, according to reports current in the outside world, the Soviet officials would be more likely to make their homes. Our hosts were the chairman of the Soviet of the Chuvash *Oblast* and the chief of the Militia of the *Oblast*, both by their youth maintaining the tradition which I have found fulfilled in the persons of most Soviet officials that it is by enthusiasm and energy of youth that the principles of the Soviet faith may best be diffused. The former was a sharp-eyed lad of not more than twenty-five years of age and the latter of about the same age and both apparently men of unlimited nervous energy.

We were invited to a meal, which had been prepared in our honor and at which, somewhat contrary to the custom of the usual Soviet dinners, there were wines and liquors in abundance. I do not know whether any principle was observed in the dispensing of these, but as I consult my feeble recollection, I am inclined to think there was not, for champagne succeeded vodka, which was in turn followed with disconcerting celerity by cognac, brandy, and port wine until a time came it seemed when they were served in inextricable confusion. Cheboxary was formerly the place of manufacture of one of the spirit factories of the government, and hence the Soviet government has inherited here a considerable quantity of vodka. The extensive mass of red brick buildings, which formerly served as the factory, had since been converted into the office of the Extraordinary Commission of the *oblast*.

The meal was a very plain one, of soup, boiled mutton and meat cakes, "a simple peasant's meal," as the chairman of the Soviet expressed it. When it was completed, I was invited to a walk about the town and to an inspection of some of the places of interest. I needed no urging when I was invited to look in at the public sitting of the Revolutionary Tribunal of the *oblast*. The case which was being tried was that of a prominent local soviet official who had been accused of the misuse of his office for gain. Apparently the trial had attracted unusual public interest for it was being conducted in the largest public meeting place in town, the local theater, where some three hundred or more interested townspeople had assembled.

The Revolutionary Tribunal is the highest court of the Soviet government, and I was interested in learning how the composition of its members was determined. In answer to my inquiries the chairman of the Chuvash *Oblast* soviet explained that the soviet of the *oblast* put forward certain candidates which were voted upon by the people. To be quite frank, he stated, the Communist Party of the *Oblast* Soviet expressed to the *Oblast* Soviet its choice of candidates, and it was from these that the choice of the *oblast* soviet was generally made. The term of membership in the tribunal was limited to one year as was that of the officers of the soviet, but the members might be at any time recalled by the will of the people although it was not made very clear to me how this will of the people might be expressed, and I concluded that it was probably through the expression of the will of the Communist Party. There is not much doubt that it is the Communist Party, which controls all elections in Russia and in as effectual a manner as elections are controlled in New York by Tammany Hall or as American presidential candidates are engineered to election by a Penrose or a Smoot[69] in a national convention.

From the Tribunal we moved on to a delightful promenade on the cliff above the Volga banks, and which at the hour, 9:00 PM, was thronged by the young people of the town. The place was reminiscent of a similar little park upon the Danube in Belgrade. We were walking upstream so that the waters of the Volga were to our right and on the left there was to be seen one of the familiar wooden pyramidical monuments erected by the Bolsheviks to the revolutionary leader of one of the peasant uprisings of the locality in the 18th century. A little farther on was a motion picture theater which had just opened its doors and which, when we entered it was showing a film of the old story of a wife's unrequited love for her husband. In the flickering of the picture and the pause which intervened between the changing of each reel, I was transplanted to the crude dime movies of ten or twelve years ago in the

---

[69] Boise Penrose and Reed Smoot were two Republican US Senators who were major powers in the Republican Party at the time.

cities of America. Perhaps in Freedom, Wyoming, I reflected such imperfect examples of the moving picture art were still being exhibited.

But the movie did not claim my attention for long, and we were proceeding on again, this time for a look-in at the prison of the district. It was like any other prison, a great stone structure of iron-barred windows and surrounded by a high wall. The warden met us on our entrance, and I was conducted to the kitchen, a neat well kept place and cleaner, I reflected, than some of our own American kitchens in Russia. The daily prison fare was said to consist of two *funts* of bread and a small quantity of gruel, fish, tea and sugar—surely a diet commending itself to many hungry peasants outside the prison walls.

I was shown one of the cells, a room some twenty-five feet by thirty and in which five prisoners were incarcerated. Their beds were made of wood and contained mattresses, sheets and blankets. The prisoners were seated about a table in the center of the room as I entered, when they arose and stood silently. It was with difficulty that I could distinguish their features, but they all seemed plain simple-looking men, not at all of savage aspect. Of the one nearest to me, a middle-aged man, standing in his shirt sleeves, I inquired the reason for his imprisonment. Quite frankly and briefly, he answered that he had misappropriated a few *puds* of foodstuffs belonging to the government. I did not pursue my investigations, but I was satisfied with the statement of the soviet chairman that there was none at the present time out of the twenty-six inmates of the prison who had been sentenced for political offence unless, as he added, two of the higher church dignitaries of the community might be included in this category.

These two had been charged with seeking to obstruct the requisition of church property by the state and had been sentenced to death, a sentence that had been recently commuted upon an order from Moscow and which was likely to be further commuted, it was thought. Since the two had been arrested, the chief of militia explained to me, there has been no trouble experienced by the local authorities in the requisition of gold and silver from the churches. On that day he stated [that] one of the churches had delivered to him voluntarily more than five *funts* of gold and several *puds* of silver. The lower clergy, I was informed, recruited mostly from the peasants of the lower classes, were in apparent sympathy with the governmental order for the requisition of church property or at least manifested no such open opposition as that which had been displayed by the higher order of the church. If the version of these Soviet officials could be accepted as impartial, one would believe there was as much class feeling between the lower and the higher order of the clergy as there existed between the bourgeoisie and the proletariat.

Cheboxary, May 28, [1922]—[Childs spent the early part of the day with a local historian who informed him of the history and culture of the Chuvash people.]…

I turned from my inquire into the romantic history and character of the Chuvash people, to that of the more realistic and for that reason more tragic and repulsive present. In company with a plump lovely-faced lady, who seemed to be one of those indefatigable laborers for the distressed whom one finds here and there among every people, I proceeded to an inspection of the children's homes and hospitals of the town.

The children's institutions which were visited seemed to be well administrated in comparison with the average in the Tatar Republic. While the children could not in general actually be said to be starving, there was a pallor of the cheeks and a listlessness about them which gave very strong evidence that the food which they were receiving was insufficient for their normal and proper development. In one home I viewed four very pitiful boys who had been brought to the home some week or two previous in as reduced a physical state due to starvation as any I have seen during my nine months' experience in Russia. The food given by the institution had been insufficient to restore the vitality of one of the boys who was lying huddled up in his rags, almost nothing but skin and bones, slowly sinking to an inevitable death. From the homes I went to a hospital which provided about seventy-six beds and where there were seventy-eight patients. The majority of the patients were ill with typhus or some ailment brought on by hunger; I was pointed out patient after patient who was denominated by the doctor as a hunger case and whose pinched face and bony limbs gave every evidence as to their lack of proper nourishment. The hospital was situated in an airy and commodious building, and one might say that there was everything for the comfort of the patients except proper food and medicine.

Perhaps the most pathetic sight which I had occasion to witness was that in the babies' home in Cheboxary where thirty-six babies were being provided for. There was no milk for them other than that afforded by seven nurses in attendance. The death rate in this home was stated to be something like eighty percent. In passing into the home I say lying out in the hall four pitiful emaciated forms of very young babies which had been brought in to the home on that day. Two of them were already dead. The evening of the same day at about midnight, I took the steamboat, the *Third International*, en route from Nizhnyi Novgorod for Astrakhan and found myself in Kazan upon awaking next morning.

Kazan, May 28, [1922]—An interesting sidelight on the growing sympathetic attitude toward America on the part even of the workers of the Soviet government was given me today by one of the employees of our office. A few days ago at a meeting of the workers in one of the large military factories in Kazan, a resolution was proposed by one of the commissars present that the failure of the Genoa Conference was attributable to America. This resolution provoked a perfect storm of indignant protest and inspired several Communists to rise to the defense of America's alleged complicity in the failure of the Genoa Conference, pointing out that such a resolution was hardly the proper return for the great assistance rendered Russia by America in the form of relief.

Several such defenses of America, in consideration of the relief extended by her to Russia, which were offered by those present, finally provoked the author of the revolution in question to arise and make the statement in defense of his position that, although it had never been made public, it was common enough knowledge that the supplies distributed by the ARA in Russia were being paid for out of funds gathered by the Russian relief. This assertion evoked, I am told, a perfect chorus of boos and hisses so that the speaker was forced to take his seat and the resolution, when put to a vote, was defeated by an almost overwhelming majority. A similar resolution, proposed at one of the meetings of the local trade unions, was likewise defeated under much the same circumstances.

This all goes to demonstrate very strongly in my opinion that the work of the ARA in Russia has established a basis of good will between the United States and Russia, which is not to be destroyed by the loose talk of politicians or professional agitators. It is, of course, difficult at this time to estimate precisely the extent of the good understanding which our work has fostered. That it has attained no inconsiderable proportion has been made evident to me on more than one occasion in the conversations which I have had for months past with representative citizen of every class of the Russian population and is further attested to by the flood of messages of thanks which the ARA is receiving every day from people in the Kazan district of the ARA. And most significant of the character of the ARA influence in the cultivation of a friendly spirit among Russians toward America is that it has made itself felt not only among the great mass of workers and peasants and even among what is left of the intelligentsia but among a certain class of Communists themselves.

June 2, [1922]—There is confirmation given now almost every day in public lectures, private conversations, and in the press of the development of that friendly spirit toward America which I had occasion to note several days ago. It has grown to be even more than that for it is developing into an ever deepening desire not alone for the friendship of America, but more specifically, for the bringing about of an official understanding between the Russian Socialist Federated Soviet Republic and the United States of America....

[At a lecture, local Russian citizens suggested the creation of the United Transport Company, some sort of organization to direct and reorganize transportation in the Tatar Republic. The purpose of the presentation was to solicit American help in the enterprise. Apparently the proposal even called for the sale of shares for the attraction of foreign capital. The proponents even went so far as to suggest a military alliance between America and Russia!]

June 10, [1922]—Russia's present famine differs from all previous famines in her history in that individuals of the most severely stricken population seem to have lost their human character under the affliction of the more recent disaster. This is the opinion of a famine authority who called upon me today and presented me with the most moving and authentic account of cannibalism which I have come upon since such occurrences were brought to my notice months ago in one canton after another of the Tatar Republic. The account given to me today was drawn from the personal experience of my informant during a journey which took place through the canton of Spassk at the beginning of the year.

"The inhabitants of the village which we entered," the writer states, "informed us that we had come late in order to observe the worst ravages of the famine as seventeen cases of cannibalism had already been registered in the village. We expressed the desire to see the people who had been known to eat human flesh, and a militiaman led us to a house, the owner of which, a Christian Tatar, had eaten his seven-year old daughter. The hut was completely void of the ordinary furniture of a peasant's home, containing not even a table nor a bedstead. Nor were there clothes of any kind, nor even any rags, for everything had been disposed of long ago in order to buy dried leaves or other substitutes utilized for the making of bread. The Tatar himself, an old man of about sixty, sat blinking on a log of wood near the stove. In appearance he was very skinny with a sharply pointed nose and eyes, deeply set and sparkling unnaturally. On the hearth there were several glowing coals upon which a bone was being roasted, filling the room with a suffocating smell. We gave the old man some bread. He examined it attentively as if it were an object that he was unacquainted with. Then he placed the piece in his mouth, and without so much as chewing it, gulped it down with a spasmodic movement of the throat and inquired, 'Is that bread?' He had probably lost all sense of taste for it. We inquired if it were true that he had eaten his own little daughter. 'Yes—yes—true—have eaten her,' was the imperturbable answer. 'Why have you eaten her?' 'Why?—Because I was hungry—very hungry,' spoken in the same quiet manner and with a movement of the features which almost denoted a smile. 'But why have you eaten the child? You must have surely had *something* to eat before?' 'Ah, yes, before, I ate dry leaves and clay. Now there are no leaves to be had and clay makes me sick. We have left off eating clay!' On the stove there was to be seen a piece of dry clay somewhat in the form of a small loaf of black bread. It had come then to this from leaves and after clay, his own daughter. 'And what are you going to eat now?' was the inquiry, which was made of him. He made a tired gesture. "It is mother that we will eat.' As the woman, his wife, whom he had evidently indicated, was nowhere to be seen, we asked him if she were present. 'She's there upon the board; she is sick—and soon will be done with.' 'And so you are going to eat your sick wife?' 'Yes, as soon as she is dead—then shall begin eating.'"

These words were not only uttered with perfect composure but the tone of the voice itself conveyed a firm conviction, making it plain that his resolution was irrevocable. At this moment a militiaman entered the house with the news that another case of cannibalism had been discovered. We were invited to follow him for investigation. We had already been deeply impressed by the interview with the old Tatar and though not relishing further scenes of such horror, we resolved to proceed to the end with the uncovery of these gloomy pictures in the village. Before leaving the old Tatar we requested the first militiaman, who had been with us, to take care of the man and to secure his axe and knife that he might not be able to fulfill our gloomy apprehension that in his impatience, his wife would be sacrificed before her natural death. We also gave orders for a search of the house inasmuch as the dreadful smell of the roasting bone led us to conjecture the possibility that there might be hidden away a supply of human flesh. Having made these arrangements, we directed our steps to the other house in which the latest example of cannibalism had been discovered."

"This latest incident had for its principals two lads of twelve and fourteen, who taking advantage of their parents' absence, had killed their little sister of three years of age and were in the act of frying her as we entered. There was on the stove a baby's leg and a chop from the flesh of the child which had been killed but a few moments before. We did not linger to speak to the children; we left the house precipitately. A little later we were joined by the militiaman, whom we had left at the Tatar's house for inspection. He handed us three little bundles enclosed in rags. In them there was disclosed salted human flesh that had been discovered in the loft of the old man's hut."

"In 1901 when human beings, together with domestic animals and even wild beasts, were beset by hunger, people died calmly and without the loss of the character which raised them above the beasts and made them human. In 1921, however, under the pressure of a hunger which it must be admitted was more generally acute, fathers killed their own children and children their brothers and sisters and ate their flesh in a raw state or cooked, for the population had passed the limits of human endurance and stricken by a savage longing for food, they became beasts. During the famine in 1901 in the district of Kazan, we spoke then of that terrible Russian disaster as of a distress which could not be repeated. But we have been mistaken for the stern reality of 1921 and 1922 has not fulfilled those expectations."

June 21, [1922]—Not since last November and until today has there arisen any occasion in connection with our work of relief for the making of an incident with the Russian government. On yesterday, however, Pearson, one of the American field workers, returned from Sarapol in the Perm district, where he had been sent for the organization in that new territory of the work of relief. He brought back with him the report of a speech, which had been made by one of the local Communists at the meeting, called together by him to effect an ARA organization, which was such as to have aroused the indignation of every American here were it not for the fact that it was so palpably silly.

The report of Pearson was as follows:

Sarapol, June 14th, 1922.

Brought to Sarapol today the first boatload of food and medical supplies for the famine stricken people of this canton. At a mass meeting held this evening in the Palace of Labor, I explained that the food delivered would be sufficient to supply eighteen thousand children. The announcement of the gift was received with general applause. While the mass meeting was in progress the secretary of the local labor union [Comrade ? Iakunin], who made the only speech of acceptance other than the chairman's in an impassioned speech sought to minimize the work of the ARA in Russia, saying that America was a very rich country and that it was nothing for the Americans to undertake to feed nine million Russians as the ARA was doing. He said that it was no secret to the Russians that America does not want to have anything to do with the present Soviet government as she had been the only one of the great nations not represented at the Genoa Conference. He also prophesied that the day would come when the American proletariat would overthrow the American government and stretch out its had toward the Russian proletariat.

"I am not," he said, "going to characterize the representatives of the American people who came to feed Sarapol. By looking at them anyone could say whom they represent. We know that they will try to extract all the gold they can from the country." He asserted that the relief America was rendering was due to the insistence of the American proletariat and that it had been undertaken by the American government only to keep the proletariat quiet. "And," he concluded, "we are grateful for that relief. We are going to thank them for it, but we are going to thank also the American proletariat, who brought pressure upon the American government to render this aid to the proletariat of Russia." Mr. Pearson and Dr. [Walter] Davenport listened attentively to the address, which was followed by a burst of applause, but as it was in Russian they failed to catch the drift of the discourse until their interpreter had translated it for them after the meeting was over.

As Acting District Supervisor, I felt obliged to make an incident of the occurrence by bringing it to the attention of the representative of the central government attached as liaison officer with the Kazan district of the ARA, as well as to the attention of Colonel Haskell. Accordingly I directed the following communication to the former:

> Kazan, June 21, 1922.
> Dear Sir,
> I wish to bring to your attention the enclosed memorandum, being the substance of a report of Mr. R. W. Pearson, who recently organized the work at Sarapol. The summary of the speech of the secretary of the Labor Union in Sarapol was prepared by [the] interpreter Malev immediately upon returning from the meeting to the boat on which Mr. Pearson was traveling and was made at Mr. Pearson's request so soon as the latter had gathered from Mr. [?] Malev verbally the import of the speech. It is wholly unnecessary for me to point out to you, Mr. Muskatt, that aside from the criticism which might be made of an injection of politics into the speech of the secretary of the Labor Union—even passing over this phrase—that the speech contains not a covert but a direct insult to a representative of the American Relief Administration in the charge—not a mere imputation—that the chief interest of the Americans in this district is one of gold rather than relief.
> I need not tell you also what a painful thought this is to each and every American in the Kazan district that the labor of some of us here for ten months is requited in such a fashion as this and that our good names, as well as the good name of the American Relief Administration in Russia, is thus permitted to be publicly

besmirched. I am told by Mr. Pearson that the speaker, who was in the presence of some three hundred citizens of the community of Sarapol, was most generously applauded at the conclusion of this defamation of our character, and so I cannot but take it that the opinions were something more than the personal expression of one man.

It is true that the chairman of the Sarapol Soviet brought to Mr. Pearson before his departure a protocol deprecating the remarks of the secretary of the Labor Union. But since this insult had been made publicly and in the presence of some three hundred citizens of the town, I do not feel that the apology made after some delay and in so private a character was sufficient to wipe out the stain cast upon the ARA and the representatives of the ARA in Kazan. I am told that this speech, after some corrections had been made, was permitted to be published in the local newspaper in Sarapol. Having called the circumstances of this unfortunate occurrence to you attention I am following the only course which is open to me and am forwarding a full statement as enclosed with a copy of this letter to the American Relief Administration in Moscow. Very sincerely yours, J. Rives Childs, Acting District Supervisor.

June 24, [1922]—In reply to the foregoing letter, I received today the following answer from Mr. Muskatt:

> June 22, 1922
>
> Dear Mr. Childs,
>
> Having become acquainted with the contents of your letter and the copy of Mr. Pearson's report dated the twenty-first instant, I feel bound to express my deep regret on account of the Sarapol incident which may very erroneously interpret our conception of ARA's activity in the Soviet Republic. We have always viewed the great work of the ARA as a deed of humanity, and the speaker's attempts to imbue it with a stripe of political hue does not at all correspond with the actual state of things. With regard to the applause, I may add: 1) The incident had taken place in a district beyond the field of ARA's charitable operations, where the

population was little acquainted with the character of your work; 2) the chairman of the Sarapol Soviet, who actually reflects the public opinion of the population, has stated in his minutes his disapprobation of the speaker's remarks; 3) Much to our regret I must add that it often happens that our public, especially in the provinces, judges of the speaker's abilities more by his dialectical and oratorical effects than by the ideas expressed in his speech.

Of course it is rather difficult for me to state exactly all the particulars of the said incident, considering, moreover, that neither Mr. Pearson nor Dr. Davenport understands the Russian language. You are certainly aware, however, that our interpreters frequently garble the sense of personal discourses, even so far as regards political addresses. Should anybody try and scrutinize carefully all the particulars of the vexatious incident, he would be sure to find out that it is nothing more than a pure misunderstanding. Much to my regret, the case cannot be submitted for examination to the local authorities, Sarapol being situated beyond the territory of the Tatar Republic. Nevertheless, I shall immediately direct the whole correspondence relative to the above, to the representative of the central government for all foreign relief organizations, [Aleksandr] Eiduck, in consequence of which I hope that Moscow will give its concrete answer. Most respectively and faithfully yours, Representative of Central Government for all Foreign Relief Organizations of the Tatar Republic, Muskatt.

Meanwhile I had received specific instructions from Colonel Haskell as to how to proceed further, and these instructions I communicated in a supplementary letter to Mr. Muskatt and in which it was stated that "No further food is to be shipped to Sarapol until the secretary of the Labor Union at Sarapol, who is guilty of the public insult to the representative of the ARA and to the ARA, has been recalled to Moscow to answer for his act, and until a statement of the fact that he has been recalled, together with the reason, has been published in the local newspaper at Sarapol and until statements made by this individual publicly have been repudiated and the truth of them denied categorically by the local authorities in Sarapol in the Sarapol press. As soon as I have received assurance from that the above outlined steps have been executed, I shall be very glad to order the renewal of shipments of food to Sarapol."

From Mr. Muskatt I received verbal assurances that he would undertake to fulfill these stipulations, and it was decided to send to Sarapol for the settlement of the incident an ARA representative Mr. [H. N.] Spalding, and an assistant of Mr. Muskatt, [?] Zaitner.

June [23, 1922][70]—Spalding and Zaitner returned today from their journey to Sarapol and brought back with them copies of the *Red Kama Valley,* the local newspaper of Sarapol, devoted almost in its entirety to attempts to give us satisfaction for the incident which had occurred. There was contained in it not only the resolution of repudiation by the local authorities of the speech of Yakunin, secretary of the Labor Union; but copies of the original report of Pearson; the reply of Muskatt to my letter; and an apologetic letter of Yakunin and an editorial which attempted to make further reparation for the injury done the ARA. The resolution of the plenary session of the Soviet Executive Committee of Sarapol was as follows:

> Resolved, after discussion of Chairman [?] Horobrith's report relative to ARA's protest, presented by the representative of the Central Executive Committee, Zaitner, and called forth by an address, given at the meeting of June 14th by the responsible secretary of the Professional Unions, Iakunin, the representatives of the above organizations and workers of Sarapol consider it their duty to state that they do not agree with that part of Iakunin's address which treats of the appraisement of the humanitarian activity of the ARA in Russia. ARA's work can in no way whatever be connected with the policy of capitalistic countries toward Soviet Russia. The aim of ARA consists solely in relieving suffering humanity in the whole world. They are doing their work of relief in Sarapol *uezd,*[71] as well, by helping the population will receive a considerable support during the most critical months, and the number of children being saved by different organizations will be increased by several thousand. All reproaches, cast by Iakunin upon

[70] Childs lists this incorrectly as June 13.
[71] See footnote 25 on page 38.

ARA, have no foundation whatever. It was a great want of delicacy to try and connect the work of relief with politics. All the above is being remonstrated to Iakunin and the following action resolved to be taken: To notify Iakunin through the professional bureaus to leave immediately for Moscow, as proposed by Zaitner, for personal explanation before the representative of the central government for all foreign relief organizations of the Soviet Republic, Eiduck. Chairman Horobrith, Secretary [?] Efremov.

There follows also the letter of Iakunin and the editorial of the *Red Kama Valley:*

Having become acquainted with the copy of the stenogram of the ARA, I was surprised at the incorrect copy, or rather mistake, owing to which I was blamed for trying to reduce to a minimum the work of the ARA. I declare that my speech did not concern the work of the ARA, the aim of which is the salvation of the starving. It only concerned the American government. It is true that I said, "America is a rich country and can afford to feed the quantity of people which are being fed by the ARA." As concerns the gold mines, I must say that every capitalistic government is interested in the increasing of its riches; therefore, I simply meant all the bourgeois governments and not only the American. Concerning personalities, the following words in the stenogram have been ascribed to me: 'I don't wish to characterize the American representatives who have come to Sarapol to give relief to the starving. By looking at them one might judge what they are.' This phrase has been mistranslated.

We know that there is an overproduction in all spheres of national economy and even the foreign press relates instances of grain being used for heating steam engines. Further, about Genoa, it is quite true that America took no part in it. It is said in the stenogram that I prophesied the day of the dethronement of the American bourgeois government by the proletariat. Here I was misunderstood. I said the time would come when the American proletariat would be relieved from the yoke of capital. Yes, but this is true because the reign of capitalism is inevitably giving way to socialism. Even the representatives of the ARA delegation have said enough of the aim of their work to demonstrate this.

I finished my speech with assurances of the success of the ARA work and think that the cheers of the public were at the same time a welcome to the ARA delegates. It is possible that the American representatives will not agree to my point of view of the political and economical state of their country, but as representatives of a civilized nation, I hope they will agree with me that it is not prohibited to express one's personal opinions on the territory of the Republican Soviets.

[The article in *Red Kama Valley* titled "The Echoes" began by gushing about the "enlightened American bourgeoisie that goes perseveringly to all parts of the world...[to relieve] human suffering" and went on to state that comrade Iakunin, a workman, had "felt on his back what the whip of Russian absolution [sic] meant," and given the lack of understanding of both Pearson and Iakunin of the other's languages, understandable misunderstandings would occur. It also spoke of their "deep respect for the American people for its gift to the Soviet Republic," while noted that Yakunin, who is a "good revolutionary" was also a "bad diplomat." In general the tenor was that there were no intentional slights, only misunderstandings and lack of communication. Childs does not mention the incident again, so the explanation must have ended the matter.]

July 2, [1922]—Plans having been made for a reunion in Samara on July fourth of representatives from among the Americans of the Volga districts, six of us from Kazan, including: Turner, Boyd, Pearson, Dr. [William] Dear and [Arthur] Hillman, beside myself, left this morning aboard the steamer *Pecheretz*, a boat especially assigned by the government for ARA operations. An automobile was taken aboard for any side trips which it might be desired to make along the way. To make our journey even more comfortable, a cook formed also a part of the personnel of the party....

We left a little after eleven o'clock and at four o'clock we were at the landing stage for Spassk, where it had been decided to put ashore the automobile and to make a short inland journey by motor to the town of Spassk and afterwards to the historic village of Bolgary, which some of the Americans present had never visited. At Spassk after a conference with the

ARA committee, we proceeded to Bolgary over a road which at times was hardly to be distinguished as a road. We must have been the first to have ever entered the town in an automobile for an excited mob of children as well as adults quickly assembled around our machine to make an interested inspection of it....

July 3, [1922]—Early in the morning we reached the town of Simbirsk, the seat of the government of that name and headquarters of a district of the ARA, contiguous to that of Kazan. The city itself, which consists of some seventy-five thousand inhabitants, is perched upon the high bluffs overlooking the right bank of the Volga, and with the gilded domes of the churches and the towers of several old buildings, rises with some little majesty to greet the eye. The town is much cleaner and better kept than most of the towns or cities of Soviet Russia which I have visited,[72] and the broad avenue, which runs through the center, gives a pleasing appearance to the general aspect.

We found the living quarters of the ARA in a home which, if not as pretentious as that of ours in Kazan, appeared at least quite comfortable. [Edward R.] Fox, the district supervisor, gave us a cordial welcome and introduced us to his staff, of whom only some five were present at the time, the remainder being out on work in the district. The ARA offices are located in a large white stone building with Corinthian pillars, which give it the appearance of an American courthouse. The superficial inspection which we were able to make of the Simbirsk work did not give us any cause to feel that our own work suffered in any way by comparison.

Early in the evening in company with the Simbirsk delegation of Americans, we went aboard *Pecharetz* and headed for Samara. From Simbirsk to Samara the most beautiful section of the Volga is passed, and we sat up until late into the night to view the lovely colors cast upon the water and the shores by the rising moon. As the watercourse approaches Samara, the banks become steeper and more precipitous, and the vegetation becomes more luxuriant for we are proceeding south. Indeed we are entering upon a territory in which camels are as much utilized for beasts of burden as horses.

---

[72] The fact that Simbirsk was Lenin's birthplace and childhood home might have accounted for the better state of things.

July 4, [1922]—Fourth of July in Samara of Soviet Russia! It is certainly the strangest fourth I have ever celebrated, stranger even than the one aboard a houseboat off the coast of St. Nazaire in 1915, or that one in Saloniki in 1919, which I spent in the garden of the Roi George Restaurant by the Aegean Sea, drinking champagne at ten o'clock in the morning with the exiled manager of the Standard Oil Company. We drove up in the automobile to the ARA house and found the eight Americans of the Samara district awaiting us. Unfortunately, the Americans from the other districts of Ufa, Orenburg, and Saratov, who had been expected to participate in the gathering, had sent word that they had found it impossible to come....

In the afternoon it was necessary to complete the faithful performance of the fourth by a game of baseball. There were present just eighteen Americans or enough to fill our two nines. Opposing teams were made up, therefore, of the six Americans from Kazan and the three from Simbirsk on one side and the nine from Samara on the other. A vacant lot was found on the outskirts of the city, and there the duty was religiously executed of playing four innings or enough to legitimize the proceedings. Though I was pitching for the first time in my life, the Kazan-Simbirsk team proved victorious by the score of twelve-seven. The task for which we were there had been accomplished, and the great American professional sport had been introduced upon the Russian steppes and within the shadows of the Urals in the Soviet Republic of Russia. Assuredly we had given proof of our patriotism!...

It was late in the evening when we took our departure and turned our boat homeward. We left with no regrets but rather with pardonable pride that we were returning to a district so greatly superior to those which we had visited. And it was not alone in the living quarters and in the creature comforts that the Kazan district had raised itself in our estimation by comparison with Simbirsk and Samara. What was more important, it had been evidenced in the organization of the work which we had had occasion to observe. It was as if one had set a great smoothly running and highly organized shop on Fifth Avenue over alongside a dowdy ramshackle store of Sixth or Seventh Avenue.

Samara and Simbirsk both had complaints of the relations borne by the government towards the ARA districts. When I thought for the cordial relations which had always subsisted between the Kazan district of the ARA and the government, I wondered whether the fault lay altogether on the side of the government that Samara and Simbirsk were not equally fortunate in the degree of cooperation which they had succeeded in obtaining....

July 5, [1922]—I was appraised today, shortly after my arrival at the office, of the arrest several days previous of a young man of the name of [?] Nikiforov, manager of one of our kitchens in the city of Kazan. The charge preferred against him by the Cheka, which had made the arrest, was that of conspiring in counter-revolutionary activities, but from another of our employees I learned that he was the victim of mistaken identity. From the same source I learned that another man by the name of Nikiforov, in a recent meeting which had been held in one of the university halls to discuss church matters, including the so-called reforms of the church or the endeavors to bring it under the more effectual control of the government, had been provoked by the words of one of the speakers to cast rather indiscrete aspersions upon the policy of the Bolsheviks.

Whether there were agents of the government present at the meeting appears uncertain, but at any rate the Extraordinary Commission learned of the occurrence in due course, as it is apt generally to become acquainted sooner or later with all that is happening in Russia, and forthwith proceeded to put its hands upon each and every Nikiforov who in any way answered the description of the offender whom it sought.

The entire incident, as I heard of it, throws, I think, considerable light upon the agitation which has been aroused in certain of the more cultivated quarters of the membership of the Russian Orthodox church as a result of the efforts of the government to supplant the Patriarch Tikhon with a head of the church who may be controlled by the Soviets. It is equally interesting also as evidence of the fact that however severe the restriction may be, there are occasionally moments, even now in Russia, when the repressed spirits of men inevitably assert themselves.

[Childs recounts the effort of Nikiforov and the efforts of the Cheka to catch him, which included the arrest of all sorts of innocent people with that name. Several church meetings were held, the perpetrator of which managed to stay a step or two ahead of the police.]...

These meetings are believed by the white elements in Kazan to have been inspired by the government for the purpose of creating a sentiment favorable to the church reforms or to such changes as are commonly thought to be designed to bring the church under the control of the government.[73] Of course it is almost impossible to gather impartial testimony, but from what I have been able to learn there has occurred a very definite split in the church over the policy of resistence of the Patriarch Tikhon and other higher dignitaries of the church against the principle put into practice by the government this spring of the confiscation of the church treasurers for famine relief. There seems to exist as definite a cleavage between the higher and lower orders of the Russian clergy as there is between the old classes of society in Russia. This is a division which appears to have been brought about by the events of the Revolution when the higher dignitaries of the church, who owed a large part of their power and position to the old regime, naturally were disposed to adopt an attitude to convert if not open hostility to the Bolsheviki.[74] On the other hand the lower clergy are in great part recruited from the peasantry and retain their sympathies for the peasants and workers, and while not disposed to permit political questions of any sort to be introduced into the affairs of the church, nevertheless, are not willing to stand idly by when politics of which they are least in sympathy are allowed to actuate church policies.

In the beginning of the Revolution, the government did not feel secure enough of its strength to hazard an open quarrel with the highest church authorities. It is probable that in this the Bolsheviki displayed acute wisdom and excellent judgement of the temper of the people. For it is extremely unlikely that the people, or even the majority of the lower clergy, would have tolerated passively any such ambitious attempts at interference with the direction of the church as the government is undertaking at the present time.

By abiding its time and postponing an open breach with the church until the position of the government was more or less secure, the soviet authorities are now favored with circumstances which leave little doubt of

---

[73] The Soviet government used all sorts of schemes to control religious organizations, from creating a state-sponsored organization called "the Living Church" to infiltrating the Orthodox clergy with KGB agents. For an interesting novel on the latter ploy, see Lavr Dvomlikov [Vladimir Volkoff] *The Traitor* (New York: Doubleday, 1973).

[74] Russian plural of the word "Bolshevik."

success in any encounter which it may have with the church for supremacy. For the church itself has not only been disrupted in the meanwhile over the policy which should be pursued toward the new government, but the Russian people, who once might have been counted to rally to the support of the leaders of the national religion, are too weary of the conflicts and dissensions which have entailed four years of blood and tears to court rashly further conflict and its consequences.

July 19, [1922]—For the purpose of visiting two of the three states of Viatka, Votskaia, and Perm, which have been recently included in the Kazan district of the ARA, I left today for a brief trip which was intended to include the territories of Votskaia and Perm. With the addition in December of the *oblast* of Mahri and a part of the Chuvash *oblast* to the Tatar Republic, composing the Kazan district of the ARA, there was added in May, the *oblast* of Votskaia and parts of the territory of the governments of Perm and Viatka, thereby making of Kazan the largest of the ARA districts in Russia. With a population of 2,456,074 inhabitants in the original Kazan district of the ARA, the extension of the territory from one of 30,606 square miles to 90,024 square miles has brought about the inclusion of [an additional] 4,462,542 inhabitants falling within the scope of the relief of the Kazan office.

I had sent the day previous out boat, the *Pecherets*, with Pearson and Tetushi, and from there it had been ordered to proceed to Christpol, where I planned to join it by automobile and to continue up the Kama River by steam to the district of Perm. Leaving Kazan shortly after one o'clock in the afternoon in company with Simson, we made our way over a fairly good stretch of road which put us in Laishev, a distance of sixty *versts*, in a little more than two hours. Like untraveled roads in the west of America, the one over which we passed was sometimes hardly distinguishable so thick was it overgrown with grass and weeds. More frequently the line of telegraph poles proved a better guide than the marks left by previous travelers. Stopping for a hour in Laishev for a brief conference with the chairman of our committee, the town was left behind as we continued our way to Chistopol, where I planned to arrive early in the evening; but in my calculations, I had not counted upon the difficulties which were to be encountered in the crossing of the Kama about twenty *versts* beyond Laishev.

[Childs recounts the difficulties of crossing the river.]

But our difficulties were by no means all overcome, for having arrived at the opposite shore, it was discovered that the bank arose with disconcerting abruptness from the riverside, and not only this, but there was the further obstacle of sand on this shore to impede our progress. The automobile, however, was at length removed and found a footing upon the wooden shelf, which served as landing place. But time after time as it was directed up the sandy hill, its wheels stuck fast, and there was nothing to do but shift it back to the wooden landing place and to commence the ascent again. [Childs continues with many mishaps with the car, which finally reached Chistopol, where it was, again with many mishaps, loaded onto a boat.]

July 21, [1922]—Yesterday we were busy pulling up the river to Chelnyi, where we arrived in the afternoon and stopped for the purpose of unloading a part of our cargo. It was not until early in the morning that we left and proceeded on to Chekandar. Arriving in Chekandar, which is on the border of the Tatar Republic and Perm government, the automobile was very easily unloaded from the boat to the shore. [From here Childs proceeds to Sarapol.]

At the next *volost* seat of Karakulinsky, we stopped in the village schoolhouse, which bore a sign denoting it as an American kitchen, for the purpose of making tea and having a bite to eat. In this village as in almost all those which I passed on my way to Sarapol, I was struck with the greater modernity and substantial quality of the buildings which were to be viewed. We were now in the Perm government, and there was to be remarked a quite considerable number of two storied dwellings such as are rarely to be met with outside of Kazan. In Karakulinsky, which lies on the Kama, though the village consists of not more than a thousand inhabitants, there were probably a dozen or more brick structures.

Of course, there assembled around us in the schoolhouse while were made our lunch, the usual number of interested townspeople who always gather about us whenever we enter a community. One of these, a young boy in the early twenties, who appeared to be the secretary of the *volost* soviet, proved to be quite familiar with the Sarapol "incident," and indeed, in the general conversation which ensued concerning it, I was surprised to find that the news of it had obtained general circulation. This same young man stated with very engaging frankness that of course it was difficult for everyone to appreciate fully the work of the ARA and that even when the people of Karakulinsky *volost* were told that the food which we were distributing came from America, there were many to whom this meant nothing as they had not conception of America or of anything outside the narrow little circle in which they moved.

I am sure that from my contact with the Russian peasants that I have been given an understanding of the darkness of mind of the average Russian, but I doubt exceedingly if it is possible for one who had never been in Russia to measure fully the profundity of this darkness. One sometimes feels after conversation with them that they are little better than animals, and yet again they give manifestation of so much human feeling that one is inevitably led to the conclusion that given only the chance which human beings merit and which has been denied the Russians for so long, they will prove themselves.

The *volost* seat of Arazmas, located in a beautiful grove of trees in the basin of a valley, was our next halting place. To drive through the shaded pleasant streets of the village and to observe people going about in active movement would never be the means of giving rise to the thought that even here in this quiet countryside, where the grain was ripening in the fields within view, hunger was continuing its harassing way. Out of a population of nine hundred, we are feeding one hundred and forty-five adults and more than one hundred and sixty children, and yet there could be found in the village more than a dozen people swollen from hunger.

At the last *volost*, Mostovitsy, at which we stopped, although there are estimated to be eight thousand needy children in the *volost*, but two hundred and twenty rations for children are being received from the ARA, and last month there were almost fifty deaths among the children from starvation. Here, as in each of the four *volosts* through which we passed, the harvest was not expected for the needs of the population beyond the month of December and very earnest appeals were made that, even if our work for adults should be discontinued after the harvest, at least the child feeding be continued.

A little after nine in the evening, we drove into Sarapol, and there found that our boat had preceded us and was awaiting our arrival. Sarapol is a pleasant little river town of much the same appearance of any one of the formerly more prosperous river towns of the Volga and the Kama basins. [Childs describes the town and its leather industry. The chairman of the

ARA committee presented him with a leather case and two quarts of champagne.] In making the gifts, the chairman expressively begged that I would not connect them with the late unfortunate incident which had occurred on the occasion of the visit of Pearson to Sarapol; and by the earnest manner in which he expressed himself regarding the appreciation, evoked among the Russian people for the work of the ARA, I was given ample assurance of the sincerity of the purpose inspiring them.

The chairman appeared on the boat in a suit of white ducking and not only in his dress but in his manner and speech gave me reason to conclude that if he had not been of the bourgeoisie previous to the Revolution, he had been as perilously in proximity to this class as any Soviet officials I have met in Russia. There was evidence of intense suffering betrayed in certain flashes of his eyes as he spoke, and I was given to conclude not only by his words but by the tone of his voice and the expression of his features that there before me was a man of very deep feeling who cared little for the dogmas and dialectics of Moscow but was concerned primarily with the saving and improvement of human life.

How many such individuals I have met in Soviet Russia who by the very disinterestedness of their idealism have lent a strength to the Bolshevik government, which they would be as little likely to admit as they would that at heart they were not in sympathy with the extreme aims of Communism But there is a resignation and spiritual and mental abnegation about the Russian character which is well nigh impossible for the foreigner to appraise. That abnegation takes the form today of a subordination of the mind of thousands of men to the mind chiefly of one man, Nikolai [sic] Lenin.

As one passes from the Volga eastward toward Perm, Sarapol marks the almost definite passage of the traveler from a territory almost wholly agricultural in character, such as the Tatar Republic, to one in which industry begins to be more predominantly manifested. Sarapol is the seat of a number of factories from the manufacture of farming implements, and I know that one of these at least has been restored to operation by the government. [Childs describes the iron industry in the surrounding area and the physical features of Sarapol, including a wooden revolutionary arch of triumph, painted in red and inscribed with "Workers of the World, Unite."] Food conditions in the *uezd* of Sarapol are, despite the aid of the ARA, in a very desperate plight: Of a population of two hundred and thirty-six thousand, the ARA is administering relief to thirty-six thousand, and Russian relief is taking care of ten thousand five hundred. There are seventy-four thousand acutely needy children alone and of these, but twenty-eight thousand are being cared for by the two organizations of relief. The remainder are starving and dying. It is true that the death rate has decreased in the *uezd* since our operations were begun in May, but abdominal sickness and swelling continues among a very high proportion of the population. The seeding of this area last fall and this spring has not been as successful as in other areas of Russia for only twenty-six percent of the tillable land was planted in the fall and spring, or fifty-five thousand *desiatins*. Before my departure the chairman of the ARA committee, who is also the chairman of the *uezd* soviet, made a very strong request that at least a limited number of adults be fed throughout the fall, but as I had been informed that all adult operations of the ARA would come to an end on September 1, I told him it was my regret that I could promise him nothing.

July 22, [1922]—We resumed our journey the previous evening by boat, and in the early morning we found ourselves entering upon a heavily forested country of pines and firs, differing in this respect quite distinctly from the stretches of open country which mark the banks of the Kama in the Tatar Republic. Ranges of hills, now on one side of the stream and now on the other, serve also to break the monotony of the landscape left behind. These are the foothills of the Ural mountains, that great mountain chain which separates Europe and Asia. Siberia is only a step now to the east, and there is not only visible evidence of its proximity in the characteristics of nature, but there are also suggestions of it to be found in the features of the population who appear at the river landings at which we touch. There is mention also of it frequently in conversation, and when we stop at the village of Elova and are introduced to the local manager of the American kitchen "who has just returned from Siberia," it requires a jerking up of mental associations to rid oneself of that lifelong feeling that Siberia is at the other end of the world. It was a year ago, but now it is America, which is on the opposite side of the globe.

[From Elova Childs went by car to Ossa in the Perm government. He notes that Elova resembles a frontier town in the Rockies.] Here, as in most villages which are the seats of a *volost*, there was to be found an ambulatory in charge of a *felsher*,[75] who in the isolated rural communities of Russia fulfills as far as possible the functions of a doctor. It is rare to find a doctor outside the cantonal seat, but these *felshers*, as they are called, who have been hospital assistants or who have in some way or another picked up the rudiments of medicine, are generally men who are capable of rendering a real service to the communities. The one we met at Elova was a young man of an apparently inquiring mid, and he displayed keen interest in showing us over the local ambulatory, where a small stock of American medicines distributed by us from Kazan, were to be seen on the shelves and which formed quite the major part of the stocks on hand.

Almost immediately after leaving Elova the road led into a forest which gradually became thicker and thicker. For a distance of some thirty-five *versts* we never emerged from it. The trees were mostly pines and firs, although there were some birches, and here and there in the dark obscurity of its depths, there were to be seen small clearings, the center of activity of woodcutters....

I have enjoyed certainly no more beautiful ride since being in Russia than this one which lead through the heart of a Russian forest and where the majesty of nature had been left almost undisturbed by human hands. [After traveling for three hours, Childs emerged from the forest in sight of Ossa, the central town in a land inhabited largely by Bashkirs.][76]

The Bashkirs are of the Mohammedan faith like the Tatars, but they are much less scrupulous about the fulfillment of the forms of their religion, and many of them continue to preserve along with the tenets of Islamism the ancient nature worship of their forefathers....

Notoriously lazy, it is said of the Bashkirs that their laziness is pushed by them to such lengths that they prefer to set about the building of a new dwelling place rather than to clean the one which they have inhabited for a long while of the dirt and filth permitted by them in their laziness to accumulate. [Childs continues to discuss the customs of the Bashkirs.]

---

[75] *Felshers* were medically trained men who served largely rural needs. Their abilities fell somewhere between those of a registered nurse and a doctor.

[76] The Baskirs, an Asian people, numbered about 1.5 million in Childs's time and lived for the most part in the governments of Ufa and Samara.

The cantons of Sarapol and Ossa were not declared officially to be a part of the famine district by the central government until this spring, and yet today, despite the aid which we have been administering for more than a month, there are more than a hundred cases every day of death from hunger in the canton of Ossa out of a population of three hundred and nine thousand. A total of thirty thousand people have died from hunger in the canton since last fall, and there were none with whom I talked who could see an end to the famine for another year. A great part of the grain, which has yet another two weeks before it may be expected to ripen, has already been cut by the desperately driven peasants, and I visited home after home where it was being eaten without having even been dried except for a few hours artificially over a stove. More than twenty-five percent of the seed grain, distributed by the government in the spring, is estimated to have been consumed for food and not more than fifty percent of the people are expected to have a crop to harvest. Throughout the canton of Ossa, as well as that of Sarapol, the children and adults appear alike very undernourished, and even those I saw who were receiving our food have a far from healthy appearance. There is no doubt, however, that the population is much better off than it was the past winter for surrogates, at least, are capable of being gathered and huckleberries[77] and strawberries are plentiful. In one home which I visited the mistress of the house brought out a great pail, which must have contained fully a bushel of huckleberries and which she averred was, besides some mushrooms and a little milk, all the food which she had had for her family for two weeks.

An interesting fact to be noted of the custom of the Christian people of the country, which we had been traversing the past two days, was the presence of rude wooden altars in the fields. Here before these altars the peasants of the surrounding countryside appear three times a year to offer up prayers for the success of their crops. This is quite characteristic of the superstitions with which the mind of the Russian peasant is so deeply imbued and which find expression also in the ikons which are to be found framed and mounted upon a stand at the entrance and exit to every Russian

---

[77] These fruits are most likely black currants, which resemble huckleberries, which do not grow in Russia.

village. The purpose of these last is to keep the devils out of the villages, according to the explanation most commonly given.

In this connection I recall that yesterday as we were passing up the river, there was encountered a boat propelled by women rowers and containing a priest. In the center of the boat a little altar had been erected upon which an ikon had been placed. According to Simson, the priest we saw was a religious pilgrim, and he was making his way to some holy place. The sight and explanation took me back to the Middle Ages, but I was bound to reflect that as serfs these people had been living in a feudal state no less than sixty years ago. What wonder was it that they were amenable to the discipline of the Soviet government? Outside of the large cities of Russia and of a few of the larger towns, one may as well say that a political consciousness does not exist among the people.

July 23, [1922]—We left Ossa after midnight, headed upstream towards Perm, in the hope that a landing of the automobile might be effected opposite Chansk and that we would be able to motor thence to Perm and return. But a suitable landing was not to be found, and so the boat was permitted to continue its passage until Perm was reached in the afternoon. Perm is a city of approximately one hundred thousand inhabitants, situated upon a gently sloping hill on the left bank of the Kama.[78] Lying as it does athwart the Trans-Siberian railroad line from Petrograd or the most northern great trunk line of communications extending east and west across Russia, and connected by direct water communication with the Caspian Sea in the south, Perm forms the natural gateway to the Urals and Siberia for Russia and for Europe....

I made my way up into the town from the wharfs and found myself in a city which spread itself in a rambling way up and down several undulating hills overlooking the Kama. There were many large and important-looking stone buildings to give a dignity to the town, but these were scattered here and there apparently indiscriminately, and there were to be seen, sandwiched in between, just the plain ordinary and more often drab and

---

[78] Perm, a rather active industrial city in tsarist times, included a government arsenal; iron and copper works; rope, lumber, and chemical industries; and electric power generators. It was outside Perm that the tsar's brother Grand Duke Mikhail was shot during the Revolution.

dingy structures, which are characteristic of an industrial community whether it be Perm or Pittsburgh. It had been my intention to have a conference with the local authorities, but as it was a Sunday I was unable to find any of these and so I had to be satisfied with doing my business with the representatives of the Ufa district of the ARA, whom I found.

Later I went to a restaurant in company with Simson and Pearson,...and we managed to obtain a very satisfactory dinner of soup, veal, white and black bread and Ice cream, with a bottle of wine thrown in, for the sum of eighteen millions for the three. The wine alone accounted for ten of the eighteen millions, but it was worth it to those like us who live sometimes from one day to another on the memory of some little luxury like that.

After dinner we walked down to a small part in the center of the town, where a concert was in progress and listened to several local solos sung successively by singers of both sexes. The music was for the most part classical, and when it was not, the program consisted of popular Russian folk songs. Here in "socialist" Russia was to be heard far better music than anywhere in a public park of a city of similar size in America, where some clangy ragtime, if such might be called music, was being beaten out upon the helpless winds.

July 24, [1922]—Leaving Perm late the evening previous, we arrived in the morning at Chansk on the right bank of the Kama, seat of a canton or *uezd* in the government of Perm. From Chansk it is one hundred and twenty *versts* to Debessyi, the capital of one of the five cantons of the Votskaia *oblast*, in which relief operations were begun in the late spring by us. According to the plan I had mapped out, I proposed to take off the Cadillac here and drive overland to Debessyi and thence south to Ievsk and from there to Sarapol, where the boat, which we were taking leave of, would be rejoined. But the Cadillac suffered such severe jolting in the operations which were necessitated in order to land it that it was found to have been too damaged to make its use altogether safe in a long cross-country journey, and therefore, it was decided to put into service the Ford, which was being transported for emergency use.

Before leaving Chansk, I was called upon by the chairman of the cantonal executive committee who presented a very earnest plea that the ARA come to the relief of the *uezd* of Chansk. Out of a population of two hundred and twenty thousand, he stated that one hundred and forty thousand were in acute need and that deaths from starvation numbered two hundred every day. What I saw in passing through the canton to Debessyi was enough to lend conviction to his statements, for in every village which was passed there were visible people of every age and sex swollen from starvation. The *volost* seat of Bolshoi Sosnovka in this *uezd* was called at, and in what had once been the *zemstvo* offices,[79] we found the *volost* soviet executive committee in conference. There were four men, all in the early thirties, and a young sharp-eyed-looking girl, who appeared to be the secretary. Of a population of twelve hundred thousand [?], there had been two hundred and eighty-eight deaths from starvation recorded between January and July. But one twelfth of the normal crop had been planted in the fall and spring, and but twenty-five percent of the population were expected to harvest sufficient grain to meet their needs until the next harvest. As I finished my interrogations I noticed that one of the members of the *volost* soviet had leaned across to the chairman and had whispered something in his ear. The latter looked at us rather uneasily and with evident embarrassment, he said hesitatingly, fumbling for his words, "Excuse me, but—may I see your mandate?"

It was the second time that I had been asked for mine in Russia, and for some reason I was made particularly provoked by the request in this occasion. It was a feeling no doubt prompted by the suspicion that the pert-looking secretary, who had been engaged during our conversation in constantly passing notes to those about her, was the real author of the demand. I handed my mandate with a gesture of curtness, which I could not conceal, to the chairman and stood looking with the most studied unconcern out of the window as he regarded the mandate, not from this side and now from that. At the end of five minutes [during which] the mandate might have been read a dozen times, the chairman with all deference bowed and returned it to me.

From Chansk to Debessyi, the road is an excellent one, passing as it does over a firm hard gravel bed. Scattered over the landscape are clumps of trees which never at any moment obscure the view of the broad rolling

---

[79] The *zemstvo* was a local elected government in tsarist times, created in the Great Reforms of the 1860s. It disappeared with the Revolution, so the local *zemstvo* was hardly functioning at this time. Childs must be referring to the building.

plateau across which one passes. We did not stop for lunch but pushed directly through to Debessyi, which was reached shortly after five o'clock. While we made a light meal of eggs and honey and milk offered us by the chairman of the cantonal soviet, the latter went to fetch the members of the ARA committee whom we desired to meet.

Debessyi, which is a small rural town, has none of the comparatively modern features about it which distinguish so sharply the towns of the Perm government in general from those of the Tatar Republic. Indeed, it has only become a town quite lately with the establishment of the Votskaia *oblast*. On January 1, the population of the canton was one hundred and twenty-four thousand, and this had been decreased by deaths from famine to one hundred and eighteen thousand six hundred and fifty-four on [by?] May 1. Of this number, one hundred and four thousand are said to be acutely in need (of whom Russian relief is feeding thirty-four thousand and the ARA only fourteen thousand seven hundred and sixty). Of horses which numbered fifteen thousand and fifteen on July 1, 1921, there are left but nine thousand six hundred and fourteen; of forty-one thousand seven hundred and sixty-six *desiatins* of winter [wheat] fields, there were planted last year eighteen thousand four hundred and fifty-three *desiatins* and of forty-nine thousand nine hundred and eighty-six *desiatins* of spring [wheat] fields, there were planted thirteen thousand nine hundred and twenty-three *desiatins*. The authorities here all voiced the unanimous opinion that only a fraction of the population would harvest sufficient resources upon which to live to the next harvest.

In contradiction to the Volga basin, Votskaia and the southern district of Perm did not begin to feel the pinch of famine until the beginning of the year. Since that time, conditions have become progressively worse off than in the canton of Debessyi there have been of recorded deaths from hunger: In April—five hundred and twenty-nine; May, five hundred and ninety-three, and in June, six hundred and twenty-three.

It was seven o'clock when I had completed the inquiry into conditions in Debessyi, and as there remained yet two hours of light, it was determined to push on to the next *volost* and to spend the night there. The *volost*, Zurinsky, twenty-four *versts* from Debessyi, was reached late in the evening, and the chairman of the soviet conducted us to quarters in a peasant's family. There was a single room which contained one bed, but from a casual glance at the interior I was satisfied to put up my cot and to find a resting place for the night on it. It was just as well that I did so, because our chauffeur Anatolie, who was given the bed, was driven out from it by the permanent inhabitants of it, who for the several hours during which it was occupied, gave him no rest.

July 25, [1922]—An early rise gave us the opportunity for an extended conference with the *volost* committee of ARA. The population of the *volost* was found to have actually increased during the past year from ten thousand eight hundred to eleven thousand. The reason...was that the partial demobilization of the Red Army had been the means of returning two thousand soldiers to their homes in the *volost*. At the present time it was estimated that there were ten deaths every day in the *volost* from starvation, which had grown so acute that all livestock was disappearing. As [sic] an instance I was told that there remained but one thousand three hundred of the four thousand possessed by the peasant of the *volost* last year. But thirty percent of the fields were planted last fall and only twenty-five percent this spring. A children's home which was visited in the village disclosed forty-three children in a very miserable state, many suffering from the trachoma,[80] which is so prevalent in Votskaia *oblast*. The majority of them were swollen despite the fact that a ration of a limited nature was received from the Russian relief.

The *volost* of Igrinsky and Chutersky, which were passed in succession as we continued our way to Ievsk, brought to light conditions which were fully as deplorable as those which had been found in the preceding *volost*. In the last-named one, they were, if anything, worse for out of a population of nine thousand two hundred in January, there remained but eight thousand.

Up to this point,...the road had been fairly good, but it was now that it grew rapidly worse and it finally degenerated into the most difficult road I have ever attempted to go over in an automobile. [The state of the road greatly delayed them.]...

At such a time of the night, it was difficult to locate any of the authorities, but the secretary of the *oblast* soviet who was finally reached by telephone, directed us to the local hotel. A guide from the revolutionary

---

[80] Trachoma is an eye infection which comes from hand-eye contact in unsanitary conditions.

tribunal from which we had telephoned directed us to the house where the sleepy proprietor was aroused, and in his night clothes, led us to a room in which there were two beds. Simson gave only one look at the beds and then turning to the landlord asked whether or not were they clean. I felt that this inquiry was if anything superfluous, and the landlord must have concluded from our disgusted glances that no good would be served by being any other but frank, for he answered quite candidly: "No, not very." I was in such a nervous state from the fatigue of the day's journey that I leaned up against a wall and laughed until the tears flowed in streams down my cheeks. But there was no other place to go, and besides we had our cots and we could vouch for them.

July 26, [1922]—Ievsk, a town of forty-four thousand four hundred and thirty-six inhabitants, is the capital seat of the Autonomous Oblast of Votskaia, which lies northeast of the Tatar Republic wedged in between the government of Perm on the east and the district of Viatka on the west. The town itself was formerly know as the Ivesky works, inasmuch as it had grown about a great factory which was founded in 1760 by Count [?] Shuvalov and which was only some years ago acquired by the government and converted into use as [an] arsenal....

The office of the *oblast* ARA committee was found located in the government offices, and there was found a very keen and intelligent young man with a sharp angular face who proved to be secretary of the committee and the actual directing head of the operations in the *oblast*. We set [sic] down together and had a very long and very satisfactory conversation together about the work, satisfactory because I was convinced when it had been concluded that no more interested and energetic worker could be found for the task than this particular young man.

In recounting the initial difficulties which had been experienced in the organization of the work, the secretary said in the course of the conversation: "Here, I was as I have said, working my head off, more often than not until midnight and up again early the next morning and with only these few assistants whom you see here in this one room and along comes a telegram from the ARA in Kazan: 'We have information that you are not carrying out our instructions,' the wire said, 'and you are not putting the energy into the work which we have a right to expect.' Mind you, there I was working by myself every night and trying to do the best I could to fulfill the instructions which we were receiving from Kazan and where the instructions were not clear I was feeling my way out of the darkness as conscientiously and as best as I could and then this telegram is received, the devil take it: 'Unless you give us greater cooperation, I shall recommend to Moscow that the rations now assigned you be transferred to another district.' The devil take it, what do you think of that? And it was signed by a man named Childs, the devil take him!" [After a good laugh, Childs told the man who he was and explained that the telegram had resulted from an over-zealous reporter on the district. All was ended amicably, and Childs paid a visit to the chairman of the Peoples' Commissar of the Autonomous Oblast of Votskaia.]

I found as is usual a young man in the early thirties as the directing head of the young government. His forehead, I observed, was above the average in height and pleasant frank blue eyes were of a nature to set one instantly at ease in his presence. I stated that I had called to pay my respects to him before leaving Ievsk and that I wished to take the opportunity of thanking him for the very cordial support which the local government had accorded the ARA....

The soviet chairman replied quite aptly that it was the ARA whom the government was obliged to thank and as evidence of the feeling of the people of the Votskaia *oblast* towards the work of the ARA, he recounted incidents which had taken place at the last assembly of deputies of workers and peasants to the *oblast* council held the preceding month. At this Soviet, he said, the darkest-minded peasants of Votskaia, who never had before heard of America, rose to voice in their simple artless language the thanks of the population to America and the American people for the aid which had been administered them by the ARA....

It was one o'clock when we set out for Sarapol, and as we ascended the hill leading from the town, and I cast my eyes back over the city, there was to be seen a score or more of the great smokestacks of the Ievsk arsenal belching great clouds of smoke and attesting to an industrial activity which the world has been very far from allowing the workers of the Russian Socialist Soviet Republic.

[Childs proceeded only with difficulty due to problems with the car.]

It was eight o'clock when we drew up into the small village of Golianyi, and it required no prolonged search among the sparse number of houses to locate the telegraph office. The telegrapher was out in the fields, but he was sent for by his wife and in the meanwhile fish, potatoes, and milk were purchased to enable us to partake of the first substantial meal which we had enjoyed since leaving the boat in Chans. It was not until shortly before ten o'clock that the telegrapher put in his appearance.

I made out two telegrams: One directed to the senior telegraphy operator in Sarapol, asking that he communicate with the captain of our boat, the *Pecheretz*, by telephone and to direct him to proceed immediately to Golianyi and to inform me of the time of his departure, and the other, addressed to the chairman of the soviet of Sarapol *uezd*, requesting that he see that the order which I had given was executed. The messages were dispatched precisely at ten o'clock and five minutes the word came flashing back that attempts were being made to get into telephone communication with the captain of the *Pecheretz* and the chairman of the Sarapol soviet. At ten thirty o'clock there followed the message that the order which I had given to the captain of our boat had been delivered at ten fifteen and that the boat had put off five minutes later. At the same time a message was received from the soviet chairman requesting that he be informed of the time of the arrival of the boat at Golianyi.

Such prompt dispatch and execution of orders had only fallen within my experience previously while in the army in France, yet this was Bolshevik Russia and I was dealing with systems of communication and transportation which were said to have suffered a paralysis and break down. Perhaps they have to those who are looking only for evidences of them. But I have set myself in this diary the same impartial task of reporting which I was performing something more than a year ago in Washington for the Associated Press, and when I was held very strictly accountable for the presentation of all available evidence on either side of controversial questions. It is my sincere hope that I may be said to have so in the self-appointed reportorial task which I have set myself on Soviet Russia.

Two hours and a half after the departure of the boat from Sarapol, it docked at Golyanyi, but our troubles were not entirely over. The bridge, leading from the shore to the landing barge, consisted for more than half its length of but a single plank over which the Ford obviously could not pass. But from a pile of lumber lying on the shore, the crew of the *Pecheretz* found material with which to assist us, and in just an hour the bridge was sufficiently repaired as to permit the passage over it of the Ford. At last the troubles of motoring in Russia had been temporarily left behind and could be for the moment dismissed from memory. We could trust to the *Pecheretz* to land us safely in Kazan.

August 10, [1922]—Almost every day now there is being brought to light some further instance of the adherence of yet another member of the former intelligentsia or bourgeoisie to the Soviet government.[81] I have had occasion previously to note the great number of higher commands of the Red Army, which have been filled by officers of the old regime. I am not competent to judge whether or not there has been an increasing development of late in the extent of cooperation accorded the soviet government by the bourgeois elements of society but that such cooperation is not confined entirely to the army has been made evident enough to me in my personal contact with Russians of every class. The instances with which I was made acquainted today, however, concerning as they do an assistant minister of the former Imperial Council.[82] It is as a minister of Kerensky, far overshadow any such examples which I have previously had of participation of those of the old regime with the government of the new.

One of these is that of an assistant minister of the tsar known as [?] Antziferov, who, having fled to Kazan at the beginning of the revolution, so won the confidence of the local authorities by his services in one of the government institutions that he finally won promotion to the directorship of the government bank. Even after his identity had been discovered, he was permitted to continue to occupy the post of trust which he had succeeded in gaining without influence, suffering as an only inconvenience the slight interruption caused by his arrest and a short imprisonment from which he

---

[81] Childs should not have been surprised since the "old intelligentsia," as he calls them, were in much demand by the Soviets because they were the only educated people trained for any technical work. In the subsequent paragraph, Childs describes the work of these men with the Soviet regime as "cooperation." It was hardly that and could better be explained as taking the only jobs available to ward off starvation.

[82] It is unclear here whether Childs is referring to the tsar's cabinet or the old Imperial Council, which had been founded by Tsar Alexander I (1801–1825) to advise the Russian emperors on legislation. After the creation of the Duma in 1906, the institution became the upper house of the tsarist legislature, somewhat like a House of Lords.

was released so soon as he had been able to establish the fact that he had not engaged in any activities against the Soviet government.

The other case concerned a former minister of Kerensky, [Nikolai] Nekrassov,[83] who previous to the Revolution had been a professor in Tomsk, Siberia. Some years before the war, he had enjoyed intimate relations with Kerensky. Upon the ascension of the latter to the chief power in the government after the Revolution, the professor was made Minister of Public Works. As such, and by reason of the friendly relations which had always subsisted between the two, he wielded a great influence over Kerensky and was always left by the latter as interim president of the Council of Ministers [of the Provisional Government] when Kerensky was absent from Petrograd. Although much mystery still enshrouds the circumstances even now, it is commonly accepted today in Russia that it was Nekrassov, who was responsible for the sending of the famous telegram during Kerensky's absence from Petrograd declaring General [Lavr] Kornilov,[84] then approaching Petrograd with an army, a traitor. For this as well as other circumstances in his relations with Kerensky, Nekrassov gained the title in Russia of the "evil genius of Kerensky." [Childs gives a long

---

[83] Nikolai Nekrasov, (1879–193?) was a prominent member of the Kadet Party, a liberal faction in the State Duma. He served in the Provisional Government and remained in Russia after the October Revolution, working, as Childs points out, for the Soviets. He was convicted of sabotage in 1930 and disappeared into the Soviet prison system.

[84] General Alexander Kornilov (1870–1918) was the supreme commander of the Russian armies in August 1917, when he tried to establish his control over Petrograd and disperse the Soviet. His attempted coup failed and he eventually died when a random Bolshevik shell struck the house in which he was staying.

account of Nekrassov's post-revolutionary peregrinations that need not be repeated here.]

Of course it is difficult to draw [a] general conclusion from any number of such individual instances. Whether they portend the healing of the civil strife which has racked the body of stricken Russia these several years, it is not within my ability to judge. Perhaps it is only a part of an inevitable shifting of the principles of those, too broken any longer to batter against what seems an irresistible tide of circumstances, and propelled by the main force of events into a spirit of conciliation towards the status quo.

EDITOR'S AFTERWORD

Childs includes here in the cleaned-up version of his diary a thirty-two page analysis of the New Economic Policy and its impact, especially in the Tatar Republic. I have decided not to incorporate it here as it does not fall within the foci of the edition.

The diary, both in rough and finished form, abruptly and mysteriously ends at this point, although Childs remained in Russia for another six months. Moreover, both versions of his memoirs, *My Thirty Years in the Near East* and *Let the Credit Go*, give short shrift to these last months as well. His diary entries were becoming less and less frequent by this time anyway, probably in part because of the increased ARA work load, which peaked in August 1922. He also had become the Kazan district supervisor. Other personal distractions also doubtlessly arose after August, the month in which he married Georgina de Brylkine-Klokacheva in Petrograd.

Alas, however, Childs encountered some personal trouble with the Soviet government when he tried to smuggle out of Russia his mother-in-law's sixty-item collection of eighteenth-century gold snuff boxes. He had successfully sent abroad a personal parcel of Russian coins in the ARA pouch, and he tried to use the same conduit for these valuable boxes, but the pouch was opened and the entire cache confiscated. Clearly this action violated the agreement between the Soviet Union and the ARA against commercial transactions, and Childs became *personna non grata*. The ARA used the ruse that Childs was "in a generally run down condition,"[85] and released him from his duties. He departed from the Soviet Union with his wife and mother-in-law in spring 1923.

As the famine conditions abated in the fall of 1922, the need for ARA work declined, yet the Soviets, however, planned to use the ties with the ARA as a bridge to the West, or at any rate to the recognition of their

---

[85] Bertrand Patenaude, *The Big Show in Bololand; The American Relief Expedition to Soviet Russia in the Famine of 1921* (Stanford CA: Stanford University Press, 2002) 681.

government by the United States. Herbert Hoover, on the other hand, had hoped that the ARA would be a Trojan Horse that would undermine the Communist government, and when he realized that by 1922 the Bolshevik grip was stronger than ever, he personally decided that it was time to remove the organization. Step by step the American Relief Administration left the former famine areas, where it had been feeding at its height some 11 million people. Most of the agents had departed by the summer of 1923, although a few stragglers stayed on into the fall for various closing operations. In June, the ARA gave a farewell dinner attended by Felix Dzerzhinski, Georgii Chicherin, and his future successor Maxim Litvinov, among others. There were toasts to friendship and statements of thanks on all sides, and a month later the Soviet government returned the gesture with a dinner of its own.

Yet on the departure of the ARA, the Soviet government moved quickly to erase the memory of the work of these saviors. Physical monuments such as American names on hospitals and American emblems on buildings were removed, and the Soviet authorities never permitted the ARA help to enter Soviet history textbooks. Moreover, retribution was levied on those Russians who had been employed with the ARA, and although it cannot be documented, many of their former employees were arrested in the purges of the 1930s simply because of the "crime" of being an employee of the organization.

The official position of Soviet history on the organization, in the rare cases that it was even mentioned, was to brand it as a underhanded vehicle for spying on and planting sedition in the young Soviet republic. They also assumed the position that the Americans had made them pay for the food America distributed. When a Soviet author of the 1950s dared to write of his reminiscences as a child of "drinking ARA condensed milk" and eating "snow-white bread, as soft as cotton,"[86] he was publicly attacked by then-dictator of the Soviet Union Nikita Khrushchev. Even when Khrushchev did thank Americans for their help during the 1921–1923 famine when he visited the United States in 1959, he spoiled the moment by quickly adding that of course just a few years before the United States had invaded Russia in

---

[86] Benjamin Weisman, *Herbert Hoover and Famine Relief to Soviet Russia, 1921–23* (Stanford: Hoover Institution Press, 1974) 188–89.

an effort to support the anti-Communist forces. When Tom Barringer returned to Russia as a tourist in the 1960s, he was met with blank stares when he said the only Russian sentence that he remembered: "I am the district supervisor of the American Relief Administration." No one, not even the well-informed tour guides, had any idea of what he was speaking.[87] Even in recent times, since the fall of Soviet Communism, although I have often asked, I have yet to find one Russian citizen who knows about the help America gave the Russian people in those terrible times.

In the years that followed, the agents of the ARA had a number of reunions of their dwindling membership, but the only one held by just the Kazan staff assembled on 16 and 17 May 1937, in Newark, New Jersey. Childs was there. In the midst of its revelry, the assembled group sent a telegram to the Kazan newspapers with effusive greetings "to all our old friends" in the Kazan district. Whether or not it ever arrived is anyone's guess. We can, however, be relatively certain that it was never published in the newspapers of that city, and since the Soviet Union was in the midst of the deadly *Chistka*, it may well have called the attention of the police to several locals who had worked for the ARA, resulting in their arrest and execution.

---

[87] Tom Barringer, interview by the editor, spring 1971.

EPILOGUE

After leaving Russia in 1923, Childs stood for and passed the foreign service exam and began a thirty-year career in the American Diplomatic Corps, serving in largely Middle Eastern posts in Egypt, Palestine, Persia, Saudi Arabia, Ethiopia, and in Tangier in North Africa. He championed the Arab cause against that of Israel, which made him unpopular in most diplomatic circles. Childs's last two assignments were ambassadorial posts, one as the US ambassador to Saudi Arabia, where he became especially close to the royal family, and the other in Addis Ababa, Ethiopia, where he ended his career in 1953. He retired then to Nice, France, bought an apartment that overlooked the Mediterranean, and devoted the remainder of his life to his writings. He returned to Richmond, Virginia, in 1973 "to die," he told this editor, but lived and wrote for another fourteen years.

ADDITIONAL READING

There is not a large body of secondary literature on the American Relief Administration's work in Russia, but what exists is of very high quality. For an overall study of the ARA in all of the countries it helped, Frank M. Surface and Raymond L. Bland's *American Food in the World War and Reconstruction Period* (Stanford CA: Stanford University Press, 1931) serves well. The study abounds with statistics, and pages 239–64 deal specifically with the ARA's Russian activity. On the Russian relief work alone, there is the authorized study by the official historian of the ARA in Russia, Harold H. Fisher, *The Famine in Soviet Russia, 1919–1923* (New York: Macmillan, 1927). The study is very solid, and despite the fact that it is over three-quarters of a century old, it is still of great value. Benjamin M. Weissman's *Herbert Hoover and Famine Relief to Soviet Russia, 1921–23* (Stanford CA: Hoover Institution Press, 1974) is likewise a very good but more focused examination which concentrates on Hoover's role more than what the agents were doing in the field. The author contends that the ARA aid to the Russians contributed to the Bolshevik ability to hold onto power. One might also take a look at his article, "Herbert Hoover's 'Treaty' with the Soviet Union," *Slavic Review* (28/2 [June 1969]: 276–88). Last, but certainly far from least, is Bertrand Patenaude's encyclopedic work, *The Big Show in Bololand; The American Relief Expedition to Soviet Russia in the Famine of 1921* (Stanford CA: Stanford University Press, 2002). This 800-page tome, easily the best work on the ARA in Russia, is unbelievably thorough and detailed but is also a "good read." Moreover, it contains an exhaustive bibliography on ARA activity in Russia.

Childs spent most of his time in the Tatar Republic. For background reading, there is Azade-Ayse Rorlich's *The Volga Tatars: A Profile of National Resilience* (Stanford: The Hoover Institution Press, 1986), which gives a history of the Tatars of the Volga, an examination of their culture, and even provides a glossary of Tatar and Russian terms that appear in the work. It is also extensively documented. Orlando Figes's *Peasant Russia, Civil War: The*

Volga Countryside in Revolution (1917–1921) (Oxford, England: Oxford University Press, 1989) examines the Revolution in the area in which Childs was to work and shows how the Bolsheviks extended their control over the region, establishing the government with which Childs had to work. Edwin Ware Hullinger, a journalist who traveled over the Tatar Republic with Childs, describes local customs and culture in his *The Reforging of Russia* (New York: Dutton, 1925). He was eventually expelled from the country for his anti-Soviet criticism.

There are a surprisingly large number of general eyewitness accounts of the Russia in which Childs served. *The Middle Road* (New York: Doran, 1923) is an autobiographical novel by Sir Philip Gibbs in which the protagonist Bertram Pollard observes the economic and social dislocation in Europe after the war. Part of it takes place in famine-stricken Russia. The author knew Childs personally. There are two works by the professional leftist Emma Goldman, *My Disillusionment in Russia* (Garden City NY: Doubleday, 1923) and *My Further Disillusionment in Russia* (Garden City NY: Doubleday, 1924). The second volume consists of twelve chapters that had somehow been misplaced and not published in the first book. Someone found them after the first book had gone to press, and they were later produced as shown. The author, like many of the wooly-minded radicals who went to Russia, turned on the Soviet "paradise" for a number of obvious reasons that she describes in this work. C. E. B. Roberts, writing under the pen name of C. E. Bechhofer, has written *Through Starving Russia* (London: Methuen, 1921), which is much the same thing. A view of the Soviet experiment from the class enemy is Iu. V. Got'e's *Time of Troubles: The Diary of Iurii Vladimirovich Got'e, Moscow, July 8, 1917 tp July 23, 1922*, trans. Terence Emmons (Princeton NJ: Princeton University Press, 1988). The author was a "bourgeois" professor of history at the University of Moscow, and he gives his readers insights into the daily life during the famine. Childs frequently had to deal with these types of people whose world had forever disappeared and who were trying to survive in the nightmare of the early days of the Soviet Union. Another personal account is Charles Sarolea's *Impressions of Soviet Russia* (London: E. Nash and Grayson, 1924). Sarolea lived in Russia during the Great War and had written a blatantaly propagandistic work titled *Great Russia: Her Achievement and Promise* (New York: Knopf, 1916), in which are chapters with such laughable titles as

"Russia Stands for Democracy" and "Russia as the Liberator of Oppressed Nationalities." *Impressions* should likewise be used with caution. Another observer of the young Soviet state was Samuel Spewack, whose *Red Russia Revealed: The Truth about the Soviet Government and its Methods* (New York: The World, 1923) is a bit more reliable. The author was an American journalist who wrote for the New York *World* and was in Russia during the early days of NEP. Of a scholarly nature is Richard Stites's *Revolutionary Dreams: Utopian Vision and Experimental Life in the Russian Revolution* (New York: Oxford University Press, 1989), which views the utopianism that abounded in the first years after the Revolution with which Childs had to contend.

Of those who actually performed the relief work, there are surprisingly few titles that were published, although numerous memoirs exist in unpublished manuscript form in archives. The ARA's head man in Russia, William Haskell, who must have had lots to say, has left only a four page article, "How We Fed the Starving Russians," *Plain Talk* (July 1948): 15–19. Of greater value is Frank Golder and Lincoln Hutchinson's *On the Trail of the Russian Famine* (Stanford CA: Stanford University Press, 1927). Hutchinson was an employee of the ARA, while Golder served it unofficially, but both men, among the first to be sent to the famine front, traveled the width and breadth of the famine regions and wrote of their experiences and their conversations with the citizens there. Essentially a diary, the work includes sections on topics such as agriculture that were obviously written later. Of the same nature is *War, Revolution, and Peace in Russia: The Passages of Frank Golder*, ed. Terence Emmons and Bertrand M. Patenaude (Stanford CA: Stanford University Press, 1992). Golder was born in Russia, earned a doctorate from Harvard, and taught at Stanford. He was sent by the Hoover Institution to collect materials on Russia for their archives, and his work formed the basis for that marvelous archival source. He had close associations, however, with the ARA members and performed, as noted above, work for them unofficially on occasion. This particular piece is largely a diary but includes Golder's correspondence beginning in 1914. Of a wilder nature is Charles Veil's *Adventure's a Wench: The Autobiography of Charles Veil* (New York: Morrow, 1934). A colorful hellraiser, the author had served in the Lafayette Escadrille, worked for the American Embassy in Paris, and joined the staff of the ARA in Russia. His work at times seems to cross the line between truth and fiction with great facility and should be used with care.

Other groups joined the Americans in famine relief, most notably the Quakers. Two accounts by Quaker relief workers are Michael Asquith's *Famine: Quaker Work in Russia, 1921–1923* (London: Oxford University Press, 1943) and Muriel Payne's *Plague, Pestilence and Famine* (London: Nisbet, 1923). Neither author worked with the ARA, but they well describe the types of terrible conditions that ARA members witnessed. For an examination of Catholic relief efforts during the famine, there is Jeffery Begeal's paper, "The Papal Relief Mission to Russia, 1921–24" on deposit with the US Catholic Bishops Conference Archives, Washington DC.

Some readers might be interested in examining more of Childs's writings, of which there are a considerable number. He wrote three sets of formal memoirs. His first, *Foreign Service Farewell: My Years in the Near East* (Charlottesville: University of Virginia Press, 1969) covers his entire life yet stresses his work in Jerusalem, Bucharest, Cairo, Teheran, Spain, Tangiers, Saudi Arabia, Yemen, and Ethiopia. It falls into the typical genre of foreign service memoirs, *i.e.*, my advice was ignored and the world has been worse off for it. In retirement, he wrote his autobiography titled *Let the Credit Go: The Autobiography of J. Rives Childs* (New York: K. S. Giniger, 1983). It contains more personal information, much of which had been edited out of *Foreign Service Farewell*, including Childs's "sexcapades" and his world travel in retirement. Even further in that direction is his *Vignettes, or Autobiographical Fragments* (New York: Vantage Press, 1977). This work is comprised of personal incidents in Childs's life, including an account of his return to Russia fifty-four years after he left in which he makes comparisons between his two visits.

Childs's collected works include also a number of scholarly works on various topics. His first book, *Reliques of the Rives* (Lynchburg VA: J. P. Bell, 1929) is a 750-page genealogy of his mother's family, the Rives (Ryves) of Virginia. He had it privately published, but he told me that it had afforded him the greatest financial remuneration of any of his works. In the 1930s, after being stationed in Teheran and traveling all over the country, he wrote *Pageant of Persia* (New York: Bobbs, Merrill, 1936), an account of his travels with the history of the localities included as background. He also includes his diplomatic activities, which reflect a reverence for the somewhat autocratic regime. He had written a book on military codes and ciphers in the early 1920s, but he could never find a publisher for the manuscript. Part of that effort appeared as *German Military Ciphers* (Washington, DC: US Government Printing Office, 1935) without Childs's further input, and he never knew that it was being published until he saw it. After World War II, he was given a leave of absence and temporarily posted in the American embassy in Paris to write *The American Foreign Service* (New York: Holt, 1948), in which he traces the evolution of the State Department and gives a view into the day-to-day functioning of the Paris embassy. He also makes comparisons between the American diplomatic service on the one hand and that of the French and the British on the other.

Childs also was the first Walter Hines Page Library Visiting Lecturer at Randolph Macon College in Ashland, Virginia, and his lectures, produced as *membra disjecta* titled *Diplomatic and Literary Quests* (Richmond VA: Whittle and Shepperson, 1963), were published. Three of the four lectures reflect Childs's background. The first two examine diplomacy and Childs's role, or the lack of it, in Operation Torch, the American invasion of North Africa in 1942. The second compares American and French traits. Childs's wife was half French, and he lived in France the last twenty years of his life, so he is well qualified to write on the subject. His last piece is an excellent essay on the Russian writer Anton Chekhov.

Childs was a great collector of books, and he acquired the editions of many works by numerous authors, especially Restif de La Bretonne, a collection of whose works Childs assembled over the years, and which was bought by Harvard University. Childs also began to acquire the works of Henry Miller, and Childs's correspondence with him concerning the collection of Miller's works was published under the title *Collector's Quest: The Correspondence of Henry Miller and J. Rives Childs, 1947–65*, ed. Richard Clement Wood (Charlottesville VA: Published for Randolph-Macon College by the University of Virginia Press, 1968).

Childs was also a published novelist with two works to his credit. His first, which was an autobiographical novel that he published anonymously, was *Before the Curtain Falls* (Indianapolis IN: Bobbs-Merrill, 1932). The protagonist, Henry Filmer, a pen name Childs used for his second novel, represents the "disillusioned generation" that lived in the aftermath of the Great War. The work predicts the coming of a new social and economic order. The volume appeared in the bottom of the Depression and sold only 3,500 copies. Six years later, Childs's second and last novel, *Escape to Cairo* (Indianapolis IN: Bobbs-Merrill, 1938) came out. It is a story of a ladies' man who runs around Europe, although mainly operating in Cairo, seducing women, always leaving them without making any commitment or feeling any obligation to them, until the final one snares him. Childs probably saw himself in that role. More than *Before the Curtain Falls*, this work is, as one reviewer put it, "an honest-to-God novel."

Childs also made scholarly contributions. His greatest efforts in this area were his works on the famous eighteenth-century novelist, mathematician, scholar, and, of course, lover Giacomo Casanova. The quantity and quality of Childs's works made him the leading living authority on the man. Childs first wrote a smaller pocket book biography of the famous libertine for a German publisher, but he was quickly solicited by the British firm Allen and Unwin to write a larger, more detailed biography. The German work later appeared in French, Italian, and Japanese, but the new expanded biography was published in English as *Casanova: A Biography Based on New Documents* (London: Allen and Unwin, 1961). Eventually, Childs produced several biographies of Casanova. A large German edition appeared as *Casanova: Die Grosse Biographie* (Munich: Blanvalet, 1977), and his last effort was *Casanova: A New Perspective* (New York: Paragon House Publishers, 1988). Of great value to scholars on the subject is *Casanoviana: An Annotated Bibliography* (Vienna: Nebehey, 1956), which he published privately. He also edited a one-volume edition of Casanova's memoirs. Combing the eight-volume edition of Casanova's recollections, *The Memoirs of Jacques Casanova de Seingalt*, trans. Arthur Machen (Edinburgh: Limited Editions Club, 1940), Childs made a compilation of various parts, producing a one-volume edition to which he wrote an introduction. The volume was published as *The Memoirs of Jacques Casanova de Seingalt* (Haarlem, Holland: Limited Editions Club, 1972). Finally, for years he edited a Casanova newsletter titled *Casanova Gleanings*, which, as is typical of the genre, produced for a select audience a few snippets and little gems on the famous man. It was published annually.

His scholarly pursuits also led him to compile, in French, a bibliography of the eighteenth century writer Restif de la Bretonne, titled *Restif de la Bretonne: témoignages et judgements, bibliographie* (Paris: aux depens de l'auteur. En vente à la Librairie Briffaut, 1949). This work grew out of the aforementioned collection of his works, and it catalyzed a revival of interest in the obscure author.

INDEX